Praise for
Database Design for Mere Mortals

"[A] must have for anyone new to relational database design. Mr. Hernandez presents the often complex subject of relational database design in a clear and easily understood manner. His attention to detail is marvelous, and the explanations of the interview process are a must read by anyone, including experienced relational database designers."

—*Jim Booth*
Principal Consultant,
James Booth Consulting

"[A]n astoundingly fresh approach to the 'nasty' task of database design. Mike uses a straightforward, no-nonsense technique that doesn't get bogged down in incomprehensible mathematical rules or scientific jargon. Anyone who has anything to do with creating applications using a database product should buy this book and read it cover to cover. For novice readers, it will save hours of frustration trying to build something without a workable design. Even the most advanced database developers will find a new way to look at database design methodology– and perhaps find many of Mike's ideas useful to make the task more interesting and palatable for others on their project teams."

—*John Viescas*
President, Viescas Consulting, Inc.
Author of Running Microsoft Access 97
and coauthor of Access and SQL Server Developer's Handbook

"**Database Design for Mere Mortals** is sure to help both aspiring and practicing database designers alike! Michael delivers the major points of logical database design with a clear, common-sense approach that makes this book an excellent resource and a pleasure to read."

—*Nick Evans*
Contributing Writer, PowerBuilder Advisor

"**Database Design for Mere Mortals** is necessary reading for the ninety-five percent of database applications developers that did not study the subject in their computer science courses. Mike has done us a favor by taking an academic topic and making it logical, approachable, and comprehensible for us mortals. Anyone interested in making their database design better should read this book. It contains good information for every level of database developer."

—*Malcolm C. Rubel*
Contributing Editor, Data Based Advisor
and FoxPro Advisor Magazine

"No matter what specific database package you're using (or, perhaps, no package at all), the concepts in this book will make sense, and will apply to your database design projects."

—*From the Foreword by Ken Getz,*
MCW Technologies
Coauthor, Microsoft Access Developer's Handbook

Database Design
for
Mere Mortals

A Hands-On Guide to
Relational Database Design

Michael J. Hernandez

▲
ADDISON-WESLEY

An imprint of Addison Wesley Longman, Inc.

Reading, Massachusetts • Harlow, England • Menlo Park, California
Berkeley, California • Don Mills, Ontario • Sydney
Bonn • Amsterdam • Tokyo • Mexico City

Library of Congress Cataloging-in-Publication Data

Hernandez, Michael J. (Michael James)
    Database design for mere mortals : a hands-on guide to relational
database design / Michael J. Hernandez.
       p. cm.
    Includes index.
    ISBN 0-201-69471-9
    1. Database design. 2. Relational databases. I. Title.
QA76.9.D26H477 1997
005.75'6—dc20   96-42313
                                  CIP

Sponsoring Editor: Kathleen Tibbetts
Project Manager: John Fuller
Production Assistant: Melissa Lima
Cover design: Square One Design
Set in 10-point Bookman by Octal Publishing, Inc.

Text printed on recycled and acid-free paper.

ISBN 0201694719

9 1011121314 MA   02 01 00

9th Printing   January 2000

For my mother, Estela R. Pundt. Not exactly a symphony, but an opus nonetheless.

In loving memory of my father-in-law, LeRoy W. Bonnicksen. He always had faith in me.

Dedicated to anyone who has unsuccessfully attempted to design a relational database.

About the Author

Michael J. Hernandez, owner of DataTex Consulting Group in Seattle, Washington, is an independent consultant and trainer specializing in relational database management. Since 1988 Mike has designed relational databases and created database applications for a wide variety of organizations and businesses and has been a featured speaker at various database conferences. He was a contributing editor for the database design chapter in *Microsoft Access 2 Developer's Handbook* (Getz/Litwin/Reddick, Sybex), and a contributing author for the database design and macro chapters in *Running Microsoft Access for Windows 95* (John L. Viescas, Microsoft Press). He has also been a contributing author to Pinnacle Publishing's *Smart Access* database journal and continues to work on various database development projects and writing projects as his schedule permits. Mike is a top-rated Microsoft Access instructor for Application Developers Training Company, a national training organization, and Focal Point, Inc., a high-end software training and consulting organization based in Seattle. In addition, Mike conducts his own highly successful database design class based on the design methodology presented in this book.

In a past life Mike was a professional guitarist for fifteen years, playing a wide variety of styles. His ability to enthuse his students comes from years of entertaining. Mike has a reputation among his colleagues for being quite uninhibited: he's played the guitar for his students, subjected them to a collection of the world's worst puns, played the game Charades to illustrate a point, and caused minor uproars with his imitations of George Bush and Ross Perot.

On the rare occasions when he has free time, Mike can be found at one of four places: drinking a mocha brevé at any immediately available Starbucks, hanging out in the database section at any Barnes & Noble bookstore, speeding along the Burke-Gilman Trail on his mountain bike with his overly athletic wife, Kendra, or hitting golf balls at the local driving range and pretending he is Lee Trevino.

You can visit Mike's web site at www.datatexcg.com and contact him via e-mail at mikeh@datatexcg.com.

Contents

Part II:
The Design Process 57

Chapter 4:
Conceptual Overview 59

Chapter 5:

Starting the Process 71

Chapter 6:

Analyzing the Current Database 97

Chapter 7:

Establishing Table Structures 151

Chapter 9:

Field Specifications. 237

Chapter 10:

Table Relationships. 273

Foreword

Perhaps you're wondering why the world needs another book on database design. When Mike Hernandez first discussed this book with me, *I* wondered. But the fact is—as you may have discovered from leafing through pages before landing here in the Foreword—the world *does* need a book like this one. You can certainly find many books detailing the theories and concepts behind the science of database design, but you won't find many (if any) written from Mike's particular perspective. He has made it his goal to provide a book that is clearly based on the sturdy principles of mathematical study, but has geared it toward practical use instead of theoretical possibilities. No matter what specific database package you're using, the concepts in this book will make sense, and will apply to your database design projects.

I knew this was the book for me when I turned to the beginning of Chapter 6 and saw this suggestion:

> Do not adopt the current database structure as the basis for
> the new database structure.

If I'd had someone tell me this when I was starting out on this database developer path years ago I could have saved a *ton* of time! And that's my point here: Mike has spent many years designing databases for clients; has spent lots of time thinking, reading, and studying about the *right* way to create database applications; and has put it all here, on paper, for the rest of us.

This book is full of the right stuff, illustrated with easy-to-understand examples. That's not to say that it doesn't contain the hardcore information you need to do databases right—it does, of course. But it's geared toward real developers, not theoreticians.

I've spent some time talking with Mike about database design. Over coffee, in meetings, writing courseware, it's always the same: Mike is passionate about this material. Just as the operating system designer seeks the perfect, elegant algorithm, Mike spends his time looking for just the right way to solve a design puzzle, and—as you will read in this book—how to best explain it to others. I've learned much of what I know about database design from Mike over the years, and feel sure that I have a lot more to learn from this book. After reading through this concise, detailed presentation of the information you need to know in order to create professional databases, I'm sure you'll feel the same way.

—Ken Getz
MCW Technologies
KenG@mcwtech.com

Preface and Acknowledgments

*If the Lord Almighty had consulted
me before embarking upon Creation,
I should have recommended
something simpler.*
—Alfonso X, King of Castile and Leon

*Creating a database can be like
creating a universe, only more
complicated. At least when the
universe was created, there was no
one around to complain.*
—Michael J. Hernandez

It all started with a simple question, "How do I properly design a database?"

It was a question that propelled me into an interesting journey—a journey to find someone or some book that could provide the answer. This journey has taken me to a number of bookstores and put me in the path of many interesting and fascinating people. I've read a variety of books on the subject, from the totally incomprehensible to the sorely lacking in content, and had conversations with people ranging from those who were in my position to those who really knew their craft. I was fortunate to have a few people in the latter category become my mentors, and I learned a great deal from them.

Books were a different story. There came a moment when I realized that current books on database design were just not written for people like me. If you had a background in mathematics, a computer science degree, and had been working in the computer industry for some time, *then* you were the audience the authors of these books were trying to reach. Otherwise there was very little available. The few attempts at "simplified" texts simply failed to teach effectively, often because the authors seemed to assume that the reader was simpleminded.

I believed that there should be a book for people who did not have high levels of specialized education; a book that was straightforward and easy to read, thorough but not tedious; a book that used examples that were relatively easy to understand. So I wrote a special report on the fundamentals of database design for a local publisher, and it met with some success. Encouraged by this, I decided that someday I would write a book on the complete process of relational database design.

Early in my journey, I became a successful database developer and instructor. I've developed databases for a number of diverse organizations and businesses and have taken pleasure in instructing people on how to use a variety of database software programs. Throughout all this I've kept my sights on my goal.

It was at the 1995 Database Summit in Seattle, Washington, that I met Kathleen Tibbetts, a Developers Press editor for Addison Wesley Longman. At that moment my journey took a quite positive turn. She was looking for people with something to say, and I was definitely that type of person. Kathleen listened very patiently to the story of the journey upon which I had embarked. She determined that this would be a good time for me to work on realizing my goal—to finally commit to paper all that I had learned about database design.

The book you now hold in your hands is a result of the culmination of this particular journey. I've shaped and molded the knowledge I accumulated into what I believe is a clear and straightforward database design method. I've tried very hard to make it accessible to everyone, regardless of previous experience. I have sought a presentation that would be easier to learn and understand than traditional design methods yet would yield the same results.

I believe that learning about database design is an ongoing process. I'm always learning more and more about the intricacies and nuances of design—and so will you. Database design is more of an art than an exact science, involving as much intuition as pure theoretical and technical knowledge. It also involves communication skills and the ability to see things in the long term as well as the short term. Database design can be a fascinating subject once you really get into it.

I've discovered that writing a book is something of a cooperative effort. I am thankful that there are always editors, colleagues, friends, and family who are ready and willing to lend their help. It is these people who provide encouragement and keep you focused on the task at hand. Without them, you could easily "put it off until tomorrow."

First and foremost, I would like to thank Kathleen Tibbetts at Addison Wesley Longman for her unwavering support and for providing me with the opportunity to write this book. She has been just as enthusiastic about this project as I have been. I look forward to working with her on further projects.

Next my deepest thanks to my good friend, colleague, and technical editor, Jim Booth. I have a great deal of respect for Jim's knowledge on the subject of database design, and his comments have been invaluable. He and I have a thick porterhouse steak and a bottle of fine red wine waiting for us once this book is out on the market.

I also owe a debt of gratitude to my good friend and colleague Christopher R. Weber. In spite of a busy consulting and lecture schedule, Chris reviewed a number of chapters and provided valuable feedback. Now, if we could both find the time to sit down and discuss music. . . . (We're both musicians.)

I'd like to acknowledge some of the many people who have shared their experience and knowledge with me and have had a positive influence on my career in the field of database management: Karen Watterson, Mike Johnson, Karl Fischer, Paul Litwin, John Viescas, Ken Getz, and Gregory Piercy. My thanks to you all.

My sincerest and deepest appreciation goes to my very dear friend and mentor, Alastair Black. Not only was he gracious enough to review every word in the entire book; he and his wife, Julia, opened their home to me and treated me as one of their own. His immeasurable and invaluable help in the writing of this book cannot be overstated. I've learned more about the *craft* of writing in these past months than at any other time in my professional or personal life.

Last, but certainly not least, a special thanks to my wife, Kendra. Every married author realizes, by the end of the work, how much he owes to the patience of the spouse, and is moved to recognize the priceless contribution of interest and forbearance. But I am enjoined not to make as much of this as it deserves, because Kendra strongly opposes public displays of affection (PDA as she calls it), whether in person or in print. So the only thing I'll say is this: Thanks Ked. Now we can resume a normal life.

Introduction

Plain cooking cannot be entrusted
to plain cooks.
—COUNTESS MORPHY

In the past, the process of designing a database has been a task performed by information systems (IS) personnel and professional database developers. These people usually have mathematical, computer science, or systems design backgrounds and have typically worked with large mainframe databases. Many of them are experienced programmers and have coded a number of database application programs consisting of thousands of lines of code. (And these people are usually very overworked due to the nature and importance of their work!)

Because most of the systems these people created were meant to be used companywide, as designers they need to have a solid educational background. Even when creating databases for single departments within a company or for small businesses, database designers still required extensive formal training because of the complexity of the programming languages and database application programs that were used at the time. However, it's not as true now as it was then.

Since the mid-1980s a number of software vendors have brought database software programs to market that run on desktop computers and can be more easily programmed to collect, store, and manage data than their mainframe counterparts. They have also produced software that allows groups of people to access and use centralized data within a client/server architecture on computers connected within a local area network (LAN). No longer is anyone in a company thoroughly dependent on mainframe databases or on having their database needs met by a centralized IS department. As the years progressed, vendors added new features and enhanced the tool sets in their database software, which enabled the database developer to create more powerful and flexible database applications.

The ease with which database software can be used has inspired many people to create their own databases. It's quite easy to create fields and tables in most database software programs, and it's relatively easy to create the queries, forms, and reports that will be used to work with the data. A number of these programs now come with sample structures that can be copied and altered to suit specific needs. Many people have tried their hand at creating a database for their department or business with varying degrees of success. The software offers sample structures and apparently quick results, so the user can be deceived into making a superficial, incomplete design. Problems are later encountered in what was believed to be a dependable database.

Most problems that surface in a database fall into two categories: application problems and data problems. Application problems include such things as data entry/edit forms that are working improperly, confusing menus, confusing dialog boxes, and tedious task sequences. These problems typically arise when the database developer is inexperienced, is unfamiliar with a good application design methodology, or knows too little about the software being used to implement the database. These problems are common and important to address, but they are beyond the scope of this work. (A good course of action to follow for solving most application problems is to purchase and study third-party "developer" books covering the software being used. Such books discuss application design issues, advanced programming techniques, and various tips and tricks that can be used to improve and enhance an application. Armed with these new skills, you can revamp and fine-tune the database application so that it works correctly, smoothly, and efficiently.)

Data problems, on the other hand, include such things as missing data, incorrect data, mismatched data, and inaccurate information. Many of these problems can be attributed to poor database design. When the structure of the database has been improperly designed, the database will not fulfill the organization's information requirements. Poor design is typically due to a lack of knowledge of good database design principles, but it shouldn't be construed as reflecting negatively on the developer. Many people—including experienced programmers and database developers—have had little or no instruction in any form of database design methodology. Many are unaware that design methodologies even exist. Data problems and poor design are the issues that will be addressed in this work.

Who Should Read This Book

No previous background in database design is necessary to read this book. The reason you have this book in your hands is to learn how to design a database properly. If you're just getting into database management and you're thinking about developing your own databases, this book will be very valuable to you. It's better that you learn how to create a database properly from the beginning than that you learn by trial and error. The latter method takes much longer, believe me.

If you fall into the category of those people who have been working with database programs for a while and are ready to begin developing new databases for your company or business, you should read this book. You probably have a good feel for what a good database structure should look like but aren't quite sure how database developers arrive at an effective design. Maybe you're a programmer who has created a number of databases following a few basic guidelines but you always ended up writing a lot of code to get the database to work properly. If this is the case, this book is also for you.

It would be a good idea for you to read this book even if you already have some background in database design. You perhaps learned a design methodology back in college or attended a database class that discussed design, but your memory is vague about some details, or there were parts of the design process that you just did not completely understand. Those points with which you had difficulty will finally become clear once you learn and understand the design process presented in this book.

This book is also appropriate for those of you who are experienced database developers and programmers. Although you may already know many of the aspects of the design process that are presented here, you'll probably find that there are some elements that you've never before encountered or considered. Since many of the processes you are familiar with are presented here from a different viewpoint, reviewing them may give you fresh ideas about methods you can use to design your databases. At the very least, the material in this book can serve as a great refresher course in database design.

The Purpose of This Book

Designing a database and its attendant application can be described as a three-phase process.

The first phase is the logical design of the database, which includes determining and defining tables and their fields, establishing Primary and Foreign keys, establishing table relationships, and determining and establishing the various levels of data integrity.

The second phase is the implementation of the logical design within a specific database software program. This process includes creating the tables, establishing key fields and table relationships, and using the proper tools to implement the various levels of data integrity.

The third phase is the development of the end-user application. This application allows a single user or group of users to interact with the data stored in the database. The application development phase itself can be divided into separate processes, such as determining end-user tasks and their appropriate sequences, determining information requirements for report output, and creating a menu system for navigating the application.

This book deals with only the first phase, the logical design of a database. There are many database design books out on the market that include chapters on implementing the database within a specific database software, SQL (Structured Query Language), and various other programming topics. Some books seem to meld the design and implementation processes together, an approach with which I don't entirely agree. The main problem I have with these books is that if a reader doesn't work with the particular database software or programming language that is being discussed, it can be difficult to obtain any useful or relevant information from the implementation chapters. That is why my focus in this work is strictly on the logical design of the database.

The logical design of a database should be performed first and as completely as possible. After you've created a sound structure, you can then implement it within any database software you choose. Once you begin the implementation, you may find that you need to modify the database structure based on the pros and cons or strengths and weaknesses of the database software you've chosen. You may even decide to make structural modifications to enhance data processing performance. Performing the logical design first forces you to make certain considerations consciously during the design phase from an informed and logical viewpoint, and as a result, later modifications are less likely to be needed.

The purpose of this book is to explain the process of relational database design without using the orthodox methodologies found in an overwhelming majority of database design books. I avoid the complexities of these design methodologies by presenting a relatively straightforward commonsense approach to the design process. I also use a simple and straightforward data modeling method as an adjunct to this approach. The entire process is presented as clearly as possible with a minimum of technical jargon.

This book should be easier to read than other books you may have encountered. Many of the database design books on the market are highly technical and can be difficult to assimilate. I think most of these books can be confusing and overwhelming if you are not a computer science major, database theorist, or experienced database developer. The design principles you'll learn within these pages will be easy to understand and remember, and the examples will be common and generic enough to be relevant to a wide variety of situations.

Most people I've met in my travels around the country have told me that they just want to learn how to create a sound database structure without having to learn about normal forms or advanced mathematical theories. Many people are not as worried about implementing a structure within a specific database software as they are about learning how to optimize their data structures and how to impose data integrity. In this book, you'll learn how to create efficient database structures, how to impose *several* levels of data integrity, as well as how to relate tables together to obtain information in an almost infinite number of ways. All this will be accomplished by understanding a few key terms and by learning and using a specific set of commonsense techniques and concepts.

You'll also learn how to analyze and leverage an existing database, determine information requirements, and determine and implement business rules. These topics are important because many of you will probably inherit old databases that you'll need to revamp using what you'll learn by reading this book. These topics will be just as important when you create a new database from scratch.

When you finish reading this book, you'll have the knowledge and tools necessary to be able to create a good relational database structure. I'm confident that this entire approach will work for a majority of developers and the databases they need to create.

How to Read This Book

I strongly recommend that you read this book in sequence from beginning to end, regardless of whether you are a novice or a professional. You'll keep everything in context this way and avoid the confusion that generally comes from being unable to see the "big picture" first. It's also a good idea to learn the process as a whole before you begin to focus on any one part.

If you are reading this book to refresh your design skills, you could read just those sections that are of interest to you. As much as possible, I've tried to write each chapter so that it could stand on its own. Nonetheless, I would still recommend glancing through each of the chapters to make sure that you're not missing any new ideas or points on design that you may not have considered up to now.

How This Book Is Organized

Here's a brief overview of what you'll find in each part and each chapter.

Part One: Relational Database Design

This section provides an introduction to databases, the idea of database design, and some of the terminology you'll need to be familiar with in order to learn and understand the design process presented in this book.

Chapter 1, What Is a Relational Database? provides a brief discussion of the types of databases you'll encounter, common database models, and a brief history of the relational database.

Chapter 2, Design Objectives, explores why you should be concerned with design, points out the objectives and advantages of good design, and provides a brief discussion on Normalization and Normal Forms.

Chapter 3, Terminology, covers the terms you need to know in order to learn and understand the design methodology presented in this book.

Part Two: The Design Process

Each aspect of the database design process is discussed in detail in Part Two, including establishing table structures, assigning Primary keys, setting field specifications, establishing table relationships, setting up Views, and establishing various levels of data integrity.

Chapter 4, Conceptual Overview, provides an overview of the design process, showing you how the different components of the process fit together.

Chapter 5, Starting the Process, covers how to define a Mission Statement and Mission Objectives for the database, both of which provide you with an initial focus for creating your database.

Chapter 6: Analyzing the Current Database, covers issues concerning the existing database. We look at reasons for analyzing the current database, how to look at current methods of collecting and presenting data, why and how to conduct interviews with users and management, and how to compile initial field lists.

Chapter 7, Establishing Table Structures, describes tables, the foundation of any relational database. How to determine and define what subjects will be tracked by the database, associating fields with tables, and refining table structures—all these topics are covered in this chapter.

Chapter 8, Keys, covers the concept of keys and their importance to the design process, as well as how to define Candidate and Primary keys for each table.

Chapter 9, Field Specifications, covers a topic that is typically glossed over by a number of database developers. In this chapter you learn that along with dictating how each field is created, Field Specifications determine the very nature of the values a field contains. Topics discussed include the importance of Field Specifications, types of specification characteristics, and how to define specifications for each field in the database.

Chapter 10, Table Relationships, explains the importance of table relationships, types of relationships, setting up relationships, and establishing Relationship Characteristics.

Chapter 11, Business Rules, covers types of Business Rules, determining and establishing Business Rules, and using Validation Tables. Business Rules are very important in any database because they provide a distinct level of data integrity.

Chapter 12, Views, looks into the concept of Views and why they are important, types of Views, and how to determine and set up Views.

Chapter 13, Reviewing Data Integrity, reviews each of the levels of integrity that have been defined and discussed in previous chapters. Here you learn that it's a good idea to review the final design of the database structure to ensure that you've imposed data integrity as completely as you can.

Part Three: Other Database Design Issues

This section deals with topics such as avoiding bad design and bending the rules set forth in the design process.

Chapter 14, Bad Design—What Not To Do, covers the types of designs you should avoid, such as a flat file design and a spreadsheet design.

Chapter 15, Bending or Breaking the Rules, discusses those rare instances in which it may be necessary to stray from the techniques and concepts of the design process. This chapter tells you when you should consider bending the rules, as well as how it should be done.

IMPORTANT: READ THIS SECTION!

A Word About the Examples and Techniques in This Book

You'll notice that there are a wide variety of examples in this book. I've made sure that they are as generic and relevant as possible. However, you may have noticed that several of the examples are rather simplified, incomplete, or even on occasion incorrect. Believe it or not, I created them that way on purpose.

I've created some examples with errors so that I could illustrate specific concepts and techniques. Without these examples, you wouldn't see how the concepts or techniques are put to use, as well as the results you should expect from using them. Other examples are simple because, once again, the focus is on the technique or concept and not on the example itself. For instance, there are many ways that you can design an Order Tracking database. However, the structure of the sample Order Tracking database I use in this book is simple because the focus is specifically on the *design process,* not on creating an elaborate Order Tracking database system.

So what I'm really trying to emphasize here is this:

Focus on the concept or technique and its intended results, *not on the example used to illustrate it.*

A New Approach to Learning

Here's an approach to learning the design process (or pretty much anything else, for that matter) that I've found very useful in my database design classes.

Think of all the techniques used in the design process as a set of tools; each tool (or technique) is used for a specific purpose. The idea here is that once you learn generically how a tool is used, you can then use that tool in any number of situations. The reason you can do this is *because you use the tool the same way in each situation.*

Take a Crescent wrench, for example. Generically speaking, you use a Crescent wrench to fasten and unfasten a nut to a bolt. You open or close the jaw of the wrench to fit a given bolt by using the adjusting screw located on the head of the wrench. Now that you have that clear, try it out on a few bolts. Try it on the legs of an outdoor chair, or the valve cover on an engine, or the side panel of an outdoor cooling unit, or the hinge plates of an iron gate. Do you notice that regardless of where you encounter a nut and bolt, you can always fasten and unfasten the nut by using the Crescent wrench in the same manner?

The tools used to design a database work in *exactly* the same way. Once you understand how a tool is used generically, it will work the same way regardless of the circumstances under which it is used. For instance, consider the tool (or technique) for determining a One-to-Many relationship. Say you have a pair of tables called TABLE_A and TABLE_B. A one-to-many relationship exists between TABLE_A and TABLE_B when a single record in TABLE_A can be related to one or more records in TABLE_B (Figure I-1) and a single record in TABLE_B is related to *only one record* in TABLE_A (Figure I-2). Using this tool, you can determine whether there is a one-to-many relationship between a pair of tables.

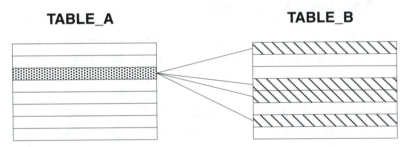

Figure I-1. *A one-to-many relationship from the viewpoint of TABLE_A.*

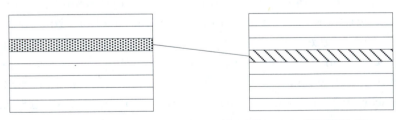

Figure I-2. *A one-to-many relationship from the viewpoint of TABLE_B.*

❖ **Note** A One-to-Many relationship is typically abbreviated as *1:N.*

❖ **Reminder** Relationships are discussed in greater detail in Chapter 10, "Table Relationships."

Now that you've learned this tool (or technique), you will find you can apply it to any pair of tables. Figure I-3 shows pairs of tables from various types of databases. As you can see, determining whether a one-to-many relationship exists between a pair of tables is performed in the same manner regardless of the type of database in which the tables reside.

Type of Database	Tables	Is there a 1:N relationship?	Reason
Order Tracking	Customers Orders	Yes	A single customer can be associated with any number of orders, but a single order is associated with only one customer.
Service Tracking	Limos Drivers	Yes	A single limousine will be assigned at most three drivers, but a single driver is assigned to only one limousine.

Type of Database	Tables	Is there a 1:N relationship?	Reason
Student Scheduling	Classes Students	No (It's a many-to-many relationship.)	A single class can have up to twenty-five students, and a single student can attend up to eight classes in a given semester.
Project Management	Managers Projects	Yes	A single manager will be assigned to several projects, but a single project is associated with only one manager

Figure I-3. *Determining One-to-Many relationships.*

All the techniques ("tools") within the design process presented in this book can be used in the same manner. You'll be able to design a sound database structure using these techniques regardless of the type of database you need to create. Remember: Focus on the concept or technique being presented and its intended results, *not on the example used to illustrate it.*

Part I

Relational Database Design

1

What Is a Relational Database?

A fish must swim three times—
in water, in butter, and in wine.
—POLISH PROVERB

Topics Covered in This Chapter

Types of Databases

Early Database Models

The Relational Database Model: A Brief History

Relational Database Management Systems

Summary

Types of Databases

There are two types of databases found in database management today, *operational databases* and *analytical databases*.

Operational databases are used in the day-to-day life of an organization, institution, or business. They are primarily used wherever there is a need to collect, maintain, and modify data. This type of database stores *dynamic* data, which means that the data changes constantly and reflects up-to-the-minute information. Examples of operational databases include inventory databases, order maintenance databases, patient-tracking databases, and periodical subscription databases.

Analytical databases, on the other hand, are used to store and track historical and time-dependent data. Whenever a business or organization needs to track trends, view statistical data over a long period of time, or make long-term projections, it will use an analytical database to store the requisite data. The data in an analytical database is *static*, meaning that the data is never (or at least rarely) modified, and the information reflected by the database is applicable to a specific point in time. Examples of analytical databases include chemical test databases, geological sample databases, and survey databases.

Early Database Models

In the days before the relational database model, two data models were commonly used to maintain and manipulate data—the *hierarchical database model* and the *network database model*.

> ❖ **Note** Although a detailed, in-depth discussion of these two models is beyond the scope of this book, I do provide a brief overview of each model here. In the overview I briefly describe how the data in each model is structured and accessed, how the relationship between a pair of tables is represented, and one or two of the advantages or disadvantages of each model.

The Hierarchical Database Model

In a hierarchical database model (hereafter referred to as an HDM), data is structured hierarchically. This model can be easily visualized as an inverted tree. In an HDM a single table will act as the "root" of the inverted tree, and other tables will act as the branches flowing from the root. Figure 1-1 shows a diagram of an HDM structure.

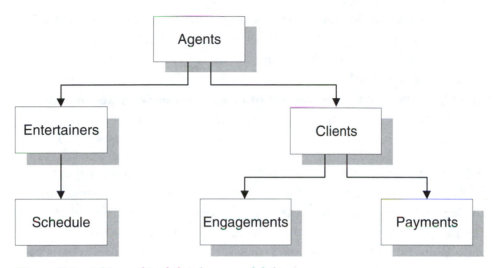

Figure 1-1. *A hierarchical database model diagram.*

Agents Database In the example shown in Figure 1-1, an agent books several entertainers, and each entertainer has his own schedule. An agent also has a number of clients whose entertainment needs are met by the agent. A client books engagements through the agent and makes payments to the agent for his services.

Relationships in an HDM are represented in terms of *parent / child.* This means that a parent table can be associated with many child tables, but a single child table can have only one parent table. These tables are explicitly linked via a *pointer* or by the physical arrangement of the records within the tables. To access any data within this model a user always needs to begin from the *root* table and work down through the tree to the target data. A user has to be very familiar with the structure of the database in order to access data in this manner.

One advantage of this type of database is that data can be retrieved very quickly because the table structures are explicitly linked. Another advantage is that *referential integrity* is built in and automatically enforced. What this basically means is that a record in a child table must be linked to an *existing* record in a parent table. It also means that if a record is deleted in a Parent table, all associated records in any child tables to which that record is linked will be deleted as well.

A problem occurs in an HDM when there is a need to store a record in a child table that is currently unrelated to any record in a parent table. In Figure 1-1, for example, a new entertainer cannot be entered in the Entertainers table until the entertainer is assigned to an agent in the Agents table. Yet it is common for an entertainer to sign up with the booking agency before a specific agent is assigned to that entertainer. This scenario is difficult to model in an HDM. However, the rules can be bent without breaking them if a "dummy" agent record is inserted in the Agents table. But this option is not really optimal.

Redundant data is another problem in the HDM because this model cannot support complex relationships. For example, in Figure 1-1 there is a many-to-many relationship between clients and entertainers; an entertainer will perform for many clients, and a client will hire many entertainers. Since this type of relationship can't be directly modeled in an HDM, redundant data must be introduced into both the Schedule table and the Engagements table. The Schedule table will have client data (such as client name, address, and phone number) to show where each entertainer is performing, but this data also (and more properly) appears in the Clients table. Likewise, the Engagements table will have data on entertainers (such as entertainer name, phone number, and type of entertainer) to show which entertainers are performing for a given client. The same data is also (and correctly) listed in the Entertainers table. The problem with this redundancy is that it opens up the possibility of entering a single piece of data inconsistently. This, in turn, can result in retrieving inaccurate information.

This problem can be solved in a roundabout manner by creating an HDM specifically for entertainers and another HDM specifically for agents. The new Entertainers database will only contain the Entertainers table and the revised Agents database will contain the Agents, Clients, Payments, and Engagements tables. The Schedule table is no longer needed in the Entertainers database because a *logical child relationship* can be defined between the Engagements table in the Agents database and the Entertainers table in the Entertainers database. With this relationship in place, information such as a list of booked entertainers for a given client or a performance schedule for a given entertainer can be produced. A diagram of the new model is shown in Figure 1-2.

Once in place, this device operates satisfactorily. But the database designer must recognize the need to build in an explicit statement of

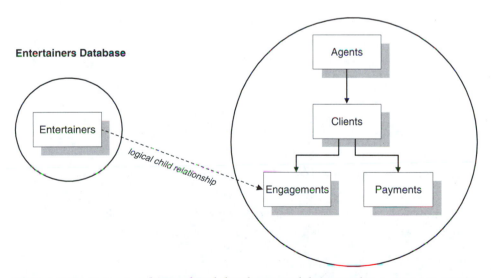

Figure 1-2. *Using two hierarchical database models to resolve a many-to-many relationship.*

this relationship. Here the need was relatively obvious, but many relationships are more obscure and may not be discovered until very late in the design process or, more disturbingly, well after the database has been put into operation.

The hierarchical database model lent itself well to the tape storage systems used by mainframes in the 1970s and was very popular in companies that used those systems. But despite the fact that the HDM provided fast and direct access to data and was a useful model in a number of circumstances, it was clear that a new database model was needed to address the problems of data redundancy and complex relationships among data.

The Network Database Model

The network database model (hereafter referred to as NDM) was in some part developed in an attempt to address some of the problems of the hierarchical database model. As with the hierarchical database model, the structure of an NDM can be visualized as an inverted tree. However, there can be several inverted trees that share branches, all of which are part of the same database structure. Figure 1-3 shows a diagram of an NDM structure.

> **Agents Database** In the example shown in Figure 1-3, an agent represents a number of clients and manages a number of entertainers. Each client schedules any number of engagements and makes payments to the agent for his or her services. Each entertainer performs a number of engagements and may play a variety of musical styles.

Relationships in an NDM are established and represented by a *set structure*. A set structure is a transparent construction that relates a

Agents Database

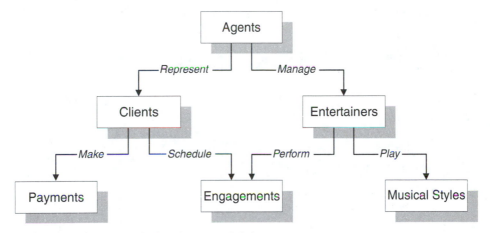

Figure 1-3. *A network database model diagram.*

pair of tables together, using one table as an *owner* and the other table as a *member*. (This is a valuable improvement on the parent/child relationship.) Set structures support a one-to-many relationship, which means that within a specific set, a record in the owner table can be related to many records in the member table, but a single record in the member table is related to *only one record* in the owner table. Also a record in the member table cannot exist *without* being related to an existing record in the owner table. For example, a client must be assigned to an agent, although an agent with no clients may still be listed. Figure 1-4 shows a diagram of a basic set structure.

Any number of sets (connections) can be defined between a specific pair of tables, and a single table can also be involved in any number of other sets with other tables in the database. In Figure 1-3, for example, the Clients table is related to the Payments table via the *Make* set structure. It is also related to the Engagements table via the *Schedule* set structure. Along with being related to the Clients table, the Engagements table is related to the Entertainers table via the *Perform* set structure.

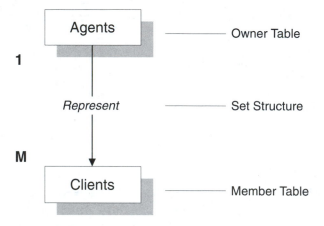

Figure 1-4. *A basic set structure.*

Data can be accessed within the NDM by working through the appropriate set structures. Unlike the hierarchical database model, where a
user must begin to access data from the root table, a user can access
data from the NDM starting from any table and work backward or forward through related sets. Consider the Agents database in Figure 1-3
once again. Say a user wants to find the agent who booked a specific
engagement. The user starts by finding the appropriate engagement
record in the Engagements table and then finding out which client
"owns" that engagement record via the *Schedule* set structure. Finally,
the user finds out which agent "owns" the client record via the *Represent* set structure. A wide variety of questions can be answered *as long
as the user navigates properly through the appropriate set structures.*

Data can be accessed very rapidly in a Network Database Model,
which is one of the model's advantages. A user can fashion more complex queries with the NDM than with the hierarchical database model.
One of the disadvantages of the NDM is that, as with the HDM, a user
has to be very familiar with the structure of the database in order to
work through the set structures. In Figure 1-3, for example, it is

incumbent on the user to be familiar with the appropriate set structures in order to find out whether a particular engagement has been paid. Another disadvantage is that it is not easy to change the database structure without affecting the application programs that interact with it. For example, relationships are explicitly defined as set structures in an NDM. A set structure cannot be changed without affecting an application program because set structures are used by the application to navigate through the data. If a set structure is changed, *all* references made from within the application program to that set structure will have to be modified.

Although the network database model was clearly a step up from the hierarchical database model, a few people in the database community believed that there must be a better way to manage and maintain large amounts of data. As each model emerged, users found that they could ask more complex questions. As the complexity of the questions increased, more demands were made on the database. And so we come to the relational database model.

The Relational Database Model: A Brief History

During the late 1960s, Dr. E. F. Codd, an IBM research scientist, was looking into new ways to handle large amounts of data. Dissatisfied with the database models and database products of the time, he had the idea that applying the disciplines and structures of mathematics to data management would help to solve many of the problems encountered when using other database models, such as data redundancy, too much dependence on physical implementation, and weak data integrity. Because he was a mathematician, it was only natural that he would take this approach.

In June of 1970 Dr. Codd presented his now landmark work titled "A Relational Model of Data for Large Shared Databanks."[*] In this work he first presented the relational database model (hereafter referred to as RDM). He based this model on two branches of mathematics—set theory and first order predicate logic. In fact, the RDM derives its name from the term "relation," which is a part of set theory. A general misconception is that the RDM derives its name from the fact that tables in the database can be "related" to one another.

In an RDM, data is stored in *relations*, which are perceived by the user as tables. Each relation is composed of *tuples*, or records, and *attributes*, or fields. (The terms "tables," "records," and "fields" will be used throughout the remainder of the book.) The physical order of the records or fields in a table is completely immaterial. Each record in the table is identified by a field that contains a unique value. These two characteristics of an RDM allow the data to exist independent of the way it is physically stored in the computer. In other words, a user isn't required to know the physical location of a record in order to retrieve its data. In this way the RDM is unlike the hierarchical and network database models, in which knowing the layout of the structures is very important if a user is going to retrieve any data. Figure 1-5 shows a diagram of an RDM structure.

> **Agents Database** In the example shown in Figure 1-5, an agent represents a number of clients and entertainers. Furthermore, clients and entertainers are associated with each other through the Engagements table, since a client will hire any number of entertainers, and an entertainer will perform for any number of clients. An entertainer may play one or more musical styles, which is reflected in the Entertainer Styles table.

---

[*]Communications of the ACM, June 1970, 377–87.

Agents Database

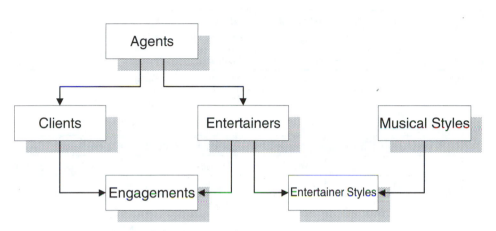

Figure 1-5. *A relational database model diagram.*

Relationships in an RDM are categorized as one-to-one, one-to-many, and many-to-many. (These relationship types are covered in detail in Chapter 10.) A relationship between a pair of tables is established implicitly through matching values of a shared field. For example, in Figure 1-6 the AGENTS table and the CLIENTS tables are related via an AGENTID field. A specific client is associated with an agent through a matching AGENTID. Likewise, the ENTERTAINERS table is related to the ENGAGEMENTS table via an EntertainerID. A record in the ENGAGEMENTS table can be associated with a record in the ENTER-TAINERS table by referring to a matching EntertainerID.

As long as a user is familiar with the relationships among the tables in the database, he can access data in an almost unlimited number of ways. He can access data from tables that are directly related as well as from tables that are indirectly related. Consider the Agents database in Figure 1-5. Although the Clients table is indirectly related to the MUSICAL STYLES table (and *very* indirectly related at that), the user can produce a list of a client's musical preferences. The user can do this easily because Musical Styles is directly related to Entertainer

Agents

Agent ID	Agent First Name	Agent Last Name	Date of Hire	Agent Home Phone
100	Mike	Hernandez	05/16/95	553-3992
101	Greg	Piercy	10/15/95	790-3992
102	Katherine	Ehrlich	03/01/96	551-4993

Clients

Client ID	Agent ID	Client First Name	Client Last Name	Client Home Phone	......
9001	100	Stewart	Jameson	553-3992	......
9002	101	Shannon	McLain	790-3992	......
9003	102	Estela	Pundt	551-4993	......

Entertainers

Entertainer ID	Agent ID	Entertainer First Name	Entertainer Last Name	......
3000	100	John	Slade	......
3001	101	Mark	Jebavy	......
3002	102	Teresa	Weiss	......

Engagements

Client ID	Entertainer ID	Engagement Date	Start Time	Stop Time
9003	3001	04/01/96	1:00 PM	3:30 PM
9009	3000	04/13/96	9:00 PM	1:30 AM
9001	3002	05/02/96	3:00 PM	6:00 PM

Figure 1-6. *Examples of related tables in an RDM.*

Styles; Entertainers is directly related to Entertainer Styles; Entertainers is directly related to Engagements; and Clients is directly related to Engagements.

You retrieve data in an RDM by specifying the appropriate fields and the table(s) to which they belong. One method of retrieving data is by using *Structured Query Language*, or *SQL*. SQL is the standard language used to create, modify, maintain, and query relational databases. For example, an SQL query like the one shown in Figure 1-7 is used to produce a list of all clients in the city of El Paso.

```
SELECT ClientLastName, ClientFirstName, ClientPhoneNumber
FROM Clients
WHERE City = "El Paso"
ORDER BY ClientLastName, ClientFirstName;
```

Figure 1-7. *A sample SQL statement.*

The three components of a basic SQL query are the SELECT . . . . . . FROM statement, the WHERE clause, and the ORDER BY clause. Fields used in the query are specified with the SELECT clause, and the table(s) to which they belong are specified with the FROM clause. Criteria is imposed against one or more fields with the WHERE clause, and the results can be sorted in any sequence with the ORDER BY clause.

Because most popular database software programs provide a graphical query-building tool, a thorough knowledge of SQL isn't too important. However, understanding the rudiments of SQL can help you get an idea of what goes on behind the scenes of the query-building tools supplied in various database software programs.

Many relational database software programs have some form of SQL implementation, whether it is used directly by the user or is "inside" the database software, creating a final query from a question built by a user with a graphical query tool. For example, Microrim's R:BASE allows a user to build and execute SQL queries directly from a command prompt in order to retrieve data. In contrast, Microsoft's Access lets a user build queries using a graphical query builder, which then generates an SQL statement that in turn retrieves the data. When the query is saved, Access also saves the SQL statement.

❖ **Note** Although a detailed discussion of Structured Query Language is beyond the scope of this book, you should understand that SQL is a language directly related to the relational database model. If you have a desire or need to study SQL, refer to Appendix A, "Recommended Reading," for a list of books on SQL.

There are a number of advantages to the relational database model, such as

- *built-in multilevel integrity.* Data integrity is built into the model at the field level to ensure the accuracy of the data; at the table level to ensure that records are not duplicated and to detect missing Primary key values; at the relationship level to ensure that the relationship between a pair of tables is valid; and at the business level to ensure that the data is accurate in terms of the business itself. (Integrity is discussed in detail as the design process unfolds.)

- *logical and physical data independence from database applications.* Neither changes a user makes to the logical design of the database nor changes made by the database software vendor to the physical implementation of the database will adversely affect the applications built upon it.

- *guaranteed data consistency and accuracy.* Data is consistent and accurate due to the various levels of integrity you can impose within the database.

- *easy data retrieval.* At the user's command, data can be retrieved either from a particular table or from any number of related tables within the database.

These and other advantages have proved beneficial to the business community and to all those who need to collect and manage data.

Indeed, the RDM has become the database of choice in many circumstances.

Until recently, one perceived disadvantage of the RDM was that software programs based on it ran very slowly. However, this was not a fault of the RDM itself, but of the ancillary technology available at the time of the model's introduction. Processing speed, memory, and storage were simply insufficient to provide the database software vendors with a platform on which to build a full implementation of the RDM. So the initial relational database software programs were not as robust and full-featured as desired, although the potential was there. Since the early 1990s, however, advances in both hardware technology and software engineering have made processing speed an insignificant issue and have allowed vendors to support the RDM more fully.

As you work through the design process presented in this book, you'll learn more information about the relational database model, such as how the tables are structured, how data integrity is established, and how relationships between pairs of tables are established.

Relational Database Management Systems

A *Relational Database Management System*, or *RDBMS*, is a software program that is used to create, maintain, modify, and manipulate a relational database. An RDBMS is also used to create the applications that users will use to interact with the data stored in the database. Of course, the quality of an RDBMS is a direct function of the extent to which it supports the relational database model. Even among "true" RDBMSs, support for the RDM varies among vendors, and there is yet to be a *full* implementation of the RDM's potential. Despite this, however, all RDBMSs are more full-featured and powerful than ever before.

Since the early 1970s, a number of RDBMS programs have been produced by a variety of software vendors. These programs have encompassed various types of computer hardware, operating systems, and programming environments. Today RDBMS programs can be found on just about any type of system and can be used under a wide variety of circumstances.

In the earliest days of the relational database model, RDBMSs were written for use on mainframe computers. (Didn't *everything* start on a mainframe?) Two of the RDBMS programs that could be found in the early 1970s were System R, developed by IBM at its San Jose Research Laboratory in California, and INGRES (*In*teractive *G*raphics *R*etrieval *S*ystem), developed at the University of California at Berkeley. These two RDBMS programs contributed greatly to the general appreciation of the relational database model.

As the benefits of the RDM became more widely known, many companies decided to make a slow move from hierarchical and network database models to the relational database model, thus creating a need for more and better mainframe RDBMS programs. The 1980s saw the development of various commercial RDBMSs for mainframe computers, such as Oracle, developed by Oracle Corporation, and IBM's DB2.

The early to mid-1980s saw the rise of the personal computer, and with it the development of PC-based RDBMSs. Some of the early entries in this category, such as dBase by Ashton-Tate and FoxPro from Fox Software, were nothing more than basic file-based database management systems. True PC-based RDBMSs began to emerge with the introduction of R:BASE, developed by Microrim, and Paradox, originally developed by Ansa Software. Each of these products helped to spread the idea and potential of database management from the mainframe-dominated domain of IS departments to the desktop of the common end user.

As more and more users worked with databases throughout the late 1980s and early 1990s, the need to share data became apparent. The concept of centrally located, common data available to any number of users seemed to be a very promising idea. Besides enhancing speed, having data in a centralized location would also make data management and security much easier. Database vendors filled this need by developing *client / server* RDBMSs.

Under this type of RDBMS, the data resides on a computer acting as a *database server,* and users interact with the data through applications located on their own local PC, or *database client.* Both data integrity and data security can be implemented on the database server, thus allowing a variety of user applications to be based and built on the same set of data without affecting the data's integrity or security. Both the database and the database applications are created and maintained by the client / server RDBMS software.

Client / server RDBMSs are now widely used to manage large volumes of shared data. Some of the more recent entries in the client / server RDBMS category are Microsoft SQL Server, from Microsoft Corporation; Oracle 7 Cooperative Server, from Oracle Corporation; and Sybase System 11 SQL Server, from Sybase.

Relational database management systems now have a long history, and they continue to play a huge role in the way people, businesses, and organizations interact with their data. It is inevitable that these programs will expand their influence in the near future by integrating the services they provide with the services provided by the Internet.

Summary

We opened this chapter by defining the two categories of databases currently used in database management, operational databases and analytical databases.

We then briefly discussed the hierarchical database model and the network database model. Our discussion covered the data structures, relationships, and data access methods used in both models, as well as their chief disadvantages. These models were widely used in the early days of database management and led to the eventual development and introduction of the relational database model.

Next we provided a detailed discussion of the relational database model, its history and features. We noted that it is based on specific branches of mathematics, and that this mathematical foundation is what makes the model so structurally sound. Then we explored the model's data structures and relationships, as well as the role of SQL in accessing data within the model. You'll remember, no doubt, that SQL is the standard language used to work with relational databases. We ended this section by reviewing the advantages the relational database model provides.

We closed this chapter with a short discussion of relational database management systems, or RDBMSs. We presented a brief history of the RDBMS, beginning with the mainframe systems of the early 1970s and progressing through the PC-based systems of the 1980s and the client/server systems of the 1990s. At this point you should have a sense of the progression of circumstances that have lead to the development of the robust systems we use today.

2

Design Objectives

Everything factual is, in a sense, theory.
The blue of the sky exhibits the basic
laws of chromatics. There is no sense
in looking for something behind
phenomena; they are theory.
*—*GOETHE

Topics Covered in This Chapter

Why Should You Be Concerned with Database Design?

The Importance of Theory

The Advantage of Learning Good Design Methodology

Objectives of Good Design

Advantages of Good Design

Database Design Methods

Summary

Why Should You Be Concerned with Database Design?

A number of people who work with RDBMS software programs seem to wonder why they should be concerned with database design. After all, most of the RDBMS programs come with sample databases that can be copied and modified to suit a specific set of needs, and tables within the sample databases can even be cut and pasted into a new database. There are even some programs that come with "Wizards" or "Experts," which are tools that walk a user through the process of defining and creating tables. However, these tools don't actually help you *design* a database—they merely help you create the physical tables that you will include in the database.

What most people don't seem to understand is that these tools are best used *after the database has been logically designed*. Tools such as the "Wizards" and the sample databases are provided to minimize the time it takes to *implement* the database structure physically. The idea is that by cutting the time it takes to implement the database structure once the logical design has been created there will be more time to focus on creating and building the applications that will be used to interact with the data in the database.

Yet, the reason to be concerned with database design is that it's crucial to the consistency, integrity, and accuracy of the data in a database. If a database is designed improperly, users will have difficulty in retrieving certain types of information, and there is the added risk that searches will produce inaccurate information. *Inaccurate information is probably the most detrimental result of improper database design. It can adversely affect the bottom line of a business.* In fact, if the data kept and used in a database is going to affect the way a business performs its day-to-day operations or if it's going to influence the future direction of the business, database design *must* be a concern.

Let's put this in a different perspective for a moment. Say our database is like a custom home and that we are going to have one built for us. What's the first thing we're going to do? Certainly we're not going to hire a contractor immediately and let him build our home however he wishes. *Surely* we will first engage an architect to design our new home *and then* hire a contractor to build it. The architect will express our needs as a set of blueprints, recording decisions about size and shape, and requirements for various systems (structural, mechanical, electrical). Next the contractor will procure the labor and materials, including the listed systems, and then assemble them according to the drawings and specifications.

Now let's return to our database perspective and think of the logical database design as the architectural blueprints and the physical database implementation as the completed home. The logical database design describes the size, shape, and necessary systems for a database; it addresses the informational needs and operational needs of our business. We then build the physical implementation of the logical database design, using our RDBMS software program. Once we've created our tables, set up table relationships, and established the appropriate levels of data integrity, our database is complete. Now we're ready to create applications that allow us to interact easily with the data stored in the database, and we can be confident that these applications will provide us with timely and, above all, accurate information.

It is possible to implement a poor design in an RDBMS, but a well designed database will yield accurate information, store data more efficiently and effectively, and will be easier to manage and maintain.

The Importance of Theory

In this chapter, "theory" is used in its primary sense to mean "general propositions used as principles." The word is not used in the colloquial sense of "conjecture or proposal."

A number of major disciplines (and their associated design methodologies) have some type of theoretical bases. Structural engineers design an unlimited variety of structures using the theories of physics. Composers create beautiful symphonies and orchestral pieces using the concepts found in music theory. The automobile industry uses aerodynamics theories to design more fuel-efficient automobiles. The airplane industry uses the same theories to design airplane wings that reduce wind drag.

These examples demonstrate that theory is relevant and very important. The chief advantage of theory is that it makes things predictable; it allows us to predict what will happen if we perform a certain action or series of actions. We know if we drop a stone, it will fall to the ground. If we are agile, we can get our toes out of the way of Newton's theory of gravitation. The point is, it works *every time*. If we chisel a stone flat and place it on another flat stone, we can predict it will stay where we put it. This theory allows us to design pyramids and cathedrals and brick outhouses. Now consider a database example. We know that if a pair of tables shares a relationship, we can draw data from both tables simultaneously simply because of the way relational database theory works. The data drawn from both tables will be based on matching values of a shared field between the tables themselves. Again, our actions have a predictable result.

The relational database model is based on the branches of mathematics known as set theory and first order predicate logic. The fact that it is based on established mathematical theory makes the RDM so structurally sound and able to guarantee accurate information. At the same time, these branches of mathematics provide the building blocks necessary to create a good relational database structure as well as the guidelines that are used to formulate good design methodologies.

There is an understandable reluctance to study complicated mathematical concepts simply to carry out a rather limited task. Therefore, it is common to hear claims that the mathematical theories on which RDM and its associated design methodologies are based don't have any relevance to the "real world," or that they are somehow "impractical." This is not true: math is central to the relational database model. But cheer up—the fact of the matter is that it isn't necessary to learn anything about set theory or first order predicate logic in order to use a relational database! That would be like saying it's absolutely essential to know all the details of aerodynamics just to drive an automobile. Aerodynamic theories may help one understand and appreciate how an automobile can get better gas mileage, but it's certainly not necessary in order to operate the vehicle.

Mathematical theory provides the foundation for the relational database model, and thus makes the model predictable, reliable, and sound. Theory describes the basic building blocks used to create a relational database and provides guidelines on how it should be arranged. Arranging building blocks to achieve a desired result is defined as "design."

The Advantage of Learning Good Design Methodology

You could learn how to design a database properly by trial and error, but it would take you a very long time, and you would probably have to repair many mistakes along the way. There are at least three main advantages to learning a good design methodology. First and foremost, it will give you the skills you need to design a sound database structure. Second, a good design methodology will provide you with an organized set of techniques that will guide you step-by-step through the design process. Third, learning and following a design methodology keeps your missteps and design reiterations to a minimum. Of course, you will naturally make some mistakes when you're designing a database, but a good methodology lets you recognize the errors before you've made a major investment of time in them.

The Importance of Understanding Database Design

Aside from making design easier and faster, a good methodology improves the end product—the database itself. First, a well-designed database allows you to retrieve information in an almost unlimited number of ways. Second, with your improved comprehension of the database design, you will be able to understand and use your RDBMS software more fully. The more you understand how a database is designed and used, the more you'll understand *why* a given element is provided in the RDBMS and *how* it is used to help implement the database structure within the RDBMS.

Third, a large number of data processing problems can be attributed to the presence of redundant data, duplicate data, and invalid data, or the absence of required data. All of these problems produce erroneous information and make certain queries and reports difficult to run. Most, if not all, of these problems can be easily avoided if you design the database properly from the beginning.

Objectives of Good Design

There are distinct objectives you'll want to achieve in order to design a good, sound database structure. If you keep these objectives in mind and constantly focus on them while you're designing your database, you'll avoid many of the problems previously mentioned.

To design a database properly, you must ensure that it

- *supports required and ad hoc information retrieval.* Information requirements and possible ad hoc information requests are determined during the design process, and the database must store the data necessary to support those requirements and requests.

- *contains efficiently constructed table structures.* Each of the tables in the database describes only one subject, has relatively distinct fields, contains an absolute minimum amount of redundant data, and is identified by a field with unique values.

- *imposes data integrity at the field, table, and relationship levels.* Once you have established these levels of integrity, data structures and their values will be valid and accurate at all times.

- *supports appropriate Business Rules.* The data provides valid and accurate information that is always meaningful to the business.

- *lends itself to future growth.* The database structure will be easy to modify or expand as the information requirements of the business change and grow.

Advantages of Good Design

The time you invest in designing a sound database structure is time well spent. Achieving the objectives associated with good design *saves* you time in the long run because you do not have to constantly revamp a quickly and poorly designed structure. There are several advantages to be gained from taking the time to design a database properly.

Once you have created a well-designed database

- *it is easy to modify and maintain the structure.* Modifications made to a field or table will not adversely affect other fields or tables in the database.

- *it is easy to modify data.* Changes made to the value of a given field in a table do not adversely affect the values of other fields within the table. In a well-defined structure, changes made to a specific value need only be made in one location.

- *it is easy to retrieve information.* Tables are well constructed, and any relationships between them are properly established.

- *it is easy to develop and build user applications.* Programming time can be spent addressing the data manipulation tasks at hand instead of working around the inevitable problems that arise when working with a poorly designed database.

Database Design Methods

Traditional Design Methods

In general, traditional methods of database design involve three phases: a *requirements analysis* phase, a *data modeling* phase, and a *normalization* phase.

The *requirements analysis* phase involves examining the business being modeled, interviewing users and management to assess the current system and to analyze future needs, and determining information requirements for the business as a whole. This process is relatively straightforward, and, indeed, the design process presented in this book follows the same line of thinking.

The *data modeling* phase involves modeling the database structure itself. This involves using a data modeling method such as entity relationship diagramming (ER diagramming), semantic object modeling, or object role modeling. Each of these modeling methods provides a means of visually representing various aspects of the database structure, such as the tables, table relationships, and relationship characteristics. In fact, the modeling method used in this book is a basic version of ER diagramming. Figure 2-1 shows an example of a basic ER diagram.

> ❖ **Note** In this book, the data modeling method is incorporated into the design process itself rather than being considered separately. Each modeling technique will be explained in conjunction with its associated design technique.

The diagram in Figure 2-1 represents several aspects of the database. First, it conveys the fact that there are two tables in this database, one called Agents and the other called Clients; each of the tables is represented by a rectangle. The diamond represents the fact that there is a relationship between these two tables, and the "1:N" within the diamond indicates that the relationship is a one-to-many relationship. Finally, the diagram conveys the fact that a client must be associated with an agent (indicated by the vertical line next to the AGENTS table), but an agent doesn't necessarily have to be associated with a client (as indicated by the circle next to the CLIENTS table).

Fields are also defined and associated with the appropriate tables during the data modeling phase. Tables are assigned *Primary keys*, various levels of data integrity are determined and implemented, and relationships are established by assigning appropriate *Foreign keys*. Once the initial table structures are complete and the relationships have been established according to the data model, the database is ready to go through the normalization phase.

Agent–Client

Figure 2-1. *An example of a basic ER diagram.*

Normalization is the process of decomposing large tables into smaller tables in order to eliminate redundant data and duplicate data, and to avoid problems with inserting, updating, or deleting data. During the normalization process, table structures are tested against *normal forms,* and modified if any of the aforementioned problems are found. A normal form is a specific set of rules that can be used to test a table structure to ensure that the structure is sound and free of problems. There are a number of normal forms, each one used to test for a specific set of problems. The normal forms currently in use are *First Normal Form* through *Fifth Normal Form, Boyce-Codd Normal Form,* and *Domain / Key Normal Form.*

The Design Method Presented in This Book

The design method presented in this book incorporates a requirements analysis. It uses a simple ER Diagramming method to diagram the database structure. It does *not* use the traditional normalization process of using normal forms. The reason is simple: normal forms can be confusing to anyone who has not taken the time to study formal relational database theory. For example, examine the following definition of Third Normal Form:

> A *relation* is in third normal form (3NF) if and only if, for all time, each *tuple* consists of a *primary key* value that identifies some *entity,* together with a set of zero or more mutually independent *attribute* values that describe that entity in some way.[*]

Unless the reader understands the terms "relation," "tuple," "primary key," "entity," and "attribute," this description is relatively meaningless.

---

[*]*An Introduction to Database Systems* 6th ed. C.J. Date, 1995, 296; emphasis added.

The process of designing a database is not and should not be hard to understand. As long as the process is presented in a straightforward manner and each concept or technique is clearly explained, anyone should be able to design a database properly. For example, most people will find the following definition clear and easy to understand:

> A table should have a field that uniquely identifies each of its records, and each field in the table should describe the subject that the table represents.

This definition is derived from the *results* of using Third Normal Form against a table structure. The design process presented in this book uses this same type of technique to translate the traditional normalization processes into a series of concepts and rules that are easy to understand and apply. These concepts and rules are integrated throughout the entire design process and help to ensure that you learn to design a database properly.

Summary

At the beginning of this chapter we looked at the importance of being concerned with database design. You now understand that database design is crucial to the integrity and consistency of the data contained in a database. We have seen that the chief problem resulting from improper or poor design is *inaccurate information*. Adequate design is of paramount concern because bad design can adversely affect the information used by an organization.

Next we entered into a discussion on the importance of theory as well as the relevance of theory to the relational database model. You learned that the model's foundation in mathematical theory makes it a very sound and reliable structure.

Following this discussion, we looked at the advantages gained by learning a design methodology. Among other things, using a good methodology yields an efficient and reliable database structure. We sharpened our focus from "concern" to "understanding," and as we looked at the importance of understanding database design, you learned that a solid comprehension of design allows you to avoid the typical problems that result from poor design.

Next we listed the objectives of good design. Meeting these objectives is crucial to the success of the database design process because they help you ensure that the database structure is sound. We then enumerated the advantages of good design, and you learned that the time you invest in designing a sound database structure is time well spent.

We closed this chapter with a short discussion of traditional database design methods and an explanation of the premise behind the design method presented in this book. By now, you understand that traditional design methods are complex and will take some time to learn and comprehend. On the other hand, while the design method used in this book is based on traditional relational database theory, it is presented in a clear and straightforward manner.

3

Terminology

*"When I use a word," Humpty Dumpty
said in rather a scornful tone, "it means
just what I choose it to mean—
neither more nor less."*
—LEWIS CARROLL
"THROUGH THE LOOKING GLASS"

Topics Covered in This Chapter

Why This Terminology Is Important

Value-related Terms

Structure-related Terms

Relationship-related Terms

Integrity-related Terms

Summary

Why This Terminology Is Important

Relational database design has its own unique set of terms just as any
other profession, trade, or discipline does. Learning this terminology is
important because

- *it is used to express and define the special ideas and concepts
  of the relational database model.* Much of the terminology is
  derived from the mathematical branches of set theory and

first order predicate logic, which form the basis of the relational database model.

- *it is used to express and define the database design process itself.* A number of terms are used to help define certain steps within the design process, and knowing them makes this process clearer and easier to understand.

- *it is used anywhere a relational database or RDBMS is discussed.* This terminology is used in such publications as educational course materials, trade magazine articles, RDBMS software manuals, and commercial RDBMS software books, as well as in conversations between practitioners.

Each term in this chapter is defined and then discussed in some detail. Pertinent details or further discussion of a given term will be added later, at the point where the term is expressly used within a specific technique in the design process.

A majority of the terms used to define the ideas and concepts of the design process are included here. But there are a few terms that are introduced and discussed later in the book, because they are more easily understood within the context of the specific idea or concept to which they are related.

Four categories of terms are defined in this chapter: *value-related*, *structure-related*, *relationship-related*, and *integrity-related*.

Value-related Terms

Data

Data are the values that are stored in the database. Data are static in the sense that they remain in the same state until they are modified by some manual or automated process. For example, consider the data shown in Figure 3-1.

```
George Edleman   92883   05/16/96   95.00
```

Figure 3-1. *An example of basic data.*

On the surface, this data is meaningless. We cannot learn, simply by inspection, what "92883" represents. Is it a zip code? Is it a part number? Even if we know it represents a service code, is it a code associated with George Edleman? There's just no way of knowing until the data is processed.

Information

Information is data that has been processed in a way that makes it meaningful and therefore useful to the person working with or viewing it. Information is dynamic in the sense that it constantly changes relative to the data stored in the database, and also in the sense that it can be processed in an unlimited number of ways.

Figure 3-2 shows the data from the previous example but processed and transformed into information. The data has been manipulated in such a way—in this case as part of a Patient Invoice report—that it is now meaningful to anyone who views it.

Information can be presented in a variety of forms. It can be shown as the result of a query, displayed on an on-screen form, or printed on a variety of reports. But the point to remember is that *data must be processed in some manner in order to become meaningful.*

It is very important to understand the difference between data and information. A database is designed to provide meaningful *information* to someone within a business or organization. This information can be provided only if the appropriate *data* exists in the database and the

Eastside Medical Clinic	Patient Name:	George Edelman
7743 Kingman Dr.	Patient ID:	10884
Seattle, WA 98032		
(206) 555-9982	Visit Date:	05/16/96
	Physician:	Daniel Chavez

Doctors Services	Service Code	Fee		Nursing Services	Service Code	Fee
[X] Consultation	92883	119.00	[ ]	R.N. Exam	89327	
[X] EKG	92773	95.00	[ ]	Supplies	82372	
[ ] Physical	98377		[ ]	Nurse Instruction	88332	
[ ] Ultrasound	97399		[ ]	Insurance Report	81368	

Figure 3-2. *An example of data transformed into information.*

database is structured in such a way to support that information. When this concept is fully understood, the logic behind the database design process becomes crystal clear.

> ❖ **Note** Unfortunately, *data* and *information* are two terms that are frequently used interchangeably throughout the database industry. This error is found in numerous trade magazines and commercial database books; the terms are even used erroneously by authors who should know better.

Null

Whenever a value is missing or unknown, it is said to be *Null*. A null value represents neither zero (in the case of numeric data) nor blank (represented by one or more spaces in the case of textual data). Zero

Clients

Client ID	Client First Name	Client Last Name	Client City	Client County	State	.....
9001	Stewart	Jameson	Seattle	King	WA	.....
9002	Shannon	McLain	Poulsbo		WA	.....
9003	Estela	Pundt	Fremont	Alameda	CA	.....
9004	Timothy	Ennis	Bellevue	King	WA	.....
9005	Marvin	Russo	Washington		DC	.....
9006	Kendra	Bonnicksen	Portland		OR	.....

Figure 3-3. *An example of null values.*

and blank are actual values and can be meaningful in some way under certain circumstances. For example, a zero can represent the current state of an ACCOUNT BALANCE; a blank in a MIDDLE INITIAL field can represent the fact that an employee has no middle initial in his or her name. In Figure 3-3, a blank represents the fact that Washington, D.C., is not located in any county whatsoever.

A null value is typically used to represent an unknown value in a field. In Figure 3-3, for example, there are null values in the COUNTY field. Shannon McLain did not know what county she lived in at the time her data was entered into the database, so no entry was made into the COUNTY field. As a result, the COUNTY field contains a null value. This value can be changed, however, once Shannon finds out what county she lives in.

A null value is also used to represent a missing value in a field. If the person who entered the data for Shannon McLain failed to ask her for the name of the county she lives in, the data is considered *missing* since no entry was made into the COUNTY field due to operator error. Once the error is recognized, it can be easily corrected by obtaining the appropriate value from Ms. McLain.

Products

Product ID	Product Desc	Category	SRP	Qty On Hand	Total Value
70001	Shur-Lok U-Lock	Accessories	75.00		
70002	SpeedRite Cyclecomputer		65.00	20	1,300.00
70003	SteelHead Microshell Helmet	Accessories	36.00	33	1,118.00
70004	SureStop 133-MB Brakes	Components	23.50	16	376.00
70005	Diablo ATM Mountain Bike	Bikes	1,200.00		
70006	UltraVision Helmet Mount Mirrors		7.45	10	74.50

Figure 3-4. *Nulls used in a mathematical expression.*

A drawback to null values is that they cannot be evaluated by mathematical expressions or aggregate functions. If a null value is used in a mathematical expression, that expression will evaluate to Null. In Figure 3-4, TOTAL VALUE is derived from the mathematical expression "[SRP] * [QTY ON HAND]." Note, however, that the value for the TOTAL VALUE field is missing where the QTY ON HAND value is Null, resulting in a null value for the TOTAL VALUE field as well. This is logically reasonable—if the number is unknown, the value will necessarily be unknown. Also there is a serious *undetected* error that occurs if all the values in the TOTAL VALUE field are then added together: an inaccurate total. The only way to obtain an accurate total is to provide a value for the entries in the QTY ON HAND field that are currently Null.

The result of an aggregate function, such as "COUNT()," will be Null if it is based on a field that contains null values. For example, Figure 3-5 shows the results of a summary query that counts the total number of occurrences of each category in the PRODUCTS table shown above. The value of TOTAL OCCURRENCES in the summary query is the result of the function expression "COUNT([TOTAL OCCURRENCES])." Notice that the summary query shows 0 occurrences of an unspecified Category, implying that each product has been assigned a category. This information is clearly inaccurate because there are two products in the PRODUCTS table that *have not* been assigned a category.

Category Summary

Category	Total Occurrences
	0
Accessories	2
Bikes	1
Components	1

Figure 3-5. *Nulls used in an aggregate function.*

The issues of missing values, unknown values, and whether a value will be used in a mathematical expression or aggregate function are all taken into consideration in the database design process, and we will revisit and further discuss these issues in later chapters.

Structure-related Terms

Table

A *table* (known as a *relation* in relational database theory) is the chief structure in a relational database. It is composed of *fields* and *records*, the order of which is completely unimportant. A table always represents a single, specific subject, which can be either an object or an event. A typical table structure is shown in Figure 3-6.

When a table represents an *object*, it represents *something that is tangible*, such as a person, place, or thing. An object has a set of characteristics that can be stored as data, which can then be processed as information in a variety of ways. Examples of objects include vendors, customers, products, patients, materials, components, properties, and locations. The table in Figure 3-6 is an example of a table that represents an object (client).

Clients

Client ID	Client First Name	Client Last Name	Client City	.....
9001	Stewart	Jameson	Seattle	.....
9002	Shannon	McLain	Poulsbo	.....
9003	Estela	Pundt	Tacoma	.....
9004	Timothy	Ennis	Seattle	.....
9005	Marvin	Russo	Bellingham	.....
9006	Kendra	Bonnicksen	Tacoma	.....

Records

Fields

Figure 3-6. *A typical table structure.*

When the subject of a table is an *event*, it represents *something that occurs at a specific point in time.* Facts about the event, like the characteristics of an object, can be stored as data and processed later as information. Examples of events include appointments, transactions, inquiries, sales, visits, and transfers. Figure 3-7 shows a table that represents an event.

Patient Visit

Patient ID	Visit Date	Visit Time	Physician	Blood Pressure	.....
92001	05/01/96	10:30	Hernandez	120 / 80	.....
97002	05/01/96	13:00	Piercy	112 / 74	.....
99014	05/02/96	09:30	Rolson	120 / 80	.....
96105	05/02/96	11:00	Hernandez	160 / 90	.....
96203	05/02/96	14:00	Hernandez	110 / 75	.....
98003	05/03/96	09:30	Rolson	120 / 80	.....

Figure 3-7. *A table representing an event.*

Categories

Category ID	Category
10000	Accessories
20000	Bikes
30000	Clothing
40000	Components

Figure 3-8. *An example of a validation table.*

A table that stores data used to supply information is called a *data table*; it is the most common type of table in a relational database. Data in this type of table is dynamic because it is manipulated (modified, deleted, and so forth) and processed into information in some form or fashion. Users constantly interact with these types of tables while performing their work on a day-to-day basis.

When a table holds data specifically used to implement data integrity, it is known as a *validation table*. A validation table usually represents subjects such as city names, skill categories, product codes, and project identification numbers. Data in this type of table is static because it will very rarely change at all. Although there is very little *direct* user interaction with these tables, these tables are frequently used indirectly to validate values that a user customarily enters into a data table. Figure 3-8 shows an example of a validation table.

Validation tables are discussed in more detail in Chapter 11, "Business Rules."

Field

A *field* (known as an *attribute* in relational database theory) is the smallest structure in a relational database. A field is used to store data in the database and it represents a characteristic of the subject of the

Clients

| | | Calculated Field | | Multipart Field | Multivalued Field |

Client ID	Client First Name	Client Last Name	Client Full Name	Address	Client City, State, Zip	Account Rep
9001	Stewart	Jameson	Stewart Jameson	.....	Seattle, WA 98125	John, Sandi
9002	Shannon	McLain	Shannon McLain	.....	Poulsbo, WA 98370	Frits
9003	Estela	Pundt	Estela Pundt	.....	Bellevue, WA 98005	John
9004	Timothy	Ennis	Timothy Ennis	.....	Seattle, WA 98115	Frits, Sandi
9005	Marvin	Russo	Marvin Russo	.....	Bellingham, WA 98225	Frits, John
9006	Kendra	Bonnicksen	Kendra Bonnicksen	.....	Olympia, WA 98504	Sandi

Figure 3-9. *A table containing regular, calculated, multipart, and multivalued fields.*

table in which the field resides. If a field contains more than one type of *distinct* value, it is considered a *multipart* field; a field that contains multiple instances of the *same* type of value is considered a *multivalued* field. A field that contains a concatenated string value or the result of a mathematical expression is called a *calculated* field. Figure 3-9 shows a table with an example of each of these types of fields.

Calculated, multipart, and multivalued fields will be discussed in greater detail in Chapter 7, "Establishing Table Structures."

Record

A *record* (known as a *tuple* in relational database theory) is a structure within a table that represents a unique instance of the subject of the table. It is composed of the entire set of fields in a table, regardless of whether or not the fields contain any values. In Figure 3-9, for example, "Timothy Ennis" represents a unique instance of the subject "Clients." Ennis's record, then, is the total collection of fields, treated as a unit. The values of those fields represent relevant facts about Ennis that are important to someone in the organization.

View

A *View* is a *virtual table* that is composed of the fields of one or more data or validation tables. A View is considered "virtual" because it doesn't store any data on its own; instead it draws its data from the tables on which it is based. Views are commonly implemented as *saved queries* in a majority of RDBMS programs. Figure 3-10 shows an example of a View.

Students

Student ID	Student First Name	Student Last Name	Student Phone	...
60003	Zachary	Erlich	553-3992	...
60928	Susan	McLain	790-3992	...
60765	Joe	Rosales	551-4993	...

Instruments

Instrument ID	Student ID	Instrument Type	Instrument Desc	...
11128	60003	Guitar	Stratocaster	...
11185	60928	Drums	Ludwig Pro	...
11147	60765	Guitar	Les Paul	...

Student Instruments (View)

Student First Name	Student Last Name	Instrument Desc
Zachary	Erlich	Stratocaster
Susan	McLain	Ludwig Pro
Joe	Rosales	Les Paul

Figure 3-10. *An example of a View.*

In this example, the STUDENT INSTRUMENTS View is composed of fields taken from both the STUDENTS table and the INSTRUMENTS table. Data displayed in the View is drawn from both tables simultaneously, based on matching values between the STUDENT ID field in the STUDENTS table and the STUDENT ID field in the INSTRUMENTS table.

Views are important for at least three reasons. First, they allow you to draw data from multiple tables. (In order for a View to draw data from multiple tables, it is necessary for the tables to have connections, or *relationships*, to each other.) Second, Views are important because they provide a means of preventing specified fields within a table (or group of tables) from being manipulated or seen by certain users. This capability can be very advantageous in terms of security. Third, views can be used to implement data integrity; this type of View is known as a *Validation View*. Designing and using Views is discussed in greater detail in Chapter 12, "Views."

Keys

Keys are special fields that serve specific purposes within a table, and the *type* of key determines its use within the table. For example, a *Primary key* is a field that *uniquely identifies* a record within a table. Another type is a *Foreign key*, which is a field that is used to *establish a relationship* between a pair of tables. Figure 3-11 shows an example of each of these types of key fields.

In Figure 3-11, AGENT ID is the Primary key of AGENTS because it uniquely identifies each record in that table. Likewise, CLIENT ID is the Primary key of CLIENTS because it uniquely identifies each of the table's records. In contrast, the AGENT ID field in the CLIENTS table is a Foreign key because it is used to establish a relationship between the CLIENTS table and the AGENTS table.

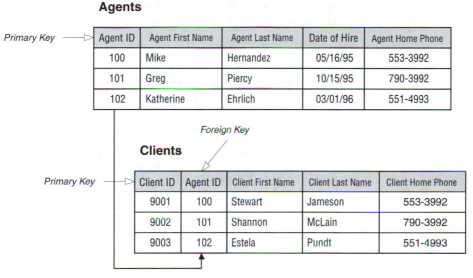

Figure 3-11. *An example of Primary and Foreign key fields.*

Key fields are a very important part of a relational database because they help to establish various levels of data integrity, and they are used to establish relationships between tables. Primary keys are discussed in greater detail in Chapter 8, "Keys," and Foreign keys are discussed in Chapter 10, "Table Relationships."

Index

An *index* is a structure within an RDBMS that is used to improve data processing. The way an index is used and how it works is strictly dependent on the RDBMS program. However, *an index has absolutely nothing to do with the logical database structure!* The only reason that the term *index* is mentioned here is because it is very often confused with the term *key*.

Unfortunately, *key* and *index* are two terms that are frequently used interchangeably throughout the database industry, yet another major error that is found in numerous trade magazines and commercial database books. (Remember *data* and *information*?) The best way to remember the difference between the two is that keys are *logical structures* used to identify records within a table, and indexes are *physical structures* used to optimize data processing.

Relationship-related Terms

Relationships

A connection established between a pair of tables is known as a *relationship*. A relationship exists when a pair of tables is connected by a Primary key and a Foreign key (as shown in Figure 3-11) or is linked together by a third table, known as a *linking table*. Figure 3-12 shows a relationship established between two tables through a linking table.

Relationships are very important to data integrity because they help reduce redundant data and duplicate data. They also provide the means to define views.

Every relationship can be characterized by the *type of relationship* that exists between the tables, the *type of participation* each table has within the relationship, and the *degree of participation* each table has within the relationship.

Types of Relationships

When two tables are related, there is always a specific *type of relationship* (traditionally known as *cardinality*) that exists between them. There are three possible types of relationships: *one-to-one*, *one-to-many*, and *many-to-many*.

Students

Student ID	Student First Name	Student Last Name	Student Phone	..
60003	Zachary	Erlich	553-3992	...
60928	Susan	McLain	790-3992	...
60765	Joe	Rosales	551-4993	...

Student Schedule *(linking table)*

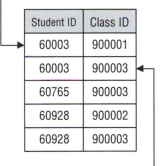

Student ID	Class ID
60003	900001
60003	900003
60765	900003
60928	900002
60928	900003

Classes

Class ID	Class Name	Instructor ID	....
900001	Intro. to Political Science	220087	...
900002	Adv. Music Theory	220039	...
900003	American History	220148	...

Figure 3-12. *A relationship established between two tables with the help of a linking table.*

One-to-One Relationships

A *one-to-one* relationship exists between a pair of tables if a single record in the first table is related to *only* one record in the second table, and a single record in the second table is related to *only* one record in the first table. Figure 3-13 shows an example of a one-to-one relationship involving an EMPLOYEES table and a COMPENSATION table. In this example, a single record in the EMPLOYEES table is related to only one record in the COMPENSATION table; likewise, a single record in the COMPENSATION table is related to only one record in the EMPLOYEES table.

Employees

Employee ID	Employee First Name	Employee Last Name	Home Phone	...
100	Zachary	Erlich	553-3992	...
101	Susan	McLain	790-3992	...
102	Joe	Rosales	551-4993	...

Compensation

Employee ID	Hourly Rate	Commission Rate	...
100	25.00	5.0 %	...
101	19.75	3.5 %	...
102	22.50	5.0 %	...

Figure 3-13. *An example of a one-to-one relationship.*

One-to-Many Relationships

A *one-to-many* relationship exists between a pair of tables if a *single* record in the first table can be related to *one or more* records in the second table, but a *single* record in the second table can be related to *only one* record in the first table. A one-to-many relationship involving a STUDENTS table and an INSTRUMENTS table is shown in Figure 3-14. In this case, a single record in the STUDENTS table can be related to one or more records in the INSTRUMENTS table, but a single record in the INSTRUMENTS table is related to only one record in the STUDENTS table.

This is by far the most common relationship that exists between a pair of tables in a database. A one-to-many relationship is very important because it helps to eliminate duplicate data and to keep redundant data to an absolute minimum.

Students

Student ID	Student First Name	Student Last Name	Student Phone	...
60003	Zachary	Erlich	553-3992	...
60928	Susan	McLain	790-3992	...
60765	Joe	Rosales	551-4993	...

Instruments

Instrument ID	Student ID	Instrument Type	Instrument Desc	...
11128	60003	Guitar	Stratocaster	...
11185	60765	Drums	Ludwig Pro	...
11147	60765	Guitar	Les Paul	...

Figure 3-14. *An example of a one-to-many relationship.*

Many-to-Many Relationships

A *many-to-many* relationship exists between a pair of tables if a *single* record in the first table can be related to *one or more* records in the second table, *and* a *single* record in the second table can be related to *one or more* records in the first table. Figure 3-15 shows a classic many-to-many relationship. In this example, a single record in the STUDENTS table can be related to one or more records in the CLASSES table; likewise, a single record in the CLASSES table can be related to one or more records in the STUDENTS table.

Establishing a direct connection between these two tables is difficult because it will produce a large amount of redundant data in one of the tables. There is also a problem with inserting, updating, and deleting data in this type of relationship. However, these problems can be surmounted, and the solution is provided in Chapter 10, "Table Relationships."

Students

Student ID	Student First Name	Student Last Name	Student Phone	...
60003	Zachary	Erlich	553-3992	...
60928	Susan	McLain	790-3992	...
60765	Joe	Rosales	551-4993	...

Classes

How do you show which students attend a specific class? It's difficult at best!

Class ID	Class Name	Instructor ID	...
900001	Intro. to Political Science	220087	...
900002	Adv. Music Theory	220039	...
900003	American History	220148	...

Figure 3-15. *An example of a many-to-many relationship.*

It's important to know what type of relationship exists between a pair of tables, because the type of relationship determines how the tables are related, whether or not records between the tables are interdependent, and the minimum and maximum number of related records that can exist within the relationship.

Types of Participation

There are two types of participation that a table can have within a relationship: *mandatory* and *optional.* Say there is a relationship between two tables called TABLE A and TABLE B. If records in TABLE A must exist before any new records can be entered into TABLE B, TABLE A's participation within the relationship is *mandatory.* However, if it isn't necessary for records in TABLE A to exist in order to enter any new records into TABLE B, TABLE A's participation within the relationship is *optional.* Each table within a relationship can participate in either manner. The type of participation each table has within a relationship is typically determined by the way the data in each table is related and how the data is being used.

Consider the relationship between the AGENTS and CLIENTS tables in Figure 3-16. The AGENTS table has a mandatory participation within the relationship *if agents must exist* before a new client can be entered into the CLIENTS table. But the AGENTS table's participation is optional *if it isn't necessary* to have agents in the AGENTS table before a new client can be entered into the CLIENTS table. The type of participation established for the AGENTS table is determined by the way its data is being used in relation to the data in the CLIENTS table. For example, if

Agents

Agent ID	Agent First Name	Agent Last Name	Date of Hire	Agent Home Phone
100	Mike	Hernandez	05/16/95	553-3992
101	Greg	Piercy	10/15/95	790-3992
102	Katherine	Ehrlich	03/01/96	551-4993

Clients

Client ID	Agent ID	Client First Name	Client Last Name	Client Home Phone
9001	100	Stewart	Jameson	553-3992
9002	101	Shannon	McLain	790-3992
9003	102	Estela	Pundt	551-4993

Figure 3-16. *The AGENTS and CLIENTS tables.*

it is necessary to ensure that each client is assigned an available agent, then the participation of the AGENTS table within the relationship should be mandatory.

Degree of Participation

Each table in a relationship has a *degree of participation*, which is the minimum and maximum number of records in one table that can be related to a single record in the other table. Consider, once again, a relationship between two tables called TABLE A and TABLE B. The degree of participation for TABLE B is established by indicating a minimum and maximum number of records in TABLE B that can be related to a single record in TABLE A. If a single record in TABLE A can be related to a minimum of one record up to a maximum of ten records in TABLE B, then the degree of participation for TABLE B is 1,10. (The degree of participation is notated with the minimum number on the left, the maximum number on the right, separated by a comma.) The degree of participation for TABLE A is established in the same manner. The degree of participation for each table in a relationship is typically determined by the way the data in each table is related and how the data is being used.

Consider the AGENTS and CLIENTS table in Figure 3-16 once more. If, for example, we say that an agent should handle *at least* one client but certainly no more than eight, then the degree of participation for the CLIENTS table is 1,8. If we further say that each client can only be assigned to one agent, then the degree of participation for the AGENTS table is 1,1.

Integrity-related Terms

Field Specification

A *Field Specification* (traditionally known as a *domain*) represents all the elements of a field. Each Field Specification has three types of elements: *general*, *physical*, and *logical*.

A field's *general* elements comprise the most fundamental information about a field in a database and include items such as field name, description, and source table. If a field is used in more than one table, these items will remain the same. *Physical* elements determine how a field is built and how it is represented to the person using it; they include items such as data type, length, and display format. *Logical* elements describe the values stored in a field; they include items such as Required Value, Range of Values, and Default Value. All elements associated with a Field Specification, including those mentioned here, are covered in greater detail in Chapter 9, "Field Specifications."

Data Integrity

Data integrity refers to the validity, consistency, and accuracy of the data in a database. It cannot be overstated that the level of accuracy of the information retrieved from the database is in direct proportion to the level of data integrity imposed within the database. Data integrity is one of the most important aspects of the database design process, and it should not be underestimated, overlooked, or even partially neglected. To make any of these mistakes would result in a high risk of undetectable errors. This, in turn, would result in users making poor strategic decisions based on inaccurate information.

Four types of data integrity are implemented during the database design process. Three types of data integrity are based on various aspects of the database structure and are labeled according to the area (level) in which they operate. The fourth type of data integrity is based on the way the data is viewed and used by an organization. Here are the types of data integrity and their descriptions:

- *Table-level integrity* ensures that the field that identifies each record within the table, is unique and is never missing its value.

- *Field-level integrity* ensures that the structure of every field is sound, that the values in each field are valid, consistent, and accurate, and that fields of the same type (such as City fields) are consistently defined throughout the database.

- *Relationship-level integrity* (traditionally known as *referential integrity*) ensures that the relationship between a pair of tables is sound and that there is synchronization between the two tables whenever data is entered, updated, or deleted.

- *Business rules* impose restrictions or limitations on certain aspects of a database based on the ways an organization perceives and uses its data. These restrictions can affect aspects of database design such as the range and types of values stored in a field, the type of participation and the degree of participation of each table within a relationship, and the type of synchronization used for relationship-level integrity in certain relationships. All of these restrictions are discussed in more detail in Chapter 11, "Business Rules." Since business rules affect integrity, they must be considered along with the other three types of data integrity during the design process.

Summary

We opened this chapter by explaining why terminology is important for defining, discussing, or reading about the relational database model and the database design process.

The discussion about *value-related terms* showed you that there is a distinct difference between "data" and "information," and that understanding this difference is crucial to understanding the database design process. You now know about *Nulls* and their affect on information retrieved from the database.

Next we discussed *structure-related terms*. You learned that the core structures of every relational database are *fields*, *records*, and *tables*. You now know that *Views* are "virtual" tables that are used, in part, to draw data from two or more tables simultaneously. We then looked at *key fields*, which are used to uniquely identify records within a table and to establish a relationship between a pair of tables. Finally, you learned the difference between a *key field* and an *index*. Now you know that an index is strictly a software device used to optimize data processing.

In our coverage of *relationship-related* terms we established that a connection between a pair of tables is a *relationship*. A relationship is used to help ensure various aspects of data integrity, and it is the mechanism used by a View to draw data from multiple tables. We then discussed the three characteristics of table relationships. The first characteristic is the *type of relationship* (one-to-one, one-to-many, many-to-many); the second characteristic is the *type of participation* (optional or mandatory); and the third characteristic is the *degree of participation* (minimum/maximum number of related records).

The chapter ended with a discussion of *integrity-related terms*. We saw that a *Field Specification* establishes the general, physical, and logical characteristics of a field—characteristics that are an integral part of every field in the database. We then learned that *data integrity* is one of the most important aspects of the database design process because of its positive effect on the data in the database. Also, you now know that there are four types of data integrity—three based on database structure and one that is based on the way the organization perceives and uses its data. These levels of integrity ensure the quality of your database design and the accuracy of the information you retrieve from it.

Part II
The Design Process

Conceptual Overview

*I don't pretend to understand the Universe—
it's a great deal bigger than I am.*
—THOMAS CARLYLE

Topics Covered in This Chapter

The Importance of Completing the Design Process

Defining a Mission Statement and Mission Objectives

Analyzing the Current Database

Creating the Data Structures

Determining and Establishing Table Relationships

Determining and Defining Business Rules

Determining and Establishing Views

Reviewing Data Integrity

Summary

Understanding how to design a relational database isn't quite as hard as understanding the universe; in fact, it's much easier. It is important, however, to have an overall idea of the way the database design process works and a general idea of the steps involved within the process. The purpose of this chapter is to provide an overview of the database design process.

For the purpose of this overview, all the techniques used in the design process are consolidated into seven phases, and each phase is discussed in general terms. This discussion provides a good overall picture of the database design process, and I hope it will give you a much clearer understanding of each of the design techniques discussed in Chapters 5–13.

> ❖ **Note** A database can be designed by a single individual or a design team composed of two or more individuals. Throughout the remainder of the book, the phrase "database developer" is used to refer to the person designing the database.

The Importance of Completing the Design Process

One thing I want to make perfectly clear at this point is the importance of completing the design process. I'm often asked if it's truly necessary to go through the entire design process. My answer is always a resounding Yes! Then I'm asked whether it's still necessary if someone is only going to create a "simple" database. ("Simple" is one of the most dangerous words known to a database developer. *Nothing* is ever "simple.") Again, my answer is "Yes! It's *still* necessary." The type, size, or purpose of the database is totally irrelevant to the value of undertaking a fully developed design. The database design process should be implemented and followed from beginning to end.

As has been shown—more examples will follow—designing a database without undergoing a complete database design process is a very bad idea. Many database problems can be attributed to poor database design. And *partially* following the design process is just about as bad as not using it at all. An incomplete design is a poor design. Only following through with a whole, unabbreviated design process assures a sound structure and data integrity.

An important point to keep in mind is that the level of structural integrity and data integrity is in direct proportion to how thoroughly the design process is followed. The less time spent on the design process, the greater the risk of encountering problems with the database. While thoroughly following the database design process may not eliminate *all* of the problems you may encounter when designing a database, it will greatly help to minimize them. Also in an RDBMS software program a well-designed database is easier to implement than a poorly designed database.

Databases are not hard to design; it just takes a little time to design them properly. Whenever it seems as if the design process is taking too long, don't use shortcuts—just be patient and remember what a wise old sage once said: "There's *never* time to do it right, but there's *always* time to do it over!"

Defining a Mission Statement and Mission Objectives

The first phase in the database design process is to define a *mission statement* and *mission objectives* for the database. The mission statement establishes the purpose of the database and provides a focus for the database developer.

Every database is created for a specific purpose, whether it's to solve a specific business problem, to manage the daily transactions of a business or organization, or to be used as part of an information system. By identifying the purpose of the database and defining it in a *mission statement*, you will ensure that the appropriate design is created and the appropriate data is collected to support the intended purpose of the database.

Along with the mission statement, *mission objectives* are defined in this phase. Mission objectives are statements representing the general tasks to be performed against the data collected in the database. These objectives are used to support the defined mission statement and aid in determining various aspects of the structure of the database.

There are two separate groups of people who will be involved in defining the mission statement and the mission objectives. The first group, which includes the database developer, the owner or head of the organization, and management personnel, is responsible for defining the mission statement. The second group which includes the database developer, management personnel, and end users, will be responsible for the definition of the mission objectives.

Analyzing the Current Database

The second phase in the database design process involves analyzing the current database, if one exists. Depending on the organization, the database will typically be a *legacy database* or a *paper-based database*. A database that has been in existence and in use for several years or more is considered a legacy database (also known as an *inherited* database). And, as many people know, a paper-based database is a loose collection of forms, index cards, manila folders, and the like. Whatever the database type or condition, analyzing it will yield valuable information about the way data is currently being managed and used. In addition, the analysis involves reviewing the way data is currently collected and presented. As the database developer you will look at how paper is used to collect data (via forms) and present data (via reports). Similarly, if some software application program is being used to manage and manipulate data for the database, you will study the way data is collected and presented on-screen.

Another part of the analysis involves conducting interviews with users and management to identify how they interact with the database on a daily basis. As the database developer you ask users how they work with the database and what their information requirements are at the current time. You then interview management personnel and ask them about the information they currently receive, and about their perception of the overall information requirements of their organization.

You then compile a list of fields and calculations, using the information gathered from the analysis and the interviews. This list then constitutes the fundamental data requirements of the organization and provides a starting point for the design of a new database. It can be anticipated that this list will be extended or refined as the design is developed.

Once the list has been compiled, it is briefly reviewed by users and management for refinement. You encourage feedback and take into consideration any suggestions for modifications. If you think the suggestions are reasonable and well-supported, you make the modifications, record the list in its current state, and move on to the next phase.

Creating the Data Structures

Creating the data structures for the database is the third phase in the database design process. You define tables and fields, establish keys, and define field specifications for every field.

Tables are the first structures you define in the database. The various subjects that each of the tables represents are determined from the mission objectives stated in the first phase of the design process, together with the data requirements gathered in the second phase of the design process. Once you have identified the subjects, you establish them as tables, and then you associate each field from the field list compiled in the second phase with an appropriate table. You then review each table to ensure that it represents only one subject and that it contains no duplicate fields.

Next you go on to review the fields within each table. If you find multi-part or multivalued fields in a table, you modify the table so that each field stores only a single value. A field that does not represent a characteristic of the subject of the table is moved to a more appropriate table or deleted entirely. When your review is complete, you establish a Primary key that will uniquely identify each record within the table.

The final step in this phase is to establish field specifications for each field in the database. At this point, you conduct interviews with users and management to help identify any specific field characteristics that may be important to them. You also review and discuss any characteristics that they may be unfamiliar with. When the interviews are completed, you define and document field specifications for each field. You then review the table structures and field specifications with users and management once more for possible refinements. When the refinements, if any, are completed, your tables are ready for the next phase.

Determining and Establishing Table Relationships

In the fourth phase of the database design process you establish table relationships. You conduct interviews with users and management once again, identify relationships, identify relationship characteristics, and establish relationship-level integrity.

Working with users and management to identify relationships is extremely helpful because you cannot possibly be familiar with every aspect of the data being used by the organization. Most people have a good perspective of the data they work with and can usually identify relationships among the data rather easily. Therefore interviewing users yields very useful information.

Once the relationships have been identified, you need to establish the logical connection for each relationship. Depending on the type of relationship, you use either a Primary key or a "linking" table to make the connection between a pair of tables based on the type of relationship you want to establish. Next you'll determine the type of participation and the degree of participation for each relationship. In some cases, these participation characteristics will be obvious due to the nature of the data stored in the tables. In other cases, the type of participation and degree of participation will be based on specific Business Rules.

Determining and Defining Business Rules

Determining and defining Business Rules is the fifth phase of the database design process. As the database developer you hold interviews, identify limitations on various aspects of the database, establish Business Rules, and define and implement Validation Tables.

The way an organization views and uses its data will dictate a set of limitations and requirements that have to be built into the database. Your interviews with users and management will determine what specific limitations and requirements will be imposed on the data, data structures, or relationships. You then establish and document these specifications as Business Rules.

The interviews held with users will reveal *specific* limitations on various aspects of the database. For example, a user working with an Order Processing database is very aware of specific details, such as the fact that a Ship Date must be later than an Order Date, that there must always be a Daytime Phone Number, and that a Method of Shipment should always be indicated. On the other hand, management interviews are intended to reveal *general* limitations on various aspects of the database.

The office manager for an entertainment agency, for example, is familiar with general issues, such as the fact that an agent can represent no more than twenty entertainers and that promotional information for each entertainer must be updated every year.

Next, you define and implement Validation Tables, if necessary, to support certain Business Rules. For example, if certain fields are found to have a finite range of values owing to the manner in which they are used by the organization, Validation Tables are used to ensure the consistency and validity of the values stored in those fields.

The level of integrity established by Business Rules at this point is significant because it relates directly to the way the organization views and uses its data. As the organization grows, its perspective on the data will change, which means that the Business Rules must change as well. This means that determining and establishing Business Rules is an ongoing, iterative process. Constant diligence is necessary at all times to maintain this level of integrity properly.

Determining and Establishing Views

Determining and establishing Views is the sixth phase of the database design process. Once more, you'll need to conduct interviews, identify various ways of looking at the data, and establish the Views.

You'll ask users and management to identify the various ways that they look at the data in the database. Whereas one group may view the data from a shared perspective, another group within the organization may use a different perspective; some individuals have unique ways of visualizing the data based on the work they perform. For example, some individuals need to retrieve data from several tables at the same time in order to see summary information; others only need to see specific fields from a certain table.

Once you have identified the various ways of seeing the data, you establish them formally as Views. Each view is defined using the appropriate table or tables, and, in the case of multitable Views, fields from the appropriate tables are assigned to the View. Once you have established all of the Views, you'll need to identify criteria for certain Views so that they will only display specific records.

Reviewing Data Integrity

The seventh and last phase in the database design process is reviewing the final database structure for data integrity. First, you'll review each table to ensure that it meets the criteria of a properly designed table, and you will initially check the fields within each table for proper structure. Any inconsistencies or problems will be resolved and reviewed once more. After the appropriate refinements are made, you'll check table-level integrity.

Second, you review and check field specifications for each field. You then make refinements to fields as necessary and check field-level integrity after any needed refinements have been made. This review reaffirms the field-level integrity identified and established earlier in the database design process.

Third, you have to review the validity of each relationship, confirming the type of relationship, as well as the type of participation and degree of participation for each table within the relationship. You then study relationship integrity to ensure that there are matching values between shared fields, and that there are no problems inserting, updating, or deleting data in any of the tables within the relationship.

Finally, you go over the Business Rules to confirm the limitations placed on various aspects of the database, as identified earlier in the database design process. If there are any other limitations that have come to light since the last set of personnel interviews, you establish them as new Business Rules and add them to the existing set of Business Rules.

Once the entire database design process is complete, the logical database structure is ready to be implemented in an RDBMS software program. However, the process is never *really* complete because the database structure will always need refinement as the organization grows.

Summary

We began this chapter with a discussion of the importance of completing the design process. Designing a database without the benefit of a good design method leads to poor and improper design. We also discussed the fact that the level of structural integrity and data integrity is totally dependent on how thoroughly the design process was followed. Inconsistent data and inaccurate information are two problems typically encountered with poorly designed databases.

Next we looked at an overview of the entire database design process. To provide a clear overall picture, the process was consolidated into the following phases:

1. *Define a mission statement and mission objectives for the database.* The mission statement defines the purpose of the database. The mission objectives define the tasks that are to be performed by users against the data in the database.

2. *Analyze the current database.* You identify the data requirements of the organization by reviewing the way data is currently collected and presented and by conducting interviews with users and management to determine how they use the database on a daily basis.

3. *Create the data structures.* You establish tables by identifying the subjects that will be tracked by the database. Next you assign each table fields that best characterize its subject, and you designate a Primary key as well. Then you establish field specifications for every field in the table.

4. *Determine and establish table relationships.* You'll identify relationships that exist between the tables in the database and then establish the logical connection for each relationship using Primary keys and Foreign keys, or linking tables. Finally, you'll set the various characteristics for each relationship.

5. *Determine and define Business Rules.* Next you conduct interviews with users and management to identify constraints on the data in the database based on the way the organization views and uses its data. These constraints are then declared as Business Rules, which will serve to establish various levels of data integrity.

6. *Determine and establish Views.* Users and management are interviewed to identify the various ways they look at the data in the database. After these various perspectives have been identified, you establish them as Views. Each View is defined using the appropriate table or tables, and certain Views use criteria that limit the records that they display.

7. *Review data integrity.* This phase involves four steps. First, you review each table to ensure that it meets proper design criteria. Second, you review and check all field specifications. Third, you test the validity of each relationship. Fourth, you go over and confirm the business rules.

5

Starting the Process

*"Where shall I begin, please your
Majesty?" he asked. "Begin at the
beginning," the King said gravely,
"and go on till you come to the end:
then stop."*
—LEWIS CARROLL
ALICE'S ADVENTURES IN WONDERLAND

Topics Covered in This Chapter

Conducting Interviews

The Case Study: Mike's Bikes

Defining the Mission Statement

Defining the Mission Objectives

Summary

Everything has a beginning, and the database design process is no different. Interestingly enough, you start the process by defining the end result. It is in the very first step of the database design process that you identify and declare the purpose of the database. You also define and declare a list of the tasks that can be performed against the data in the database. Both of these items provide a focus and direction for developing a database, and they help ensure that the final database structure supports the stated purpose and tasks.

Conducting Interviews

Interviews are a very important part of database design process, and
they are used at several key points within the process itself. Assuming
that you work within some organization and have a need to design a
database to support the work that you and your fellow employees do,
you'll need to conduct interviews in the manner described in this book.
This means that throughout the design process, you'll interact with
some of your fellow employees, management personnel, and (depending on the size of the organization) the owner himself. If you work for a
small organization that employs only a handful of people, or if you are
only creating a database for yourself, you'll conduct "self-interviews."
In other words, you'll still conduct the interviews described in this
book, but you will act as the interviewer *and* the interviewee. *You* will
be the one who provides the answers to the questions.

*The reason interviews are important is because they provide valuable
information that can affect the design of the database structure.* When
you're working with table relationships, for example, it is sometimes
difficult to determine the type of participation and degree of participation for a specific relationship. The only way for you to determine the
proper values for these relationship characteristics is by conducting
an interview with the appropriate people. Once the interview is complete, you can use the information you gathered to set the relationship
characteristics. Using an interview as an information-gathering tool,
you can gain new insights from participants regarding part of the database or clarify facts that you don't understand. It's important to note
that you must always conduct each of the interviews discussed in this
design process regardless of the type of database you're designing or
the number of people involved. Failure to do so means you neglect
some information. Clearly, this can adversely affect the final structure
of the database.

Because interviews can provide such vital information, it is important to learn how to conduct them. Interviewing is much easier if you have a set of prepared questions. (Coming up with questions "off the top of your head" is rarely a good idea, unless you're an experienced interviewer and are highly skilled at producing ad hoc questions.) Having a prepared list of questions allows you to provide a focus and direction for the interview, and it provides the participant with a continuity of thought. The interview flows more smoothly and is more productive when the questions move easily from topic to topic.

As you prepare your list of interview questions, make sure that you ask *open-ended* questions. For example, "Did you feel our service was (a) Poor, (b) Average, (c) Good" is a *closed* question. There's no room for the respondent to give an objective opinion or further elaborate because a finite set of answers is provided as the only form of response. "How do you feel about our service?" is an open-ended question because it gives the participant an opportunity to provide a complete and objective answer to the question. It also provides him with the option to elaborate further on the answer. There are times when you may need to use closed questions, but it's better to use them intentionally, sparingly, and with a specific purpose in mind.

> ❖ **Note** Throughout the remaining chapters, examples of open-ended questions are provided whenever conducting an interview is part of the concept or technique being presented. You can use these examples as a guide for formulating your own questions for the required interview.

When you conduct an interview with users or management, be sure to begin by setting up a few guidelines. If everyone knows how the interview is going to be conducted and what is expected of each person, they will be willing participants and will be quite responsive to your questions. Tell the participants the subject of discussion, the names of the other participants, the intended time of the session, and whether this interview is part of an ongoing series of interviews. Above all, reassure the participants that your interview is not a disguised assessment of their performance.

In addition to the guidelines you convey to the participants, there are general guidelines you can set for yourself, as the interviewer. Here are a few suggestions:

- *Set a limit of six people or less for each interview.* Limiting the number of participants promotes a more relaxed atmosphere and makes it easier for you to encourage everyone to participate. One problem you'll find in conducting an interview with a large number of people is that the intimidation level of some of the participants will rise in direct proportion to the number of participants taking part in the interview as a whole. Some people are just afraid of looking ignorant or incompetent in front of their colleagues, whether or not there's truly any justification for such feelings. So you do have a very good reason to restrict the number of participants in an interview.

- *As much as possible, conduct separate interviews for users and management.* Separating the two groups is a good idea for any number of reasons, including the "fear factor" noted above, but the main reason is that each group has a different perspective of the organization and how the data the organization maintains is used on a daily basis. Therefore, if you separate the groups you can leverage their unique perspectives to your advantage as you work through the database design process. Another reason for keeping the interviews separate is to eliminate the conflicts that can arise when there is disagreement between users and management regarding certain aspects of the organization. It's not unusual for there to be a lack of communication between these two groups of individuals, and the odds are fifty-fifty that the interview will bring such failings to the surface. The airing of such problems may impel staff and management to establish better lines of communication, or it may exacerbate the problem further. In any case, it can extend your interview and diffuse the results. Use your knowledge of the potential interview participants and the organization itself to help you judge whether or not to keep the interviews separate. If you need to conduct an interview with both groups at the same time, do so *intentionally* and with a specific purpose in mind, and be prepared for distractions.

- *Whenever you have to interview several groups of people, designate a group leader for each group.* The group leader will help you ensure that the interview runs smoothly. It will be the responsibility of the group leader to prepare each member of his group for the interview. A group leader will also be responsible for providing you with any new information obtained from the members of his group that came to light outside of the interview. During the interview, the group leader can direct your questions to the member of his group best equipped to answer them. However, as much as possible, avoid letting the group leader answer every question.

- *Prior to the actual interview, let the participants know what you're going to discuss and how the interview will be conducted.* Many people are leery of interviews. They don't like to be "put on the spot" and they don't want to be asked any "trick" questions. People are apt to be more at ease and willing to participate if they know in advance what is expected of them and what they should expect from the interview. You can do much to alleviate their fears and suspicions by providing them with this information.

- *Make sure that all participants understand that you appreciate their taking part in the interview and that their responses to the interview questions are valuable to the overall design project.* Earlier experiences are likely to make some people believe that whatever input they provide goes unnoticed and unappreciated at work. Even when their input made a significant impact on a specific project in the past, rarely did they get so much as a thank-you. In light of this, there's no real motivation for them to participate in your interview. Many, if not all, of your participants will start out with this attitude. But you can really change their motivation by letting them know that you truly and *honestly* appreciate their participation and are very interested in their responses. Assure them that their feedback is truly valuable to the design process, and that in many cases their responses can substantiate and validate decisions made throughout the design process. If you can make yourself credible through genuine sincerity, participants will help you in any way they can. Your job will be much easier and everyone will participate voluntarily and enthusiastically. It's very effective to show, on a second interview, how you have already used participants' earlier contributions.

- *Conduct the interview in a well-lit room, separated from distracting noise, with a large table and comfortable chairs, and have coffee and munchies on hand.* To conduct a successful interview, you'll want to pay close attention to atmosphere. In a well-lit room it is easy for everyone to read the materials used during the interview. A large table ensures that everyone has space to work, and comfortable chairs help everyone to concentrate on the task at hand, unencumbered by the aches and pains associated with "bad" chairs. It's always good to have plenty of coffee on hand; it seems to be the preferred beverage of businesspeople everywhere. Finally, a good supply of munchies helps to keep everyone in a good mood. People actually seem to think better when they have something to munch on. It keeps their mouths occupied while they're thinking.

- *If you're not very good at taking notes, either assign that task to a dependable transcriber for each interview or get the group's permission to use a tape recorder to record the interview.* Whenever you conduct an interview, you're doing so in order to gather specific information about the organization, so it's important to have a detailed record of the interview. It's unusual to be able to conduct an interview *and* take good notes at the same time. Lacking this ability, you may enlist one of the participants to take notes for you. This is one good way to encourage participation from people who are normally quiet or reserved. But if the transcriber is distracted by the proceedings, the notes may suffer. For accurate transcription, you can use a tape recorder to record the interview. This method has the advantage of allowing you to review the proceedings quite easily afterward.

- *Give everyone your equal and undivided attention.* This is a crucial point for you to remember. Whenever you conduct an interview, make sure you're paying complete attention to the person who is speaking. There will be many times when the person you're interviewing responds to your questions with vague or incomplete answers. A participant may respond this way for several reasons. It may be that he doesn't quite know how to express the ideas he wants to convey or that he's not at liberty to divulge certain information. It could also be that he's just not comfortable talking about himself and what he does, or that he is suspicious of you for some reason. In any case, you'll have to be patient and make him feel at ease so that he will provide you with the information you need.

Here's another point to consider. If you give a participant the impression that you're bored, uninterested, or preoccupied, he will immediately reduce his level of participation within the interview. On the other hand, if the participant sees that you are interested in what he is saying and has your undivided attention, he will participate quite enthusiastically. Your personal attitude and the attention you give to each of the participants can make a real difference to the success of the interview.

- *Make sure everyone understands that you are the official arbitrator if and when a dispute arises.* It's inevitable that minor disputes will arise during an interview, and that there will be some amount of tension until such disputes are resolved. You can avoid this situation by arbitrating these disputes yourself. As the database developer, you're in the best position to arbitrate a dispute because you have an objective viewpoint and can see both sides of an issue. Also the decision you make will always be in the best interests of the database structure. Always remember that any disputes that have to do with something other than the database structure can be referred to a more appropriate authority, if one exists.

- *Keep the pace of the interview moving.* You've probably attended meetings during which a particular point was belabored or much time was spent trying to extract information from a reluctant participant. You can prevent this from happening during your interviews by mentally putting a cap on the time you'll allow for a question to be answered and the time you'll spend on a specific topic. Don't inform the participants about this limit; instead try to promote a sense of urgency.

- *Always maintain control of the interview.* This is the single most important guideline for any interview you will conduct. The moment you lose control of the interview something will inevitably go wrong. One typical scenario that occurs in this situation is that one of the participants takes control of the direction of the interview and begins to discuss issues that have little or no relevance to the original purpose of the interview. In some cases, you can reestablish control of the situation and move the focus of the discussion back to the original subjects. However, in other cases, it's best to declare your portion of the interview "complete" and let the participants carry on with their discussion. If you want to avoid situations like this, just be sure to maintain control of the interview.

Interviews are used throughout the design process, so they will be discussed in the next several chapters. Sample dialog is provided to illustrate typical interview scenarios, along with examples of questions you might use during a given interview. The questions provided in the examples always relate to the type of interview being conducted.

> ❖ **Note** Whenever an example of an interview is provided, the dialog is only sketched in, transcribed in fragments. The purpose of the example is to illustrate the *technique* involved in conducting a specific type of interview. The dialog within the example provides ideas for the types of questions that can be used in the interview.

THE CASE STUDY: MIKE'S BIKES

There are numerous examples throughout the book that illustrate the concepts and techniques used in the database design process. The examples are drawn from various types of databases and are used in an arbitrary fashion. They are used in this manner to illustrate that

once you have learned how to apply a concept or technique generically, you can apply it to working with any type of database. The focus
should be on the concept or technique being presented, not on the
example itself.

Nevertheless, in order to illustrate the steps involved in the design process with some degree of continuity, a single database example is used
as a case study. As the database design process unfolds, each technique is applied to designing the database for the fictitious company in
the case study. Only a few details about the company are provided in
this chapter. Further details are revealed as each new concept or technique is presented.

Mike's Bikes, our case study business, is a new bike shop located in a
small suburb called Greenlake, not far from downtown Seattle. It has
been open for only two months, and business is growing steadily. Mike,
the shop's owner, has been conducting his daily business on paper.
Sales are recorded on preprinted forms, employee and vendor information is recorded on sheets of paper and kept in manila folders, and
information on regular customers is kept on index cards. As a result,
Mike spends a lot of time maintaining all this data. He owns a computer but uses it mainly to play games, write letters, and "surf the
'net." The only business-related task he performs on the computer is
keeping track of the bike shop's inventory using a spreadsheet program.

Recently, Mike learned that using a database would be a good way to
store and work with data related to his business. Using a database
would greatly diminish the amount of time he currently spends maintaining his data, and he could always ensure that the data is up-to-
date and that the information is always accurate. Although he thinks a
database is a good idea, he's aware of the fact that he doesn't know the
first thing about properly designing a database. Undaunted, Mike has
decided to hire a database consultant to design the database for him.

You are, in this fable, the consultant he has hired for the project. As the database design process unfolds throughout the next several chapters, you'll apply each technique to design the database for Mike's Bikes. And, as each concept or technique is introduced, Mike will supply any further information that is needed in order for you to complete the design of the database.

Defining the Mission Statement

In the previous chapter, we noted that the *mission statement* declares the specific purpose of the database in general terms and that it is defined at the beginning of the database design process. In more detail, it provides you with a focus for your design efforts and keeps you from getting diverted and making the database structure unnecessarily large or complex.

The Well-Written Mission Statement

A good mission statement is succinct and to the point. Verbose statements have a tendency to be confusing, ambiguous, or vague; they do more to obscure the purpose of the database than to clarify it. The following sentence is an example of a typical mission statement:

> "The purpose of the New Starz Talent Agency database is to maintain the data we use and provide the information we need to run the day-to-day affairs of our business."

This mission statement is well defined and uncluttered by any unnecessary statements or details. It is a very general statement, just as it should be. Think of a mission statement as the flame of a candle located at the end of a dark tunnel. The light produced by the flame guides you to the end of the tunnel, so long as you focus on it. In the same manner, the mission statement guides you to the end of the "tunnel," that is, the database design process. Guided by your mission statement, you can focus on designing a database structure that will support the declared purpose of the database.

A well-written mission statement is free of any phrases or sentences that explicitly describe *specific tasks*. If your mission statement contains any such phrases or sentences, remove them and rewrite the statement. Be sure to keep the discarded phrases handy, though, because you may be able to use them to formulate mission objectives. (Mission objectives are discussed in the next section.) The following sentence is an example of a poorly worded mission statement:

> "The purpose of the Whatcom County Hearing Examiner's database is to keep track of applications for land use, maintain data on applicants, keep a record of all hearings, and maintain data for office use."

It should be immediately apparent that there are a few things wrong with this mission statement.

- *It's slightly verbose.* Remember that the ideal mission statement should be succinct and to the point.

- *The specific purpose of the database is unclear.* The manner in which this mission statement is written makes it difficult to ascertain the specific purpose of the database.

- *It describes several specific tasks.* Two issues arise when a mission statement is written in this manner. First, the description of the tasks does nothing to define the specific purpose of the database. Second, the statement somehow appears to be incomplete. It seems to beg the question: "Are there any tasks we've forgotten to include in the mission statement?"

You can fix this mission statement by removing the references to specific tasks (be sure to save them for the next step), and rewriting the statement. Here is an example of one of the possible ways you could rewrite this mission statement.

> "The purpose of the Whatcom County Hearing Examiner's database is to maintain the data we use in support of the services this office provides to the citizens of this county."

Notice how the purpose of the database has become much clearer in this version. Also note that the statement is more succinct and doesn't give the impression of being incomplete. If you can formulate your mission statements in this manner, you'll always have a clear focus during the database design process.

Composing a Mission Statement

The process of creating a mission statement involves conducting an interview with the owner or manager of the organization, learning about the organization, and determining the purpose of the new database.

The interview for this step is conducted with the owner of the organization or, if he directs, the appropriate staff. Either will be able to help you with the statement of purpose, bringing an overall understanding of the organization and a general comprehension of why the database is necessary in the first place. Besides helping you to define the mission statement, this interview will also provide a great deal of information about the organization itself. This information is valuable because you can use it later in the design process.

As you conduct the interview, encourage the interview participant to discuss as many facets of the organization as he can, even if the discussion relates to issues that aren't directly relevant to the database.

The idea here is to understand what the organization does and how it functions; the more you understand an organization, the better prepared you will be to design a database that will fulfill its needs. Once you have a better understanding of the organization, its general need for a database will become clear, and you can then translate this need into a mission statement.

Be sure to ask open-ended questions during the interview. In some cases, a good question can prompt the participant to state the purpose of the database without much effort. For example, say you posed the following question:

> "How would you describe the purpose of your organization to a new client?"

This is a good open-ended question because it focuses on the issue yet gives the participant the freedom to respond with what he feels is a complete answer. Furthermore, with this type of question you're very likely to get a response that you can translate directly into a mission statement.

Now assume you received the following reply:

> "We supply entertainment services to our clientele for any and all occasions. We take care of all the details for the engagement so that it is as worry-free for the client as possible."

This type of response can easily be rewritten and turned into a mission statement. In fact, when a response such as this one consists of two or more sentences or phrases, one of the sentences or phrases typically indicates the purpose of the database. In the reply above, the first sentence can be used to construct the mission statement. The following mission statement illustrates one of several ways you could rewrite the reply:

"The purpose of the All-Star Talent database is to maintain the data we use in support of the entertainment services we provide to our clientele."

The most important point to remember is that the mission statement should make sense to you (the database developer) and to those for whom you are designing the database. Different groups of people have different ways of phrasing statements, and the specific wording of the statement can depend greatly on industry-specific terminology. Your mission statement is complete when you have a sentence that describes the specific purpose of the database and that is understood and agreed upon by everyone concerned.

Here are a few sample questions that you can use to arrive at your mission statement:

"How would you describe the purpose of your organization to a new client?"

"What would you say is the purpose of your organization?"

"What is the major function of your organization?"

"How would you describe what your organization does?"

"Will you define the single most important reason for the existence of your organization?"

"What is the main focus of your organization?"

You may have noticed that some of these questions seem to be the same question rewritten in a different manner. Keep in mind that the observation regarding the phrasing of mission statements applies to any interview questions you'll use throughout the database design process. You can pose the *same question* to several people and receive different responses because each person may interpret the meaning of the question a little differently. In some cases, you may just get a long,

"I haven't had my first espresso yet" type of stare. Experiment with the way you phrase questions and find out what type of phrasing works best for you. Your method of constructing and posing questions may be different than someone else's, but it doesn't matter so long as you have a method that works for you.

Case Study

Now you need to define a mission statement for Mike's Bikes. Before you can define the mission statement, you need to conduct an interview with him to gather information about his business. Assume you have an assistant named Zachary who is conducting the interview for you. The interview may go something like this:

ZACHARY: Can you tell me why you believe you need a database?

MIKE: I think we need a database just to keep track of all our inventory. I'd also like to keep track of all our sales as well.

ZACHARY: I'm sure the database will address those issues. Now, what would you say is the single most important function of your business?

MIKE: To provide a wide array of bicycle products and bicycle-related services to our customers. We have a lot of great customers. And regular ones, too! They're our biggest asset.

(The interview continues until Zachary has finished asking all the questions on his list.)

After the interview, review the information you have gathered and define the mission statement. You have ascertained a few points from the previous dialog with Mike, such as the fact that he'll need to be able to track products, customers, and customer sales. But the most valuable point is provided by his reply to the second question. The first sentence in that reply can be used to formulate the mission statement. Taking into account some of the other points that were identified in the interview, you can rewrite Mike's reply to create the following mission statement:

> "The purpose of the Mike's Bikes database is to maintain the data we use to support our retail sales business and our customer-service operations."

When you feel you have a good mission statement, review it with Mike and make sure that he understands and agrees with the declared purpose of the database. When you and Mike are satisfied with the mission statement, you can go on to the next step, which is defining the mission objectives.

Defining The Mission Objectives

To expand upon the overview in the previous chapter, *mission objectives* are statements that represent the *general* tasks supported by the data maintained in the database. Each mission objective represents a *single* task. Together the mission objectives provide information that is used throughout the database design process. For example, mission objectives are used to help define table structures, field specifications, relationship characteristics, and Views. They are also used to help establish data integrity and to define Business Rules. Finally, mission objectives guide database development and ensure that the final database structure supports the mission statement.

Well-Written Mission Objectives

A well-written mission objective is a declarative sentence that clearly defines a general task and is free from unnecessary details. It is written in general terms and is succinct and to the point. The following sentences are examples of typical mission objectives:

"We need to maintain complete patient address information."

"We need to keep track of all customer sales."

"We need to make sure an account representative is responsible for no more than twenty accounts at any given time."

"We need to keep track of vehicle maintenance."

"We need to produce employee phone directories."

These mission objectives are well defined and easy to understand. Each mission objective represents a single general task and defines the task clearly, without unnecessary details. For example, the last mission objective in the list states that employee directories need to be produced, but it doesn't indicate *how* they are to be produced. It is not necessary to indicate how the employee lists will be produced because that issue is part of the application development process. Remember that the purpose of a mission objective is to help define various structures within the database and to help guide the overall direction of the database's development.

If a mission objective represents more than one general task, it should be broken into two or more mission objectives. Following is an example of a poorly written mission objective:

"We need to keep track of the entertainers we represent and the type of entertainment they provide, as well as the engagements that we book for them."

There are two problems with this mission objective:

- *It defines more than a single general task.* It is clear that there are two tasks represented in this statement: keeping track of entertainers and keeping track of engagements.

- *It contains unnecessary detail.* It's unnecessary to refer to the entertainer's "type of entertainment" in this mission objective. The phrase "type of entertainment" either refers to a distinct piece of the overall entertainer information, or it represents a new task that should be declared as a mission objective. If it refers to a distinct part of the overall entertainer information, it should be removed from the statement; if it represents a new task, it should be used as the basis for a new mission objective.

You can fix this mission objective by removing the unnecessary detail and rewriting it as two mission objectives. Here is an example of one possible revision:

"We need to maintain complete entertainer information."

"We need to keep track of all the engagements we book."

Notice that each mission objective now clearly defines a single general task and is easy to understand as well. Mission objectives such as these are easy to use as you design the database.

Composing Mission Objectives

Defining mission objectives is an easy process that involves conducting interviews with users and management, and then writing appropriate mission objectives based on the information gathered from the interviews.

The purpose of the interview is to determine what types of general tasks need to be supported by the data in the database. You accomplish this end by asking the participants open-ended questions and allowing them to elaborate on their replies if necessary. The mission statement and mission objectives interviews are the easiest you'll conduct during the design process because everyone is usually enthusiastic about participating. It's pretty easy to get people to discuss what they do on a daily basis and to give their perspective on the function of the organization. Also this is one of the few interviews you'll conduct where it's acceptable to involve both users and management in the same interview; there should be a lot of common ground between the two groups due to the general nature of the interview.

One very important point to remember is that *the interviews you conduct here contain very general discussions*. The discussions are more conceptual than analytical. In other words, the intent here is not to analyze the current database or database application but to get an overall idea of the general tasks the database should support. Remember that one of the purposes of the mission objectives is to help guide the development of the database structure.

As you conduct the interview, be sure, once again, to ask open-ended questions. Remember that open-ended questions are apt to elicit better responses from your participants. Ask the participants questions regarding their daily work, how the organization functions, and what type of issues they feel need to be addressed by the database. Encourage them to discuss as many facets of their work and the organization as they possibly can. As they reply, try to record each response as a declarative sentence. If you can do this, it is much easier to transform a sentence into a mission objective. Here are just a few examples of the types of questions you could pose during the interview:

"What kind of work do you perform on a daily basis?"

"How would you define your job description?"

"What kind of data do you work with?"

"What types of reports do you generate?"

"What types of things do you keep track of?"

"What types of services does your organization provide?"

"How would you describe the type of work you do?"

Any of these questions is likely to evoke a good, lengthy response from the participant. One of the advantages of questions like these is that they easily provide the opportunity for you to ask follow-up questions. For example, say you received the following response to the last question in the list:

"First, I try to determine the general problem with the vehicle. Then, I fill out a work order and note my assessment of the problem. Finally, I send the vehicle to the next available service team."

You'll immediately notice that it's a lengthy response, which is fine. Also, note that you could easily ask a follow-up question, such as the following:

"Is there any customer information you work with in regards to the procedure you just described?"

Even if the reply is no, the question is still open-ended enough for the participant to further elaborate on his original response. This type of follow-up question could also jar the participant's memory and cause him to relay other information, which may or may not be related to the subject of the original response.

Following is a set of mission objectives that could be derived from the participant's original response:

"We need to maintain information on customer vehicles."

"We need to keep track of work orders."

"We need to maintain information on our service teams."

"We need to maintain information on our mechanics."

"We need to maintain information on our customers."

Three of these objectives are derived directly from the response. They were easy to determine because their subjects are explicitly stated in the response. The last two mission objectives are determined from *assumptions* based on the response. This technique, which can be thought of as "reading between the lines," is used quite often. It relies on the ability to determine what information a response conveys *implicitly* as well as what it conveys *explicitly*. So pay attention. Listen for implications. Without good assumptions, your overall set of mission objectives could be incomplete.

Review the following response and determine whether or not there is any implicit information hidden within the response itself:

> "I book entertainment for our clientele, which consists of commercial and noncommercial clients. Our noncommercial clients are typically individuals or small groups who book weddings, birthdays, anniversaries, and the like. Our commercial clients, on the other hand, consist of businesses such as nightclubs and corporations. The nightclubs book entertainment in six-week slots; the corporations book things such as corporate parties, product rollouts, and various types of promotional functions."

Aside from the explicit information that this response conveys, there are at least two pieces of implicit information that can be uncovered in this response. The first piece of implicit information is the fact that there is a need to maintain information on the entertainers booked for the engagements. An agent needs to know things such as the name of the entertainer, his phone number, and where to mail the contract. The second piece of implicit information is the fact that there is a need to maintain information on the engagements themselves. An agent must know all the details concerning the engagement in order ensure that the engagement runs smoothly.

Now that you know how important it is to look for implicit information, keep it in mind when you're defining mission objectives.

The "final words" regarding mission objectives are these: make sure that mission objectives are both properly defined and well defined, that each objective makes sense to you and to those for whom you are designing the database, and make sure you look for any implicit information hidden within every participant's response.

Case Study

Now's the time to interview Mike and his staff so that they can help you define the mission objectives for the Mike's Bikes database. Here's a partial transcript of the interview with Mike. Once again, your assistant, Zachary, is conducting the interview.

> ZACHARY: Can you give me an idea of the things you'd like to track in the database?
>
> MIKE: Oh sure, that's pretty easy. I want to keep track of our inventory, our customers, and our sales.
>
> ZACHARY: Is there anything else that you can think of that is related to these subjects?
>
> MIKE Well, I guess if we're going to keep track of our inventory, we should know who our suppliers are.
>
> ZACHARY: What about the sales reps involved in each sale?
>
> MIKE: Oh yeah, we should definitely keep information about our employees. If nothing else, it's a good idea to do this from a human resources point of view. At least, that's what my wife tells me!

(The interview continues until Zachary has finished asking all the questions on his list.)

When the interviews are complete, review all the information you've gathered and define any appropriate mission objectives. Be sure to keep the "final words" in mind as you define them. Here are a few possible mission objectives for the Mike's Bikes database.

"We need to maintain complete inventory information."

"We need to maintain complete customer information."

"We need to track all customer sales."

"We need to maintain complete supplier information."

"We need to maintain complete employee information."

Once you've compiled a list of mission objectives, review them with Mike and his staff. When they are satisfied that they understand the mission objectives and that the list is relatively complete, commit the list to a document in your favorite word processor and save it for later use.

Summary

This chapter opens with a discussion of the *interview process*. You learned why interviews are an important part of the database design process and why it's important to learn how to conduct an interview properly. You now know the difference between an *open-ended* question and a *closed* question, as well as when to use each kind of question. We ended this discussion by reviewing a set of guidelines that should be used for each interview to help you ensure that your interviews are productive and successful.

The *mission statement* was our next topic of discussion. We expanded upon the Chapter 4 overview by looking at how the mission statement states the specific purpose of the database. You now know that the process involves conducting interviews and learning about the organization, then formulating the mission statement from the information you gathered during these steps. We defined the characteristics of a good mission statement, and you learned that a well-defined mission statement establishes a clear focus for your design efforts.

The chapter closes with a section on the subject of *mission objectives*. Again, we got additional details over the Chapter 4 overview. As you now know, mission objectives represent the tasks performed against the data in the database, and they are defined after the mission statement. We explored how to define a mission objective. Here, you learned that interviews are conducted with users and management, and that information gathered from these interviews provides the basis for each mission statement. We discussed the characteristics of a well-written mission objective, and you learned that a clearly defined mission objective will help you define various structures within the database.

6

Analyzing the Current Database

To see what is in front of one's nose
needs a constant struggle.
—GEORGE ORWELL ,
"IN FRONT OF YOUR NOSE"

Topics Covered in This Chapter

Getting to Know the Current Database

Conducting the Analysis

Looking at How Data Is Collected

Looking at How Information Is Presented

Conducting Interviews

Conducting User Interviews

Conducting Management Interviews

Compiling a Complete List of Fields

Case Study

Summary

Getting to Know the Current Database

To determine where you should go, it's necessary to understand where you are. The database currently in use can provide a dependable resource for developing the new database. What is required is a detailed understanding of the current database, and careful judgment of the features that can remain useful, or conversely, those that should be discarded. To make such judgments, you need to answer the following questions:

What types of data does the organization use?

How does it use that data?

How does it manage and maintain that data?

The answers to these inquiries provide the basic guidelines for creating the new database structure. Armed with this information you can design a database that best suits the organization's needs.

The best way to answer these questions is by analyzing the database the organization currently uses. (It's very likely that it is using *some* type of database, whether it is a paper-based database, a legacy database, or even a system based on the memory of some of the employees.) The goal of the analysis is to determine the types of data the organization uses and how the data is managed and maintained. It also serves to identify how the data is viewed and used. If you conduct this investigation properly, it will reduce the time it takes to define the preliminary field and table structures for the new database.

This analysis requires reviewing the various ways data is collected, reviewing the ways in which the data is presented, and conducting a set of interviews with users and management. The information gathered from the analysis is then used to define a preliminary field list and help determine the tables that should be included in the initial database structure. Furthermore, if the analysis reveals that the current database is poorly designed, precautions can be implemented to guard against making the same mistakes in the new database. Despite whatever shortcomings the current database may have, it can help you identify a number of the fields and tables that you should define in the new database.

Yet there's one particularly significant point to remember as you're analyzing the current database: *do not adopt the current database structure as the basis for the new database structure*. This is a particularly bad idea, because imported errors are the most difficult to identify. Every so often, there's a point during the analysis when a novice database developer (and sometimes experienced ones as well) will stop and think, "This database doesn't look too bad. Let's just end the analysis here and use this database as the basis for the new one." The danger posed by this line of thinking is that any "hidden" problems within the current database will be transferred into the new database. These types of problems include awkward table structures, poorly defined relationships, and inconsistent field specifications. And without a doubt, these problems always surface later at the least opportune time. So by all means explore the old database for information on types of data, uses of data, and perhaps use some of the old database's data, once you have tested it. But it's always better to define a new database structure explicitly than to copy an existing structure. After all, if the old database didn't have any problems, you wouldn't be building a new one.

Two types of databases are typically analyzed during this part of the database design process: *paper-based* databases and *legacy* databases. In some cases, an organization uses either one or the other; sometimes it uses both. Although you use fundamentally the same analysis process for both types of databases, there are some minor differences in the approach you will use to analyze each type of database. These differences have more to do with the databases themselves than with the overall analysis process. Both approaches are seamlessly incorporated into the analysis process presented in this book.

Paper-based Databases

Data that is literally collected, stored, and maintained on paper is known as a *paper-based database*. The paper used in this type of database appears in a variety of shapes, sizes, and configurations. Some of the more common formats include index cards, hand-written reports, and various types of preprinted forms. Anyone who has ever worked in an office for a business or organization is very familiar with this type of database.

Analyzing this type of database can be a daunting task. One of the most immediate problems is finding someone who completely understands how the database works so you can learn its use and purpose. There are several problems with the paper-based database itself, especially in terms of the way data is collected and managed. Typically, this type of database contains inconsistent data, erroneous data, duplicate data, redundant data, incomplete entries, and data that should have been purged from the database long ago. Clearly, the only reason to analyze this type of database is to identify various items that will be incorporated into the new database. For example, individual pieces of data extracted from various sections of forms in the paper-based database will be turned into fields in the new database.

Legacy Databases

Any database that has been in existence and in use for five years or more is considered to be a *legacy database*. Mainframe databases typically fall into this category, as do older PC-based databases. "Legacy" is used as part of the name of this type of database for several reasons. First, it suggests that the database has been around for a long time, possibly longer than anyone can clearly remember. Second, the term "legacy" may mean that the individual who originally created the database has either shifted responsibilities within the organization or is working for someone else, and thus the database has become his or her legacy to the organization. Third, the term implies the disturbing possibility that no single individual completely understands the database structure or how it is implemented in the RDBMS software program.

Mainframe legacy databases present some special problems in the analysis process. One of the problems is that a number of older mainframe databases are based on hierarchical or network database models. If neither you nor the staff has a firm understanding of these models, it will take some time to decipher the structure of the database. In this case, it is very helpful to make printouts of the data in each of the database structures.

Even if a legacy database is based on the relational model, that doesn't necessarily mean that the structure is sound. Unfortunately, sometimes the people who created these databases didn't completely understand the concept of a relational database. (After you have read this book, you won't fall into that group.) As a result, many of the older database structures are improperly or inefficiently designed.

Improperly or inefficiently designed database structures are found on PC-based legacy databases as well. A very large number of PC-based databases were originally designed and implemented in dBase II and dBase III, which were nonrelational database management systems. As a result, the database structures implemented within these systems could not take advantage of the benefits provided by the relational model; for example, many of the structures contain duplicate fields and store redundant data.

Analyzing a legacy database is somewhat easier than analyzing a paper-based database because a legacy database is typically more organized and structured than a paper-based database, the structures within the database are explicitly defined, and usually the company or organization uses an application program to interact with the data in the database. (The application program can reveal a lot of information about the data structures and the tasks performed against the data in the database.) The time it will take to perform the analysis properly will depend to some degree on the platform (mainframe or PC) and the RDBMS used to implement the database.

The key point to remember when analyzing either a paper-based or a legacy database is to proceed patiently and methodically through the process in order to ensure a thorough and accurate analysis.

Conducting the Analysis

There are three steps in the analysis process: reviewing the way data is collected, reviewing the manner in which information is presented, and conducting interviews with users and management.

As you conduct the first two steps in this process, it will be necessary for you to speak to various people in the organization. *Be sure your conversations with them are related purely to the reviews you're conducting.* You'll have the opportunity to ask them other in-depth questions later. Keep in mind that these reviews are an integral part of your preparation for the interviews that will follow. Indeed, the reviews help to determine the types of questions you will need to ask in subsequent interviews.

Looking at How Data Is Collected

The first step in the analysis process involves reviewing the ways in which data is collected. This includes everything from index cards and hand-written lists to preprinted forms and data-entry screens (such as those used in a database software program).

Begin this step by reviewing all paper-based items. Find out what types of paper documents are being used to record data, and then gather a single sample of each type. Assemble these samples together in a folder for use later in the design process. As an example, say that supplier data is collected on index cards. Go through each of the index cards until you find one with an entry that is as complete as possible. When you've found an appropriate sample, make a copy of it and place

A1 Office Supplies	
Suite 133	
7739 Alpine Way SE	
Seattle, WA 98115	
Susan McLain	519-5883
FAX	519-9948

Employee Fact Sheet				
Name: George Chavez		Date Hired: June 30, 1995		
Address: 7527 Taxco Drive		City: Seattle	State: WA	Zip: 98115
Phone: 553-0399	Date of Birth: 09/22/53		SSN: 456-92-0049	

Education:

Name of Academic Organization	Location	Year Graduated
University Of Texas at El Paso	El Paso, TX	1977

Figure 6-1. *Examples of paper-based items used to collect data.*

the copy in your stack of samples. Proceed through this process for each type of paper being used. Figure 6-1 shows examples of paper currently used to collect data.

Next review the computer software programs currently being used to collect data. The objective here is to gather a set of sample screen shots that represent how the programs are used. A word of caution: many people have discovered unique and ingenious ways to use common programs, such as word processors and spreadsheets, as a way to collect and manage data. Make sure you speak with someone who is familiar with the way the computers are being used within the organization, and discover which programs are used to manage the organization's data.

Customer Information

Name (F/L): John Holmes

Address: 725 Globe Circle   Status: Active

City: El Paso   Phone: 778-9715

State: TX   Zip: 79915   FAX: 778-4497

	A	B	C	D	E
1	*Product ID*	*Product Description*	*Category*	*SRP*	*Qty On Hand*
2	9001	Shur-Lok U-Lock	Accessories	75.00	
3	9002	SpeedRite Cyclecomputer		65.00	20
4	9003	SteelHead Microshell Helmet	Accessories	36.00	33
5	9004	SureStop 133-MB Brakes	Components	23.50	16
6	9005	Diablo ATM Mountain Bike	Bikes	1,200.00	
7	9006	UltraVision Helmet Mount Mirrors		7.45	10

Figure 6-2. *A typical database screen and a typical spreadsheet screen.*

As you review how each program is being used to collect data, find a screen that best represents how the program is used. You're looking for screens like those shown in Figure 6-2. The first screen is typical of those found in database programs, and the second screen is typical of those found in spreadsheet programs. When you've found an appropriate sample, create a screen shot (use [ALT]-[PRTSC] or a screen-capture program), paste it into a document in your word processing program, and then print the document. You'll find that you will want to have several samples for each program you review. Repeat this procedure for each program.

Once you have all the appropriate screen shots gathered together, assemble them in a folder for use later in the design process. Make sure you clearly mark the folder containing the samples of paper and the folder containing the screen shots.

Looking at How Information Is Presented

The second step in the analysis process is to review any methods currently used to present information needed by the organization. This includes all hand-written documents, computer printouts, and on-screen presentations. The most common method of presenting information is by means of a *report*. A report is any hand-written, typed, or computer-generated document used to arrange and present data in such a way that it is meaningful to the person or people viewing it. Thus the report transforms the data into information!

Another method of presenting information is through on-screen presentations, also known as "slide shows." These presentations are typically used to present a variety of information by means of a computer screen or overhead projector; such presentations are generally created with programs such as Microsoft PowerPoint or Harvard Graphics.

Begin this step by reviewing all the reports generated from the database, regardless of whether they are produced by hand or generated by the computer. Identify all of the reports currently being used, gather a sample of each one, and assemble each one in a separate folder as you did with the items in the previous step. Overall, this task is easier to perform in this step than it was in the previous step because people are typically more familiar with the reports their organization uses. Usually copies of the reports are readily available, and most reports can be reprinted if necessary. Figure 6-3 shows an example of a hand-written report and a computer-generated report currently used by an organization.

Employee Phone List
as of 05/16/96

John Alcot	554-3002
Regina Allen	752-5593
George Chavez	623-3292
Ryan Erlich	554-2991

Current Product Inventory

Product ID	Product Description	Category	SRP	Quantity
9001	Shur-Lok U-Lock	Accessories	75.00	
9002	SpeedRite Cyclecomputer		65.00	20
9003	SteelHead Microshell Helmet	Accessories	36.00	33
9004	SureStop 133-MB Brakes	Components	23.50	16

Figure 6-3. *Examples of hand-written and computer-generated reports.*

The final part of this step is to review any on-screen presentations that use or incorporate the data in the database. It's unnecessary to review *every* presentation, but you do need to review those that have a direct bearing on the data in the database. For example, you *don't* need to review a presentation on the features of the organization's new product, but you *do* need to review a presentation on year-to-date sales statistics.

Once you've identified which presentations you need to review, go through each one carefully and make screen shots of the slides that use or incorporate data from the database. Then gather the screen shots together and assemble them in a folder for later use. (Write the name of the presentation on the folder; you may need to refer to it again at a later time.) *Follow this procedure separately for each presentation.* You want to make sure you don't accidentally combine two or more presentations together, because this mistake will inevitably lead to mass confusion and result in one huge mess!

Figure 6-4 shows an example of the type of slides you're looking for within a presentation.

Reviewing a presentation is difficult in some cases, and deciding whether or not a slide should be included as a sample is purely a discretionary decision. Therefore, work closely with the person most familiar with the presentation to ensure that you include all appropriate slides in the samples.

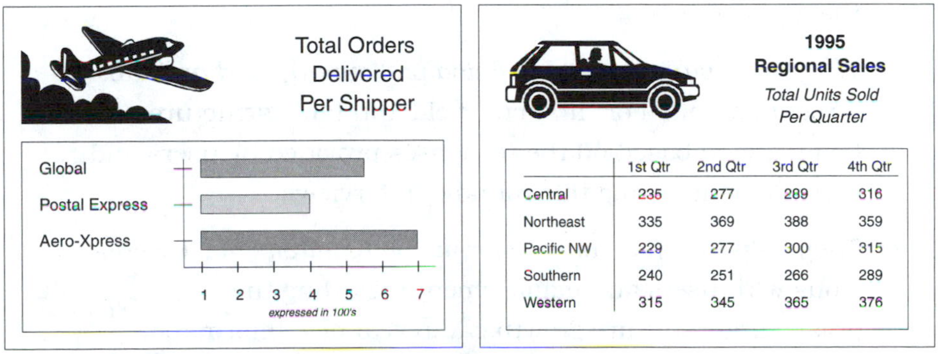

Figure 6-4. *Examples of on-screen presentation slides.*

Conducting Interviews

Now that you have a general idea of how the organization collects and presents its data, it's time to interview users and management to determine how the organization *uses* its data. Interviews are useful in the analysis phase for the following reasons:

- *They provide details about the samples you assembled in reviewing how data is collected and how information is presented.* During the reviews, the discussions you had with users and management were solely meant to identify in general terms how data used by the organization is collected and presented. During the interview phase you can ask specific questions about the samples you assembled during those reviews. You can clarify any aspects of a specific sample that you consider to be vague or ambiguous.

- *They provide information on the way the organization uses its data.* By conducting interviews you will learn how the users work with the data on a daily basis and how management uses information based on that data to manage the affairs of the organization.

- *They are instrumental in defining preliminary field and table structures.* Initial or "first cut" field and table structures can be identified based on the responses provided by users and management during this round of interviews.

- *They help to define future information requirements.* Discussions with users and management regarding the organization's future growth can reveal new information requirements that must be supported by the database.

> ❖ **Note** Throughout the remainder of the book, the term *management* is used to refer to the person or persons controlling or directing an organization.

> ❖ **Note** The following techniques are used for both user interviews and management interviews. The only differences between the two sets of interviews lie in the subject matter and the content of the questions.

Conducting interviews is a two-part process: the first part involves speaking with users, and the second part involves speaking with management. You'll speak to the users first because they represent the "front lines" of the organization. They have the clearest picture of the details connected with the day-to-day operations of the organization. Also the information you gather from the users should help you to understand the answers you receive from management.

You'll use both open-ended and closed questions throughout the interviews, alternating between each type as the interview progresses. The open-ended questions are used to focus on specific subjects; the closed questions are used to obtain specific details on a certain subject. At the beginning of the interview, for example, start with a few open-ended questions in order to establish some general subjects for discussion, then select a subject and ask more specific (closed) questions relating to that subject. For example, start with an open-ended question such as the following:

"How would you define the work that you do on a daily basis?"

This type of question usually elicits a response of three or more sentences. It's perfectly acceptable if you receive a long, descriptive response because it's easier to work with than one that is terse. To illustrate this point, assume you received the following response to the previous question:

"As an account representative, I'm responsible for ten clients. Each of my clients makes an appointment to come into the showroom to view the merchandise we have to offer for the current season. Part of my job is to answer any questions they have about our merchandise and make recommendations regarding the most popular items. Once they make a decision on the merchandise they'd like to purchase, I write up a sales order for the client. Then, I give the sales order to my assistant, who promptly fills the order and sends it to the client."

This is a very good response. The participant not only answered your question; he provided you with the opportunity to begin asking follow-up questions. The response also suggests several subjects that you can discuss later in the interview.

> ❖ **Note** When you receive a terse response (such as "I fill out customer sales orders"), you'll have to ask even more questions to obtain the information you need from the participant. Yet this type of response may indicate that a participant is just nervous or uncomfortable. In this case, you could put him at ease by discussing an unrelated topic for a few moments, or by allowing him to select a more familiar or comfortable subject.

As you ask each open-ended question, identify any subjects suggested within the response to the question. You can identify subjects by looking for *nouns* within the sentences that make up the response. Subjects are always represented by nouns and identify an object (such as a person, place, or thing) or an event (something that occurs at a given point in time). There are some nouns, however, that represent a *characteristic* of an object or event; you don't need to concern yourself with these just yet. Therefore, make sure you only look for nouns that *specifically* represent an object or event. To ensure that you account for every subject you need to discuss, mark the nouns with a double-underline as you identify them; for example,

"As an <u>account representative</u>, I'm responsible for ten <u>clients</u>."

After you've identified all of the appropriate nouns within the response, list them on a sheet of paper; this is your *list of subjects*. You'll add more subjects to the list as you continue to work through the design process. This list serves two purposes: you'll use it to discuss the subjects as the interview progresses, and you'll use it later in the design process to help define tables.

The entire procedure just described is referred to as the *subject identification technique* throughout the remainder of the book. It is a very useful tool because it helps you identify subjects that need to be addressed by the database.

Returning to the example, say you underlined the appropriate nouns within this response:

As an <u>account representative</u>, I'm responsible for ten <u>clients</u>. Each of my clients makes an <u>appointment</u> to come into the <u>showroom</u> to view the <u>merchandise</u> we have to offer for the current <u>season</u>. Part of my job is to answer any questions they have about our merchandise and make recommendations regarding the most popular <u>items</u>. Once they make a decision on the merchandise they'd like to purchase, I write up a <u>sales order</u> for the client. Then, I give the sales order to my assistant, who promptly fills the order and sends it to the client."

Based on this response, we can produce the following list of subjects:

Account representatives	Merchandise
Appointments	Sales orders
Assistant	Seasons
Clients	Showroom
Items	

You can use this list of subjects to come up with further questions during the interview.

To verify that the nouns you've underlined are genuine subjects, review the way they're used in the response. For example, consider the first two subjects on this list. The first subject, "account representatives," is suggested in the first sentence. Because of the way this noun is used in the sentence, you can assume it represents an *object* (person, place, or thing), which in this case is an individual or group of individuals collectively known as "account representatives." The second subject in the list, "appointments," is suggested in the second sentence. You can assume this noun represents an *event* (something that occurs at a given point in time) because of the way it is used in the sentence.

Once you've identified the subjects suggested within the response, pick a particular subject and begin to ask follow-up questions related to it. The purpose of this line of questioning is to obtain as much detailed information as possible about the subject you've selected. Therefore, make your follow-up questions more specific as you progress through this part of the discussion. The nature of your follow-up questions will depend on the responses you receive from the participant. Based on our sample response, for example, you can continue to ask more specific questions regarding sales orders or you could begin a new line of questioning regarding clients. However, say you asked the following question to learn more about sales orders:

> "Let's discuss sales orders for a moment. What does it take to complete a sales order for a client?"

Note that this question begins with a statement directing the interview participant to focus on a particular subject. Once you've selected a specific subject to discuss, always use a statement similar to the one in the example as a preface to your first question about the subject. The statement will guide the discussion. Also note that although the question itself is open-ended, it prompts the participant for details regarding the subject you've chosen (sales orders) and allows you to establish the focus of the participant's responses.

Now assume that the participant gave the following reply:

> "Well, I enter all the client information first, such as the client's name, address, and phone number. Then I enter the items the client wants to purchase. After I've entered all the items, I tally up the totals and I'm done. Oh, I forgot to mention: I enter the client's fax number and shipping address—if they have one."

Start your analysis of this response by using the subject identification technique to determine whether there are any further subjects suggested within the response. If so, add them to your list of subjects. Remember: list only those nouns that represent an object or event.

Once you've finished, begin looking for any *details* regarding the subject under discussion. Your objective here is to obtain as many facts about the subject as possible. *Now* you're interested in the nouns that represent *characteristics* of the subject—they *describe* a particular aspect of the subject. These nouns are easy to identify within a sentence because they are typically in singular form ("phone number," "address"). In contrast, the noun used to identify the subject is usually in possessive form ("the *client's* phone number," "the *company's* address").

As you identify nouns that represent characteristics, mark each one with a single underline. Try to account for as many characteristics of the subject as possible. Here's an example of a user response:

> "Well, I enter all the client information first, such as the cli-
> ent's <u>name</u>, <u>address</u>, and <u>phone number</u>."

As you identify the appropriate nouns within the response, list them on a sheet of paper. This becomes your *list of characteristics*. You'll add more characteristics to the list as you work through the design pro-cess, and later you'll use this list when you are determining the fields for the database. *Use a separate sheet of paper for the list of character-istics. Do not list the subjects and characteristics on the same sheet!* (The reason for keeping them on different lists will become clear when you begin to define tables for the database in Chapter 7.)

Throughout the remainder of the book, we will refer to this procedure as the *characteristic identification technique*. It's a very useful tool because it helps you determine the fields that need to be defined in the database.

To continue the example, say that you underlined the appropriate nouns within this response:

> "Well, I enter all the client information first, such as the client's
> <u>name</u>, <u>address</u>, and <u>phone number</u>. Then I enter the items the
> client wants to purchase. After I've entered all the items, I tally
> up the <u>totals</u> and I'm done. Oh, I forgot to mention that I enter
> the client's <u>fax number</u> and <u>shipping address</u>—if they have one."

You could then produce the following list (shown in alphabetical order):

Address	Phone number
Fax number	Shipping address
Name	Totals

You now have a list of characteristics for the subject under discussion. These characteristics will subsequently become fields in the database.

Verify that the nouns you've marked with a single underline are genuine characteristics by reviewing the way they're used in the response. For example, consider the two characteristics on this list. The first characteristic, "names," is suggested in the first sentence of the response. By the way the noun is used in the sentence, you can assume that it describes some aspect of the subject Client. The characteristic "Shipping address" is suggested in the last sentence of the response. You can assume this noun also represents some aspect of the subject Client by the way it is used in that sentence.

After you've finished discussing a particular subject, move on to the next subject on your subjects list and begin the same pattern of questioning. Start with open-ended questions, identify the subjects suggested in the responses, ask more specific questions as the discussion progresses, and identify as many of the subject's characteristics as possible. Continue this process in an orderly manner until you've discussed every subject on your list.

❖ **Note** Although the subject identification technique and characteristic identification technique are very useful, they do take a short amount of time to learn. With some practice, however, they become intuitive. You'll use these techniques during your interviews with users and management, and later when you're identifying fields and tables for the initial database structure.

Conducting User Interviews

The first part of the interview process involves conducting user interviews. These interviews will focus on the following four issues:

- the types of data users are currently using;

- how users are currently using their data;

- the data-collection samples, report samples, and on-screen presentation samples you assembled during the first two steps of the analysis; and

- the types of information users need in conjunction with their daily work.

Reviewing Data Type and Usage

You can usually discuss the first two issues at the same time if you carefully phrase your questions at the beginning of the interview. Your objective for this part of the interview is to identify the types of data the users are currently using and how they use that data in support of the work they do. You'll use this information later in the design process to help define field and table structures. Use the data-collection and data representation samples to help formulate questions about data. (However, don't discuss the samples just yet; they should be treated as a separate issue.) During this discussion, you'll start with open-ended questions, identify subjects within the responses, and then use specific follow-up questions to identify the characteristics of each subject.

As you begin the interview, ask each participant about the work he or she performs on a daily basis. After the participant has provided an overall description of the work he does, ask him to explain his job in more detail. Have the participant "walk you through" the job he performs on a daily basis.

Following is a dialog that is typical of what occurs during this part of
the interview:

> INTERVIEWER: What kind of work do you do on a day-to-day
> basis?
>
> PARTICIPANT: I accept land-use applications that are sub-
> mitted by various people, log them in, and
> set a hearing date with the Hearing Exam-
> iner. I also assist applicants if they have any
> questions regarding a specific application.
>
> INTERVIEWER: Let's talk about the applications for a
> moment. What type of facts are associated
> with an application?
>
> PARTICIPANT: There's quite a number, actually. There are
> facts concerning the type and name of the
> application, its designation and address, and
> its location.
>
> INTERVIEWER: Tell me about the facts concerning the appli-
> cation's type and name.
>
> PARTICIPANT: There are four things we record: the type of
> application, the name of the subdivision, the
> purpose of the project, and the description of
> the project.

Note how the interviewer starts the discussion with an open-ended
question. After the participant responds, the interviewer uses the subject identification technique to identify subjects within the response.
The interviewer then chooses a particular subject and uses another
open-ended question to focus the participant on that subject. Because
the participant's next response was stated in general terms, the interviewer uses the subject identification technique once again and selects
yet another subject. This time, however, the interviewer focuses on a
particular aspect of the subject and uses a more specific follow-up
question to elicit a detailed response from the participant.

The interviewer can continue to narrow the focus of questions as the discussion progresses. As the participant responds to each question, the interviewer continues to use the characteristic identification technique to identify characteristics of the subject that appear in the response. After all of the characteristics have been identified, the interviewer then moves on to the next subject and begins the entire process again. This procedure will be repeated until all the subjects have been discussed. You'll use exactly the same procedure when you act as interviewer.

Reviewing the Samples

The next issue you'll discuss concerns the data-collection samples, report samples, and on-screen presentation samples you assembled earlier in the analysis process. Your objectives during this discussion are to identify how the objects represented by the samples are used, to clarify any aspects of the samples you don't understand, and to assign a description to each sample.

Now that you have an idea of the types of data the participants use as well as how they use those types of data, you'll find it easy to talk to participants about the samples. Start the conversation by selecting a sample to discuss, and then begin asking questions about it. Say you've chosen to work with the data-collection sample shown in Figure 6-5.

Before you ask your first question, review your notes from the discussions held at the beginning of the interview to determine whether any of what you have already discussed is relevant to the sample you're about to discuss. For example, in one of the previous discussions, a participant indicated that part of his job is to keep track of all the organization's customers. Using that statement as a starting point, you could ask him how he uses this data-collection sample to perform that task. You could ask this question, for instance:

Customer Information

Name (F/L):	John Holmes		
Address:	725 Globe Circle	Status:	Active
City:	El Paso	Phone:	778-9715
State:	TX Zip: 79915	FAX:	778-4497

Figure 6-5. *A data-collection sample.*

"You mentioned in a previous discussion that you keep track of all the customers. How does this screen help you to carry out that task?"

This is a well-phrased question. It is prefaced with a statement that focuses on a particular subject, and the question itself then brings the participant's attention to the sample. The question is open enough to elicit a clear and complete response.

To continue this example, say the participant responds with the following reply:

"This screen allows me to enter new customers, as well as modify and maintain all the information we have on existing customers."

If this reply answers the question to your complete satisfaction, you'll use it as the basis for describing the sample. On the other hand, if this reply does not completely answer the question, continue with the appropriate line of questioning until the participant clearly identifies the purpose and use of the sample. It's necessary for each sample to have a description because you'll use the samples again later in the design process.

The description should be succinct yet give a clear indication of the purpose of the sample and how it is used. Write the description on a slip of paper and attach it to the sample. The following sentence is an example of a description you might use for the sample in Figure 6-5.

"This screen is used to collect and maintain all customer data."

It's necessary for you to understand the sample as completely as possible so that you can write a clear and concise description. If there are any aspects of a given sample you don't understand, ask the participant to clarify them for you. For example, assume you're working with the report sample shown in Figure 6-6.

If you don't know what the abbreviation "SRP" represents, you'll have to ask someone to tell you what it means. You could pose a simple question:

"What do the letters 'SRP' stand for in the 'Current Product Inventory' report?"

Current Product Inventory

Product ID	Product Description	Category	SRP	Quantity
9001	Shur-Lok U-Lock	Accessories	75.00	
9002	SpeedRite Cyclecomputer		65.00	20
9003	SteelHead Microshell Helmet	Accessories	36.00	33
9004	SureStop 133-MB Brakes	Components	23.50	16

Figure 6-6. *A report sample.*

Such a direct approach usually elicits the clear and definitive response you seek.

As you compose descriptions for each of the samples, you'll find that writing a description of a *complex* sample can be difficult. A sample is complex if it represents more than one subject. The sample in Figure 6-6, for example, only covers one subject: Products. The sample in Figure 6-7, however, covers at least three subjects: Doctor Services, Nursing Services, and Patients. With a complex sample you will often have to do more work to determine the sample's purpose and use. In some cases you'll have to use the subject identification technique to determine what subjects are represented within the sample. Once the subjects are identified, it's easier to clarify the function or functions of the sample. You can then compose a description that gives a clear picture of the sample's purpose.

For example, say you're working with the report sample shown in Figure 6-7 and you have questions regarding the nursing services. You wonder whether the organization is using this report as an indirect means of maintaining a current list of nursing services. At the same time, you want to avoid asking a participant a question whose answer is simply yes or no. You'd rather use a question that elicits a more informative response. You could use the following open-ended question to begin the discussion on this sample:

"What nursing services do you provide besides those listed in this sample?"

By using this type of question, you give the participant an opportunity to give a detailed response. Furthermore, you give yourself the opportunity to ask follow-up questions as warranted by the participant's reply. To continue the example, say you received the following answer:

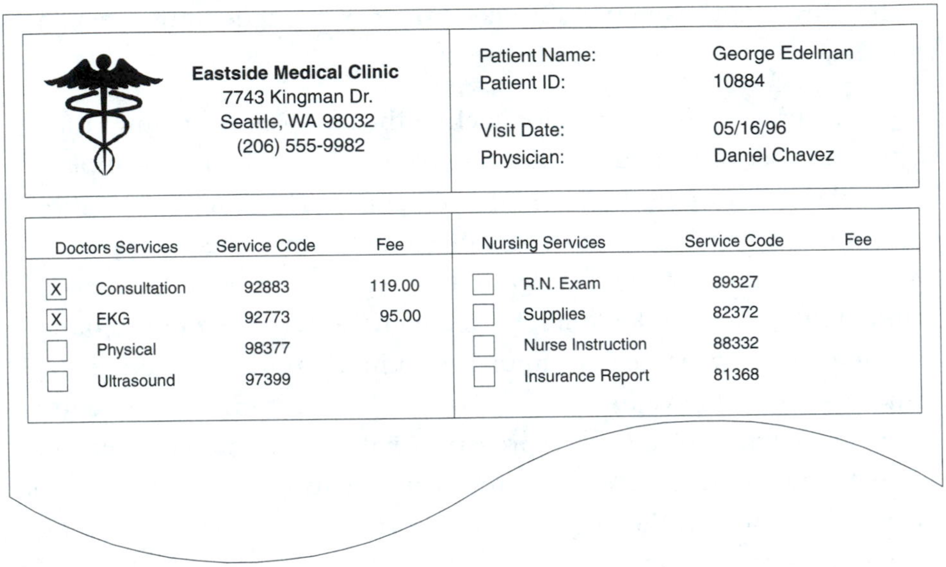

Eastside Medical Clinic
7743 Kingman Dr.
Seattle, WA 98032
(206) 555-9982

Patient Name: George Edelman
Patient ID: 10884

Visit Date: 05/16/96
Physician: Daniel Chavez

Doctors Services	Service Code	Fee
[X] Consultation	92883	119.00
[X] EKG	92773	95.00
[ ] Physical	98377	
[ ] Ultrasound	97399	

Nursing Services	Service Code	Fee
[ ] R.N. Exam	89327	
[ ] Supplies	82372	
[ ] Nurse Instruction	88332	
[ ] Insurance Report	81368	

Figure 6-7. *An example of a complex report sample.*

> "We provide various specialized services for the more complex patient. You only see the general services on this report. However, I can show you a complete list of our services that Katherine maintains on her computer."

If this reply clarifies the point in question and you now understand the purpose of this report sample, you can continue with the process of writing the description of the sample. If the point is still unclear, you can continue with follow-up questions until everything is explained to your satisfaction.

Reviewing Information Requirements

The final issue you'll discuss with users concerns their information requirements. The objectives of this discussion are to determine whether individual users receive information based on data they don't directly control or maintain, to determine what types of additional information they need, and to determine what types of information they can foresee themselves needing in the future. The information you gather during this discussion will be used later in the design process to help define and verify field and table structures. You can also use this information as yet another way of determining whether anything was accidentally overlooked during any of the previous discussions.

Current Information Requirements

Users typically receive the information they use through a variety of reports. Therefore, the best way to begin this discussion is by reviewing the report samples. This time around, though, you're not so concerned with how the report is used as you are with the data the reports are based on. It's quite common that information on some of the reports a user receives is based on data he does not personally create and maintain. If such is the case, you must determine the origin of that data so that you can identify *all* the data used by a user, whether he uses it directly or indirectly.

Start the conversation by first selecting a report from the report samples. Then work with one of the participants to determine what data is used to produce the report. Ask him if he creates and maintains the data on which the report is based. If the answer is yes, you can move on to the next sample. But if the answer is no, then you need to identify the origin of the data. The following example illustrates this process.

Say you have an assistant by the name of Kendra who is beginning a discussion with a participant named Gregory on the report sample shown in Figure 6-8. As Kendra begins the conversation, Gregory mentions that he works in the telemarketing department. When Kendra first asks about the sample report, Gregory indicates that he

Customer Phone List

Customer Name	Customer Type	Last Purchase	Phone Number
Alastair Black	Preferred	05/21/96	551-0993
Dave Cunningham	Silver	03/19/96	533-9182
Zachary Ehrlich	Preferred	05/16/96	515-3921
Frank Lerum	Gold	04/12/96	552-3884

Figure 6-8. *A sample report.*

receives it every Monday morning. So Kendra asks him the following question:

"Do you provide the data that's used to generate this report?"

Her next course of action depends on the Gregory's response to this question. If his answer is yes, she can move on to the next sample. It's a good idea, however, for her to ask a follow-up question to double-check that his answer is true. She can use a question such as the following:

"Do you personally enter and maintain this data on a daily basis?"

If his answer is still yes, she can definitely move on to the next sample.

On the other hand, if Gregory's answer to the original question is no, Kendra will need to ask a few follow-up questions. First, she will ask him whether he contributes *any* data to the report. If he does, she'll determine what data he specifically submits. Then she'll ask whether or not he knows the source of the remaining data.

To continue the example, say Gregory's reply to the original question is no and that the following dialog takes place after his response:

KENDRA: Can you tell me, then, if there is any data that you contribute to the report at all?

GREGORY: I do supply the customer's name and phone number.

KENDRA: Then you don't supply the Customer Type or the Last Purchase Date, is that correct?

GREGORY: Yes, that's correct.

KENDRA: Can you tell me who provides the Customer Type and the Last Purchase Date?

GREGORY: I'm not really sure, but . . .

KENDRA: Do you have an idea of where these items come from?

GREGORY: As a matter of fact, I do. They come from the sales department.

KENDRA: That sounds good to me. I'll make a note of that on this sample, and then we can move on to the next one.

Note that as the dialog begins, Kendra first tries to determine whether Gregory submits any data at all to the report. When Gregory reveals that he contributes two of the items for the report, she then poses a follow-up question to verify that he is not submitting any of the other data. Finally, she tries to identify the source of the remaining data by asking Gregory if he knows where the data originates. In this case, it takes only two well-phrased questions to find the answer. If Gregory could not answer the last two questions, Kendra would need to continue her investigation with other participants.

If your discussion progresses in the same manner as that of the preceding dialog, you're sure to obtain all the information you need about your report samples. Remember: follow-up questions are a crucial part of the conversation. You must phrase your questions properly to elicit the types of responses you need from the participants.

Additional Information Requirements

The next subject of discussion is *additional* information requirements. The objective here is to determine whether the users require additional information that is not being delivered to them currently. If this is the case, then you must identify what it is. If necessary, you'll define new data structures to support this extra information later in the design process.

Start this conversation by directing the participants to review the reports they currently receive. Ask them whether there is any other information they would like to see in any of the reports. Next direct them to discuss the additional information, what reports it pertains to, and the reason they believe it is necessary. Then determine whether the new information represents new subjects or new characteristics. If it does, identify each new item and add it to the appropriate list. Finally, review the comments the participants have made and determine whether there are any further issues you need to discuss with them in regards to the reports.

To illustrate this process, say you're beginning this discussion and you've just asked the participants to review the report samples they currently use. One of the participants is reviewing the sample report shown in Figure 6-9.

Now instruct this particular participant to note any additional information she would like to see on the reports as well as to give a brief statement indicating why the information is necessary. At this point, it

Current Product Inventory

Product ID	Product Description	Category	SRP	Quantity
9001	Shur-Lok U-Lock	Accessories	75.00	
9002	SpeedRite Cyclecomputer		65.00	20
9003	SteelHead Microshell Helmet	Accessories	36.00	33
9004	SureStop 133-MB Brakes	Components	23.50	16

Figure 6-9. *The sample report being reviewed by a participant.*

doesn't really matter exactly *how* the notations are made so long as they are clear and attached to the report in an obvious manner. In this case, the participant who was reviewing the sample report shown in Figure 6-9 decided to use large sticky notes as a means of document-ing her comments. On each sticky note she has specified a new field she'd like to include on the report along with the reason for its inclu-sion. She has also suggested a possible location for the field by writing its name on the report itself. Figure 6-10 shows the sample report with her comments.

Next determine whether any *new* subjects or *new* characteristics are represented in the additional information. Examine each report and apply the subject identification technique and the characteristic identi-fication technique to the comments attached to the report. We can apply these techniques to the first comment in Figure 6-10:

"Can we include the Vendor name? It would make it easier to identify a specific product."

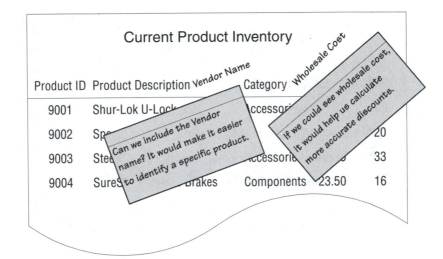

Figure 6-10. *A report sample with comments.*

Both a subject and a characteristic have been identified. (Note that the subject and characteristic aren't directly related: "Vendor name" is a characteristic of a "Vendor," not of a "product." There's no problem here, but you should be aware that this apparent mismatch of subjects and characteristics is typical. This will be addressed later in the design process.) Check your subjects list and characteristics list to determine whether you've already accounted for these items. If you have, move on to the next comment and repeat this procedure.

If this process turns up a new subject, add it to your list of subjects and then identify as many of its characteristics as possible. When you're finished, add these items to your list of characteristics, move on to the next comment, and repeat the entire procedure. In many instances, however, you'll only identify new characteristics. Don't be alarmed. People often want to add items to a report that are characteristics of subjects that are *already* represented by the information on the report.

Finally, reexamine each report and determine if you have any questions or concerns about the notes participants have made. For instance, you may question the rationale behind one participant's belief that specific fields are necessary on a given report. Or you might wonder why another participant wants to *exclude* certain fields from one of his reports. You definitely want to make sure that the fields he wants to exclude are truly unnecessary and that their removal will not adversely affect the information the report provides to other people. In either case, the inclusion or exclusion of fields will affect the final database structure.

If a report has one or more remarks that are cause for concern, review it with the appropriate participant and settle as many of the issues as you can. You can usually resolve all your concerns with a few simple questions, but in some cases the resolution to certain issues will not become apparent until later in the design process. For example, there are instances in which some fields appear on two or more reports. It's difficult to determine if they are being unnecessarily duplicated until you begin to define the field and table structures. When you encounter an issue that is difficult to resolve at the present time, make a note of it and put the report aside for later review.

Future Information Requirements

The last subject of discussion concerns *future* information requirements. Your objective here is to identify any information that the participants believe will be necessary for them to receive as the organization grows. Once such future information requirements are identified, you can ensure that the data structures needed to support that information are defined in the database.

First you'll need to make sure that every participant has some idea of how the organization is growing and in what direction it is growing. The nature of the organization's growth will determine what new information participants will require. If several people are unacquainted with these issues, you'll need to obtain this information from management and then relay it to the participants prior to the discussion. Once everyone is familiar with these matters, you can begin the conversation.

Start the discussion by directing the participants to think about the future growth of the organization and how it may affect the work they do on a daily basis. Keep in mind that some of them are going to have a difficult time envisioning this scenario. When this happens, use the following types of questions as a means of helping them focus their thoughts:

> "How will the organization's growth affect the amount of information you'll need to do your job?"
>
> "Do you think you'll need additional types of information to carry out your duties effectively as the organization grows?"
>
> "How will the growth of the organization increase the time you spend on your day-to-day tasks?"
>
> "Can you predict what types (categories, not specific items) of new information you'll need in order to carry out your duties as the organization expands?"
>
> "Do you anticipate a need for new information if your duties are increased because of the organization's growth"

Keep in mind that most of the participants' answers will be based on *speculation*. There's no accurate way for them to predict what types of information they'll really need until the organization's growth occurs. However, if you can anticipate their hypothetical information requirements, you can prepare for them by defining the necessary data structures in advance.

As the participants make their responses, use the subject identification technique to identify brand new subjects, and then add them to your list of subjects. Then use the characteristic identification technique to uncover any new details concerning existing or new subjects, and add them to your list of characteristics.

To help participants visualize the types of information they may need in the future, it is useful to sketch ideas for new reports or data entry forms, identifying any new subjects and characteristics that need to be addressed in the database structure. If you create several rough drawings of sample reports, be sure to assemble them in a separate, clearly marked folder. Then code each revision so that you can compare it with earlier revisions. Figure 6-11 shows an example of a preliminary design for a future report.

Continue the conversation with users until you're satisfied that you've accounted for as many of the participants' future information requirements as possible. When you've completed the discussion, you're ready to conduct interviews with management.

1st Quarter Customer Sales Statistics

Customer ID	Customer Name	Sales Amounts		
		Maximum	Minimum	Average
9001	Stewart Jameson	265.00	23.00	55.00
9002	Shannon McLain	550.00	125.00	70.00
9003	Estela Pundt	250.00	35.00	36.00
9004	Timothy Ennis	325.00	20.00	25.00

Figure 6-11. *An example of a design for a new report.*

> ❖ **Note** All of the techniques you learned during the user inter-
> views section can be used in the management interviews section
> as well. The following section is somewhat shorter and more con-
> cise, because I have assumed that by now you understand how
> to use the techniques described earlier.

Conducting Management Interviews

The second part of the interview process involves interviewing management personnel. These interviews will focus on the following issues:

- the types of information managers currently receive,

- the types of additional information they need to receive,

- the types of information they foresee themselves needing, and

- their perception of the business's *overall* information
  requirements.

Reviewing Current Information Requirements

Your objectives during the first part of this interview are to identify the
information that management routinely receives and to determine
whether they currently receive any reports that are not represented in
your group of report samples.

As you begin the interview, ask each participant about the work he performs and the responsibilities associated with his position. Because
most people in management positions tend to have a number of things
on their minds, your questions will help them focus their attention on
the matters at hand. Their answers will give you some idea of how they
might use the information on the reports they receive and provide you
with a perspective of their need for this information.

Next ask each participant if he uses any of the reports in your collection of report samples. If the participant doesn't use any of the reports, proceed with the next step. But if the participant does, examine each report, and ask him to identify any other subjects on the report that might have been previously overlooked. Use the subject identification technique as necessary to aid with this process. If the manager identifies a new subject, add it to your list of subjects and use the characteristic identification technique to uncover the subject's characteristics. Then add these to your list of characteristics. Repeat this procedure for each sample report.

Continue the discussion by asking each participant whether he receives any reports that are *not* represented in the group of report samples. If the answer is yes, obtain a sample of each "new" report. Next review each new report with the participant. Use the subject identification technique and the characteristic identification technique to identify the subjects represented by each new report and their associated characteristics. Then add the subjects and characteristics to their respective lists. Finally, attach a description to each new report and add the new report to your collection of report samples. Repeat this procedure until you've accounted for every new report.

Reviewing Additional Information Requirements

The next subject of discussion concerns management's need for *additional* information. Your objective is to determine whether they require some supplemental information that is currently missing from the reports they receive. If you conclude that this is the case, you must identify that additional information. Later in the design process, you'll define new data structures (if necessary) to support this extra information. However, if no additional information is required, move on to the next part of the interview.

You'll use the same techniques for this discussion that you used for this segment of the user interviews. Here are the steps you'll follow:

1. Review the report samples with the participants once again, and ask them if there is any additional information they would like to include in any of the reports.

2. Have them note the additional information—including the reasons why they believe it's necessary—on the appropriate reports. Remember that it doesn't matter how these notations are made so long as they are clear, noticeable, and are attached to the applicable report.

3. Determine if the information represents new subjects or new characteristics. If it does, identify each new item and add it to the appropriate list.

4. Review the reports and discuss any concerns you have about them with the participants. Once your concerns are resolved, this process is complete.

Reviewing Future Information Requirements

Future information requirements is the next subject of discussion. Your objective during this discussion is to determine what information management foresees itself needing in the future. Once these needs have been identified, you can ensure that the data structures are in place to support the information as the need for it arises.

As you begin the discussion, have the participants take into consideration how the organization is growing and in what direction it's growing. Then ask them what effect that growth will have on the information they require to make sound decisions and what effect it will have on the way they guide or direct the organization. Remember that their answers are going to be based on speculation, as was the case with similar questions you asked users. Until the organization's growth occurs, there's no way for management to predict their future needs accurately. However, it's always a good idea to plan for the future as much as possible.

As the participants respond, use the subject identification technique and characteristic identification technique to identify items within their replies. Then add each new item to the appropriate list.

If they have ideas about new reports they may need, make sketches of them. Then take each new report and determine what subjects and characteristics the information on the report represents. When you've identified all the items, add them to the appropriate list. Then assemble these new reports in a clearly marked folder.

When you've accounted for as many of their future requirements as possible, you're ready to move on to the last subject.

Reviewing Overall Information Requirements

The last topic of discussion concerns the organization's *overall* information requirements. In the opinion of management, what generic class of information does the organization need? In pursuing this question, you're trying to discover whether there is any data that the organization needs to maintain that has not been previously discussed, either in the user interviews or the management interviews. If you determine that there is such data, you'll need to account for it in the database structure.

To help participants answer this question, review with them both the group of sample reports and the group of new reports that you've gathered throughout the analysis and interview processes. Ask participants to consider the information provided by the reports and how that information will be used. (They'll have to have made assumptions that led to suggesting the new reports.) Next ask participants to determine whether there is any information that would be useful or valuable to the organization but that is not currently being received by *anyone* within the organization. If such information is needed, go through the normal process of identifying the information and the subjects and characteristics it represents. Sketch a sample of a new report that will contain the new information and add that sample to the group of new report samples.

For example, assume that one of the participants has identified a need for demographic information; he believes that it would help the organization identify a more specific target market for its product. But currently there is no report that provides this information. To clearly identify the information he needs, work with this participant to create a sketch of a report that will present this information. Then use the appropriate techniques to identify and note the subjects and characteristics represented by the report. Finally, add the new report to the folder of new reports. Now the data structures necessary to support the new information can be defined in the database.

Continue to repeat this procedure until participants can no longer identify any further information that could be of use or of value to the organization. Once you are reasonably confident that you have accounted for all the information the organization needs or will need, you may suspend the interview process and begin the process of compiling the preliminary field list.

In the next step, aim toward making the preliminary field list complete. But keep in mind that even though you and the participants may believe you've accounted for all the information that the organization could possibly use, you may have to revisit this process. It's common that new information continues to be identified as the database design process unfolds.

Compiling a Complete List of Fields

The Preliminary Field List

Now that you have completed your analysis of the current database and the interviews with users and management, you can create a *preliminary field list.* This list represents the fundamental data requirements of the organization and constitutes the core set of fields that will be defined in the database. You'll create the preliminary field list using the following two-step process:

1. Review and refine the list of characteristics you have compiled.

2. Determine whether there are any characteristics in the data-collection samples, report samples, and on-screen presentation samples that need to be added to the preliminary field list.

The first step is to review and refine the list of characteristics you compiled throughout the analysis and interview process. As you'll remember from its definition in Chapter 3, a *field* represents a characteristic of a particular subject. Therefore, each item on the list of characteristics should become a field. But before you can define characteristics as fields, first you need to review the list to identify and remove duplicate characteristics.

As you conducted the interviews, you used the characteristic identification technique to identify characteristics in each participant's responses. You then collected these characteristics on a list as the interview process continued. There were probably times when you mistakenly added the same characteristic to the list more than once or unknowingly added an item with a different name but representing the same characteristic as one already listed. Refine the list using the following procedure.

Look for items in the list with the same name. When you find one or more duplicates, determine whether the duplicates represent the same characteristic. If they do, remove the duplicates from the list. If they don't, determine what each occurrence of the item represents. In many instances, you'll find that each instance represents a characteristic of a *different* subject. If this is the case, rename each occurrence of the item to reflect how it relates to the appropriate subject.

For example, say the item "Name" appears three times on your list of characteristics. Because your current objective is to eliminate duplicate characteristics, your first inclination will be to remove the duplicates. But before you do so, determine what subject each instance of "Name" represents. You can easily do this by reviewing your interview notes; this will help you remember when you added the item to the list and why it was added.

Now say that after careful examination, you discover that the first occurrence of "Name" represents a characteristic of the subject Clients, the second a characteristic of the subject Employees, and the third a characteristic of the subject Contacts. To resolve the duplication, *rename* each occurrence of "Name" to reflect its true meaning. You now have three new characteristics: "Client Name," "Employee Name," and "Contact Name."

As you review your list of characteristics, you'll find that there are instances similar to "Name" that need to addressed in the same manner. It's common to see one or more occurrences of items such as "Address," "City, "State," "Zip Code," and "Phone Number." These are referred to collectively as *generic items*. The main point to remember is that you'll need to rename each instance of a generic item to reflect its true relation to a subject, thus ensuring that you have as accurate a field list as possible.

Now look for items that have different names but the *same* meaning and remove all but one. There should be only a single occurrence of a particular characteristic. For example, say that "Product #," "Product

No.," and "Product Number" appear on your list of characteristics. It's evident that these items all have the same meaning, and you only need one of them on your list. Choose the one that conveys the intended meaning clearly, completely, and unambiguously. Remove the remaining items from the list of characteristics. (In this case, the best choice is "Product Number.")

Finally, make sure that each item on your list represents a *characteristic*. It's easy to accidentally place items on the list that represent subjects. You can test each item by asking yourself questions like these:

> "Can this word be used to describe something?"

> "Does this word represent a component or detail or piece of something in particular?"

> "Does this word represent a *collection* of things?"

> "Does this word represent something that can be broken down into smaller pieces?"

Depending on the item you're working with, some questions will be easier to answer than others. If you find that an item represents a subject rather than a characteristic, remove it from the list of characteristics and add it to the list of subjects. Be sure to identify the new subject's characteristics and add them to your list of characteristics.

For example, say "Item" appears on your list and you're not quite sure whether it represents a characteristic or a subject. Use the questions listed above to help you make a determination. For instance,

> "Can 'Item' be used to describe something?"

> "Does 'Item' represent a component or detail or piece of something in particular?"

You could make a case that "Item" helps to describe a "Sale" inasmuch as it identifies what a customer purchased. On the other hand, you could also say that "Item" isn't a characteristic because it doesn't represent a *singular* aspect of a "Sale." "Date Sold," for example, represents a singular characteristic of a "Sale." So leaving the quandary surrounding these questions unresolved, you go on to the next question.

"Does 'Item' represent a collection of things?"

You can answer this question easily by looking at the plural form of the word, which in this case is "Items." If "Items" can be referred to as a collection, it *is* a subject. It's beginning to become clear that "Item" does represent a collection of some sort, and you can make a final determination by asking yourself the last question:

"Does "Items" represent something that can be broken down into smaller pieces?"

To answer this question, determine whether you can identify any characteristics for "Items." If so, then it definitely represents a subject and should be moved to the list of subjects. Also you'll need to identify its characteristics and add them to your list of characteristics.

Continue with this procedure until you've reviewed and refined the entire list of characteristics to your satisfaction. When you are through you have your first version of the *preliminary field list*. You'll add new items to it and refine it further during the next step.

The second step involves studying the data-collection samples, report samples, and on-screen presentation samples you gathered during the analysis of the current database. In this step, your objective is to determine whether there are any characteristics found on the data and report samples that need to be added to the preliminary field list.

To begin this step, highlight every characteristic you find on each sample. Then take each characteristic and determine whether it's already on the preliminary field list; if it's on the list, cross it out on the sample. Next look at the remaining characteristics and determine whether any of them has the same meaning as an existing field; if it does, cross it out on the sample. (Use the same procedure you used in the first step to make this determination.) Finally, if there are any highlighted characteristics left on the samples, add them to the Preliminary field list.

For example, say you're working with the data-collection sample shown in Figure 6-12. Highlight each characteristic you find on the sample, as shown in Figure 6-13. In some instances, you'll find duplicate characteristics. As you can see, both "Name" and "Phone No." appear twice on the sample. Because the duplicate has the same meaning as the original in each case, you can cross out the duplicates.

To continue with the example, say you've reviewed your preliminary field list and found that every characteristic on the sample is already on the preliminary field list with the exception of "Name" and "Phone

Supplier Information

Company:	Acme Power Tools		
Address:	635 Montana Ave	Status:	Active
City:	El Paso	Office Phone:	598-4455
State:	TX Zip: 79925	FAX Number:	598-5715

Contacts

Name:	George Barlett	Phone No.:	532-9228
Name:		Phone No.:	

Figure 6-12. *An example of a data-collection sample.*

Supplier Information

Company: | Acme Power Tools

Address: | 635 Montana Ave   Status: | Active

City: | El Paso   Office Phone: | 598-4455

State: | TX   Zip: | 79925   FAX Number: | 598-5715

Contacts

Name: | George Barlett   Phone No.: | 532-9228

~~Name:~~ | ~~Phone No.:~~ |

Figure 6-13. *A sample with highlighted characteristics.*

No." Cross out the existing items on the sample to show that you have accounted for them. But before you add "Name" and "Phone No." to the preliminary field list, make sure that the names of these items properly describe their relation to the subject. In this case, the two remaining fields represent characteristics of a group of people known as "Contacts." Therefore, these characteristics are renamed and added to the list as "Contact Name" and "Contact Phone Number." Repeat this procedure for each sample you've gathered until you have gone through all the samples you have collected.

The Calculated Field List

There's one final refinement you need to make to the preliminary field list before it can be considered complete: every "calculated field" must be removed and placed on a separate list. This new list becomes your *calculated field list*. A calculated field is one that stores the result of a mathematical calculation as its value. Calculated fields are listed separately because they are used in a specific manner later in the design process.

To build the calculated field list, look for any field in the preliminary field list that can be considered to be the result of a calculation. "Amount," "total," "sum," "average," "minimum," "maximum," and "count" are a few of the words typically used to name calculated fields. Common names for calculated fields include "Subtotal," "Average Age," "Discount Amount," and "Customer Count." As you identify each calculated field, remove it from the preliminary field list and place it on the calculated field list. When you've finished screening all the fields in the preliminary field list, you're then left with two complete new lists: the final version of the preliminary field list and the calculated field list.

Reviewing Both Lists with Users and Management

Conduct brief interviews with users and management to review the items that appear on the preliminary field list and the calculated field list. The purpose of the interviews is to determine whether there are any fields that have been left out of either list. If everyone believes that the lists are complete, continue with the next step in the design process. Otherwise, identify the fields that are missing and add them to the appropriate list.

Be sure to conduct interviews at this juncture; the feedback participants provide is a means of verifying the fields on both lists. To prevent distress and frustration, let me warn you again to avoid becoming too invested in the idea that these lists are complete and final. At this point you still may not have identified every field that needs to be included in the database—inadvertently, you're almost sure to miss a few fields—but if you strive to make your lists as nearly complete as you can, the inevitable additions or deletions will be quick and easy to make.

CASE STUDY

You've already defined the mission statement and mission objectives for Mike's new database. Now it's time to perform an analysis, conduct interviews, and compile a preliminary field list.

First, analyze Mike's current database. As you already know, he keeps most of his data on paper. The only exception is the product inventory he maintains on a spreadsheet program. So first you'll need to gather a sample of each type of paper-based format Mike uses to collect data. You'll also need to get a screen shot or printout of the spreadsheet he uses to maintain the product inventory. Assemble these samples together in a folder for later use. For example, Figure 6-14 shows a sample of the index cards Mike uses to collect customer information and a screen shot from his spreadsheet program.

Next identify the methods Mike uses to present information. He currently uses a number of reports to present the information he and his staff need to conduct their day-to-day affairs. Most of the reports are produced on a typewriter; the remainder are generated from the computer with a word processing program. Gather samples of all the reports and place them in a folder for later use. Figure 6-15 shows a sample report that Mike creates on his typewriter.

Now you're ready to interview Mike's staff. Here are some points to remember as you're conducting the interviews:

1. Identify the types of data staff members are using and how the data is being used. Be sure to use the subject identification technique and the characteristic identification technique to help you analyze responses and formulate follow-up questions.

2. Review the data-collection, report, and on-screen presentation samples you gathered during the beginning of the analysis process. Determine how each sample is used, write an appropriate description, and attach the description to the sample.

Steven Pundt	363-9755
Apartment 2B	
2380 Redbird Lane	
Seattle, WA 98115	
He's primarily interested in mountain bike stuff.	
Keep him abreast of the summer bike tours.	

	A	B	C	D	E
1	*Product ID*	*Product Description*	*Category*	*Price*	*Qty On Hand*
2	9001	Shur-Lok U-Lock	Accessories	75.00	12
3	9002	SpeedRite Cyclecomputer	Accessories	65.00	20
4	9003	SteelHead Microshell Helmet	Accessories	36.00	33
5	9004	SureStop 133-MB Brakes	Components	23.50	16
6	9005	Diablo ATM Mountain Bike	Bikes	1,200.00	4
7	9006	UltraVision Helmet Mount Mirrors	Accessories	7.45	10

Figure 6-14. *A paper-based and a computer-generated sample from Mike's Bikes.*

Supplier Phone List

Company Name	Contact Name	Phone Number
ACME Cycle Supplies	George Chavez	633-9910
B & M Bike Supplies	Carol Ortner	527-3817
CycleWorks	Julia Black	527-0019
Evanstone's Cycle Warehouse	Allan Davis	636-9360

Figure 6-15. *A report sample from Mike's Bikes.*

3. Identify the staff members' information requirements. Determine what information they're currently using, what additional information they need (remember to use the samples.), and what kind of information they believe they'll need as the business grows.

During the interview, one of the employees wonders whether she can add a new field to the Supplier Phone List report. Your response? You hand her the report and ask her to attach a note indicating the name of the new field and a brief explanation of why she believes it's necessary. When she's finished, return the sample to the report samples folder. Figure 6-16 shows the report sample with the attached note.

The final interview you'll conduct is with Mike. Keep the following points in mind as you speak with him:

1. Identify the reports he currently receives; you need to know what kind of information he uses to make business decisions. If he receives any reports that are not represented in your group of report samples, obtain a sample of each report and add it to the group, updating the subject and characteristic lists as needed.

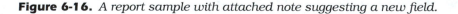

Supplier Phone List

Company Name	Contact	Phone Number
ACME Cycle Supplies	George	0
B & M Bike Supplies	Carol	7
CycleWorks	Julia Black	19
Evanstone's Cycle Warehouse	Allan Davis	360

Can we include Fax Number? We can process special orders more quickly via fax.

Figure 6-16. *A report sample with attached note suggesting a new field.*

2. Review the group of report samples with him and determine whether he can identify any subjects or characteristics that have been overlooked by his staff. Use the appropriate techniques to identify these items and add any new items to the proper list.

3. Determine whether there is any additional information Mike needs to supplement the information he currently receives.

4. Determine what types of information Mike will need as the business grows.

As you and Mike discuss his future information needs, he indicates that there is some new information he'd like to receive once the business really gets rolling: he'd like to see total bike sales by manufacturer. He believes this information would help him determine which bikes should be consistently well stocked. Such a report does not currently exist, so have Mike sketch it out on a sheet of paper. Next, identify the subjects and characteristics represented on the report and add them to the appropriate list. Then add the new report to your group of report samples. Figure 6-17 shows the sketch of Mike's new report.

Bike Sales Summary

Company Name	Bike Model	Total Units Sold
Altair Bicycles	ATB 600-A	12
	Cruiser 500	7
Bandido Bikes	Baja Delight	16
	Diablo Rojo	9

Figure 6-17. *The sketch of Mike's new report.*

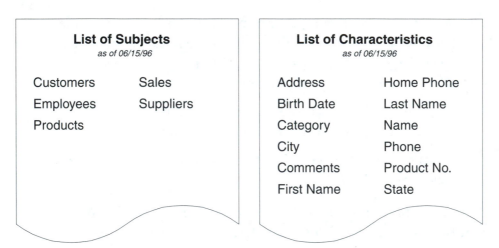

Figure 6-18. *Partial lists of subjects and characteristics for Mike's Bikes.*

Your analysis is complete: you've interviewed Mike and his staff, you've gathered all the relevant samples, and you've created a list of subjects and a list of characteristics. A *partial* list of subjects and characteristics is shown in Figure 6-18. All you need to do now is to create your preliminary field list.

As you already know, you'll need to refine your list of characteristics before it can become your first version of the preliminary field list. So remove all duplicate characteristics, delete items that have different names but that refer to the same characteristics, and refine those items that have "generic" characteristic names. (Remember the problem with the characteristic called "Name"? If you find such instances, now is the time to resolve them.) Next review all your samples and determine whether they contain characteristics that do not currently appear on the preliminary field list. If you find any, add them to the list. When you're done, you have the first version of your preliminary field list.

Now you need to remove all the calculated fields from the preliminary field list. As you know, a calculated field is one that stores the result of

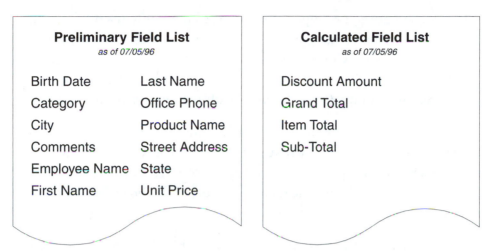

Figure 6-19. *A partial preliminary field list and a calculated field list.*

a mathematical calculation as its value. Once you've removed all the calculated fields, placed them on their own new list, which becomes your calculated field list. Figure 6-19 shows a *small portion* of your final preliminary field list and your list of calculations.

> ❖ **Note** You may have noticed that each list includes a date in the title. It's a good idea to date your lists so that you retain a clear history of their development.

Summary

This chapter begins with a discussion of the reasons that an organization's current database should be analyzed. You learned that to make that analysis, there are specific questions and answers that will identify aspects of the current database. Armed with the answers you can design a database that best suits the organization's needs. Next, we briefly looked at the two types of databases commonly used by organizations: *paper-based* databases and *legacy* databases. We ended this discussion by identifying the *three steps used in the analysis process:* reviewing the way data is collected, reviewing of the way information is presented, and conducting interviews with the organization's staff.

The chapter continues with a discussion of the review process. You learned how to review the ways an organization collects its data and how to assemble a set of *data-collection* samples. Then you learned how to *review the ways the organization presents information* and saw how to assemble a set of *report* samples.

Next, we discussed the process used to *conduct interviews,* and we saw why interviews are useful in this stage of the design process. During this discussion you learned two techniques that are crucial to the success of interviews: the *subject identification technique* and the *characteristic identification technique.*

Conducting *user interviews* was the next subject of discussion. We delved into the four issues addressed during this set of interviews along with the techniques used to address them. This section was followed by a discussion about conducting *management interviews.* You learned the issues addressed and the techniques used during this set of interviews as well.

Finally we went through the process of *compiling a list of fields* based on the list of characteristics and any characteristics that appear in sample reports. You learned that your list of fields is broken down into two separate lists: a *preliminary field list* and a *calculated field list.* The preliminary field list enumerates the fundamental data requirements of the organization and the core set of fields to be defined in the database. The calculated field list consists of fields whose values are the result of mathematical computations.

Establishing Table Structures

*It is a capital mistake to theorize
before one has data.*
—SHERLOCK HOLMES,
THE ADVENTURES OF SHERLOCK HOLMES

Topics Covered in This Chapter

Defining the Preliminary Table List

Defining the Final Table List

Associating Fields with Each Table

Refining the Fields

Refining the Table Structures

Case Study

Summary

A database is used to keep track of various subjects that are important to an organization. For example, a medical clinic needs to keep track of, among other things, its "Patients," "Doctors," and "Appointments"; an equipment-rental business must maintain such data as its "Customers," "Equipment," and "Rental Agreements"; and a registrar's office is concerned (at least) with "Students," "Teaching Staff," and "Courses." In every case—and in any other scenario you can imagine—each subject is represented by a *table* within the database. Furthermore, each table is composed of *fields*, which represent the elements that define or describe the subject of the table. Tables constitute the very foundation of the database, and when they are properly designed, a solid and sound foundation is guaranteed.

Defining the Preliminary Table List

During this portion of the database design process, you'll define a *preliminary table list* that will be used to identify and establish the tables for the new database. You'll use three procedures to develop this list. The first involves using the *preliminary field list*, the second involves using the *list of subjects* gathered during the interviewing process, and the third involves using the *mission objectives* you defined at the beginning of the database design process. You'll then move on to build the structure of each table using fields from the preliminary field list.

Determining Implied Subjects

The process of defining the tables for the database begins with a review of the preliminary field list with the objective of determining what subjects are implied by the items on the list.

You may wonder why you're reviewing the preliminary field list instead of starting with the list of subjects. The list of subjects does seem a more intuitive place to start. After all, you've carefully built this list during the interview process, and you've been influenced by the conversations you've had with the users and management. You probably believe that all this has helped you identify every subject that needs to be represented in the database. You may be correct, but if you're wrong, you could have a minor problem: missing tables.

The reason to consult the preliminary field list first is that studying the listed fields helps you to identify subjects from an unbiased viewpoint—you're letting the fields "talk" to you. It's crucial that you now look at this list as objectively as possible—as though you've never seen it before—*without* any of the biases you've collected during the inter-view process. For example, you'll discover that certain groups of fields suggest specific subjects, some of which may not have been identified during the interview process. You'll also discover that you can use the preliminary field list to verify many of the subjects on the list of sub-jects. So here you have another means of cross-checking that all the necessary subjects will be represented in the new database structure.

As you review the preliminary field list, ask yourself whether a certain set of fields defines or describes a particular subject. If nothing comes to mind readily, move on to another set of fields. If you can infer a sub-ject from the listed fields, enter that subject on the new *preliminary table list* that you are creating. Figure 7-1 shows a partial sample of a preliminary field list and an example of how a subject can be sug-gested by a set of fields.

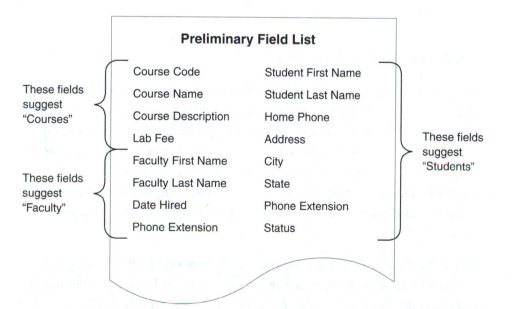

Figure 7-1. *An example of using the preliminary field list to identify subjects.*

Preliminary Table List

Classrooms

Courses

Faculty

Labs

Students

Figure 7-2. *The first version of the preliminary table list.*

Continue your review until you've scanned all the fields and identified as many subjects as possible. Be sure to add each subject you identify to the preliminary table list. This list will grow as you work with the list of subjects and mission objectives. Figure 7-2 shows an example of a first version of a preliminary table list.

Using the List of Subjects

Next you'll create a second version of the preliminary table list by merging the list of subjects (created during the interviews with users and management) with the first version of the preliminary table list (compiled by studying the preliminary field list). This new version is a more complete list of tables. Merging the two lists is a three-step process, which involves resolving duplicate items, resolving items that represent the same subject, and combining the remaining items together into one list.

For the first step, start by reviewing each item on the list of subjects and cross-checking it against the items on the preliminary table list. Your objective here is to identify duplicate items. In other words, you're looking for items on the list of subjects that already appear on the preliminary table list. If you find a duplicate item, you have to be very careful how you resolve the duplication. Begin by determining whether the items represent *different* subjects even though they share the same name. (Use your interview notes as necessary to help you make the determination.) If they do represent different subjects, rename each occurrence so that it accurately identifies the subject it represents and add both items to the preliminary table list. If they don't represent different subjects, then determine whether they truly represent the same subject. If the meaning is the same for both occurrences, cross out the item on the list of subjects and keep the one that appears on the preliminary table list. Then, resume the review until you've scanned all the items on the list of subjects and the preliminary table list.

To illustrate this process, say that you're developing a database for an equipment rental business, and you're working with the list of subjects and the preliminary table list shown in Figure 7-3.

As you review these lists, you discover two duplicate items: "Equipment" and "Rental Agreements." So you start with "Equipment" and

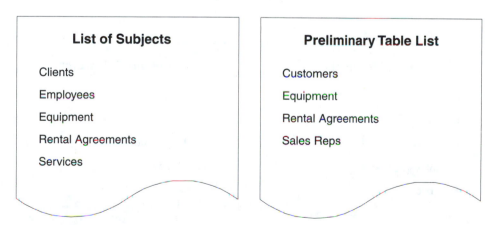

Figure 7-3. *The list of subjects and the preliminary table list for an equipment rental business.*

try to determine whether each occurrence represents a *different* subject. In reviewing your interview notes, you find that "Equipment" on the list of subjects represents items such as tools, appliances, and audiovisual equipment. But you then remember that "Equipment" on the preliminary table list also includes trucks, vans, and trailers. After you review your interview notes further, you discover that vehicle rentals are treated differently from "regular" equipment rentals. Therefore, each occurrence of "Equipment" *does* represent a different subject. You resolve the duplication by keeping one occurrence of "Equipment" and renaming the other "Vehicles." You list both items on the preliminary table list.

You go through the same process with "Rental Agreements." Fortunately, you discover that both occurrences share exactly the same meaning. The only thing you have to do in this case is cross out "Rental Agreements" on the list of subjects. Now you can continue your review until you've inspected each item on the list of subjects. Figure 7-4 shows the revised list of subjects and the preliminary table list.

In the second step of the merge process, your objective is to determine whether an item on the list of subjects and an item on the preliminary

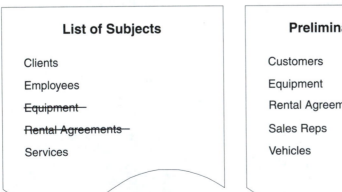

Figure 7-4. *The revised list of subjects and the revised preliminary table list.*

table list *represent the same subject* even though they have *different* names. If you identify such a set of items, select the name that best represents the subject and use it as the sole identifier for that subject. If the name you've selected already appears on the preliminary table list, cross out its counterpart on the list of subjects. If the name appears on the list of subjects, *remove* its counterpart on the preliminary table list and replace it with the name from the list of subjects. Continue with this process until you've covered all the items on the list of subjects.

To continue with the example of the equipment rental business, assume that you've discovered that "Clients" and "Employees" on the list of subjects and "Customers" and "Sales Reps" on the preliminary table list represent (respectively) the same subject (see Figure 7-4). You resolve the duplication in the first set of items by keeping "Customers" and crossing out "Clients." After reviewing your interview notes, you then determine that "Customer" is the name that best represents both the people and the organizations that rent equipment from the business. You resolve the duplication in the second set of items by keeping "Employees" and discarding "Sales Reps" because you believe that "Employees" best describes those people who are employed by the business, regardless of their position. Figure 7-5 shows a revised version of both lists with a resolution of these duplicate items.

The third step of this process is the easiest of the three. All you do is add the remaining items from the list of subjects to the preliminary table list. Then throw away the list of subjects—you won't need it anymore. The list that remains becomes the second version of the preliminary table list. That's all there is to it! Figure 7-6 shows the second version of the preliminary table list, which is the result of merging the two lists shown in Figure 7-5.

List of Subjects

~~Clients~~

~~Employees~~

~~Equipment~~

~~Rental Agreements~~

Services

Preliminary Table List

Customers

Employees

Equipment

Rental Agreements

Vehicles

Figure 7-5. *The revised list of subjects and the revised preliminary table list.*

Preliminary Table List

Customers

Employees

Equipment

Rental Agreements

Services

Vehicles

Figure 7-6. *The second version of the preliminary table list.*

Using the Mission Objectives

In this third and final procedure, you'll use the mission objectives to determine whether you have overlooked any subjects during the previous two procedures. This is your final opportunity to add tables to the preliminary table list.

Start with the first mission objective, and use the subject identification technique to identify the subjects represented in that statement. Underline each subject you identify and then cross-check it against the items on the preliminary table list. Use the same techniques here that you used in the previous procedure:

1. If the item you underlined in a mission objective statement already appears on the preliminary table list, determine whether the items represent different subjects. If they do, assign an appropriate name to each occurrence, and add them to the preliminary table list. If they are truly duplicates, cross out the duplicate item on the mission objective.

2. If the item underlined in the mission objective statement has a name that is synonymous with the name of an item on the preliminary table list and both items represent the same subject, select the name that best identifies that subject and use it in the preliminary table list.

3. If the item underlined in the mission objective statement represents a new subject, add it to the preliminary table list.

Repeat these steps until you've worked through all the mission objectives.

To see how these techniques are used to review a mission objective, say you're designing a database for a flight training school. Now, assume that you've used the subject identification technique on the following statement:

"We need to maintain data on our <u>pilots</u> and their <u>certifications</u>."

Furthermore, say that you're cross-checking the subjects you identified in this mission objective against the items in the preliminary table list shown in Figure 7-7.

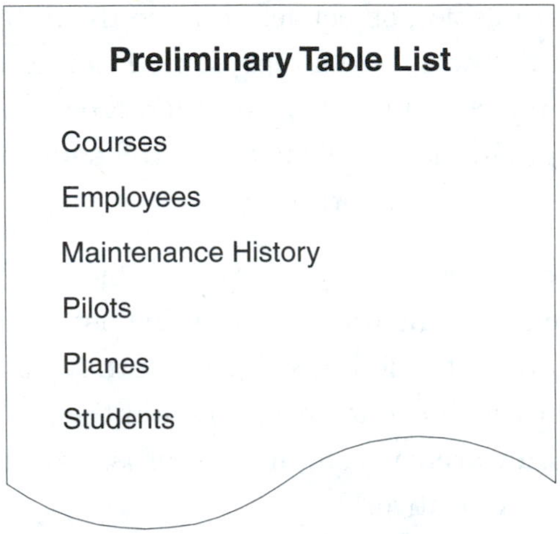

Preliminary Table List

Courses

Employees

Maintenance History

Pilots

Planes

Students

Figure 7-7. *The preliminary table list for a flight training school.*

In this case, you can cross out "pilots" in the mission objective statement because it already exists on the preliminary table list, and it
represents the same subject. But you'll have to look at "Certifications"
carefully. First, you can see that it does not appear on the preliminary
table list; second, its name is not synonymous with any item on the
preliminary table list, and it doesn't duplicate any item on the list; and
third, "Certifications" doesn't represent the same subject as any other
item on the preliminary table list. You can conclude from these obser-
vations that it is a new item and should be added to the preliminary
table list. Be sure to cross it out on the mission objective statement so
that you'll know you've already dealt with it. Figure 7-8 shows the
revised version of the preliminary table list.

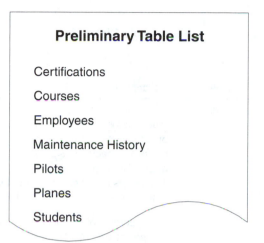

Figure 7-8. *The revised preliminary table list.*

Define the Final Table List

At this point, your preliminary table list is as complete as it can be. Now you'll transform it into a *final table list*. To do so you'll need to add two elements that are not currently on the preliminary table list: *table type* and *table description*. Figure 7-9 shows an example of a final table list.

We classify tables by "type" so that we can identify tables that function in a similar manner. There are four table types:

- *Data.* This type of table stores data used to supply information and represents a subject that is important to the organization. (This type of table is discussed in more detail later in this chapter.)

- *Linking.* This type of table is used to establish a link between two tables in a many-to-many relationship. (*Linking tables* are covered in Chapter 10.)

Final Table List

Name	Type	Description
Classrooms	Data	The spaces or areas within a facility reserved for the purpose of conducting class proceedings. Information regarding the physical aspects, on-site resources, and availability of these areas is useful because it allows us to assign classes to the facility that can make the best use of these areas.
Courses	Data	The programs of instruction conducted through courses offered by this institution. Course information must always reflect the addition of new courses, the deletion of old courses, and the continuing evolution of existing courses.

Figure 7-9. *An example of a final table list.*

- *Subset.* This type of table contains supplemental fields that are related to a particular data table and further describe the subject of that table in a very specific manner. (Subset tables are discussed in more detail later in this chapter.)

- *Validation.* This type of table is used to implement data integrity. (*Validation tables* are discussed in Chapter 11.)

The table description is used to provide a clear definition of the subject represented by the table and to state why the subject is important to the organization. There are certain guidelines governing the creation of a table description, and they'll be discussed later in this chapter. But before you transform your preliminary table list into the final table list, you have one final task to perform: refine the table names.

Refining the Table Names

Naming a table is a more complex affair than you may have first imagined. There are guidelines that govern the way a name is created, and following them is very beneficial. These guidelines ensure that a name is clear and unambiguous, that it is descriptive and meaningful, and that each table is named in a consistent manner. Following are some guidelines for creating table names:

Guidelines for Creating a Table Names

- *Create a unique, descriptive name that is meaningful to the entire organization.* Using unique names helps to ensure that each table clearly represents a different subject. (If you encounter duplicate table names at this point, resolve the problem by using the techniques described earlier in this chapter.) Choose names that are descriptive enough to be self-explanatory. "Vehicle Maintenance" is an example of a good, descriptive name.

- *Create a table name that accurately, clearly, and unambiguously identifies the subject of the table.* Vague or ambiguous names typically could represent more than one subject. When you encounter such a name, you should identify the subjects it represents and then treat each one as a separate table. "Pieces" is an example of a name that is vague. It's difficult to determine exactly what the table represents without referring to its description. If this table appeared in a preliminary table list for a boat manufacturer, you'd probably discover, upon investigation, that it represents two subjects: "Engine Components" and "Body Components." Therefore, you would remove "Pieces" and add the two more descriptive new subjects to the list.

- *Use the* minimum *number of words necessary to convey the subject of the table.* Everyone in the organization should be able to identify what the table represents without having to read its description. But at the same time you want to avoid using a minimalist approach to names. Consider, for example, the table name "TD_1." Unless you know the meaning of each character in the name, you won't have the slightest idea what this table represents. You want to avoid going to the opposite extreme as well. "Multi-Use Vehicle Maintenance Equipment" is much too long and can easily be shortened to just "Equipment."

- *Do not use words that convey physical characteristics.* Steer clear of words such as "File," "Record," and "Table"; they add a level of confusion that you don't need. Furthermore, names that incorporate this type of word commonly represent multiple subjects. Consider the name "Patient Record." On the surface, this may appear to be an acceptable name. However, two problems arise: First, the name contains a word with a data-file connotation ("Record"), which we are trying to avoid. Second, the name actually represents more than one subject: at minimum, it would include three subjects: "Patients," "Doctors," and "Examinations." In this case, "Patient Record" would be replaced by the three new subjects on the preliminary table list.

- *Do not use acronyms and abbreviations.* Acronyms are hard to decipher, abbreviations convey little or no meaning, and both violate the first guideline in this list. Take acronyms, for example. Say you're helping an organization revise its database structure and you encounter a table named "SC." You don't know what this table represents because you don't know what the letters stand for. In order to determine what "SC" refers to, you conduct a brief interview with the staff. To your disbelief, you discover that "SC" has three meanings: administrative personnel believe this to be "Steering Committees"; information systems staff says that it stands for "System Configurations"; and people from the security department are adamant that it represents "Security Codes." This example illustrates a perfect reason to avoid acronyms and abbreviations at all costs.

- *Do not use proper names and other words that will unduly restrict the data that can be entered into the table.* This guideline will keep you from falling into the trap of creating duplicate table structures. For example, a name such as "Southwest Region Employees" severely restricts the data that can be entered into this table. When the organization grows, what will be done about employees from other regions? Will there need to be a "Pacific Northwest Region Employees" table and a "Western Region Employees" table? It is poor database design practice to have duplicate structures such as these: First, it's difficult to retrieve data from all three tables simultaneously; second, it becomes incumbent on the person maintaining the database to ensure that the tables are always synchronized in terms of structural modifications and data integrity.

- *Do not use names that implicitly or explicitly identify more than one subject.* You must always ensure that each table represents only one subject. A table with an ambiguous name suggests that the subject was not clearly or accurately identified during the analysis and interview processes. To rectify this problem, review your notes and conduct further analysis and interviews as necessary. "Facility/Building" and "Space or Area" are examples of ambiguous names.

- *Use the plural form of the name.* As you know, a table represents a single subject, which can be an object or event. You can take this definition one step further and state that a table represents a *collection* of *similar* objects or events. For example, a sales rep wants to maintain data on all his customers, not just a single one; and a car rental business wants to keep track of all its vehicles, not just the blue BMW. Using the plural form of the table name is a sound idea because it makes clear your intention to refer to a collection. Collections, of course, always take the plural ("Boats," not "Boat"). In contrast, words that identify fields are always singular ("Home Phone," not "Home Phones"). By following this rule it's easy to differentiate between table names and field names in the documentation for the database. (As you rename your tables, remember that the plural form of some words does not end in *s* or *es*. For example, the singular and plural forms of "equipment" are exactly the same.)

Use these guidelines to refine each table name on the preliminary table list. When you're finished, this list becomes your final table list and remains so for the duration of the database design process. However, it's only "final" in the sense that you've accounted for all the tables that could be identified by analyzing the current database and sample reports and conducting interviews with users and management. You may still add new tables to this list based on requirements imposed by relationships, data integrity, or other information you develop.

Indicating the Table Types

As you learned earlier in this chapter, you'll indicate each table's type on the final table list. Remember that the four classifications used to identify the table type are *data*, *linking*, *subset*, and *validation*.

When you first create your final table list, every item on the list is a *data* table because it represents a subject that is important to the organization and stores data that is used to produce information. *Link-ing* tables and *validation* tables will be missing from the list because you have not yet defined any relationships or data integrity. (You will address these issues later in the design process.) *Subset* tables will be missing from the list because you define them *after* you assign fields to the data tables.

Take the final table list and identify each table as a data table. You'll assign other table types later as the database design process contin-ues to unfold.

Composing the Table Descriptions

Another aspect of the table that you'll record on the final table list is the *table description*. Table descriptions are crucial if everyone is going to understand why each table exists and why the organization is con-cerned with collecting the data for each table. In fact, the description must *explicitly define the table* and *state its importance* to the organiza-tion. It doesn't matter whether the definition comes first or whether you use more than one sentence to convey this information—both the defi-nition and the explanation of the table's importance must be in the description. The table description also serves as a device for validating the need for a table—if you are unable to explain why a table is impor-tant to the organization, then you need to investigate when and how the table was identified and whether it really is necessary at all.

Just as you had guidelines to help define table names, you also have a set of guidelines to help you compose a table description that is focused, concise, unambiguous, and clear.

Guidelines for Composing a Table Description

- *Include a definition statement that accurately identifies the table.* Everyone should be able to easily determine the identity of the table from its description without any confusion or ambiguity. Here's an example of a poor definition of a Suppliers table for a bakery database. As you can see, it's not very accurate.

"Suppliers—the companies that supply us with ingredients and equipment."

What if the bakery receives some of its ingredients from local farmers? They certainly don't qualify as a "company." And what type of equipment do these suppliers supply? Cooking utensils? Hand trucks? Delivery racks? A much better definition of suppliers follows:

"Suppliers—the people and organizations from whom we purchase ingredients and equipment."

This statement can be used in the table description as the *table definition.*

- *Include a statement that explains why this table is important to the organization.* A table contains data that is collected, maintained, manipulated, and retrieved by the organization for a *particular* reason. Your statement should explain *why* the data is important to the organization. Keeping in mind that this statement becomes part of your table description, you might be tempted to use a statement like this:

  "We need the Suppliers table to keep track of the names, addresses, phone numbers, and contact names of all our suppliers."

This statement is inadequate because it emphasizes only *what* needs to be stored in the Suppliers table instead of amplifying *why* the data is important to the business. The following example conveys a better sense of why the information is important:

> "Supplier information is vital to the bakery because it allows us to maintain a constant supply of ingredients and to ensure that our equipment is always in working order."

In this example, the importance of the data is conveyed by identifying the services the suppliers provide to the bakery. This statement implies that without the suppliers, the bakery could run out of ingredients or have a hard time keeping its equipment in top shape. This statement now reflects why the table is important to the organization.

- *Compose a description that is clear and succinct.* Don't be too brief or too verbose. Avoid restating or rephrasing the table name in your table description, as in this example:

> "Student Schedule—the class schedule of the student."

You want to make sure that everyone can identify the table and understand its importance to the organization, but at the same time you want to avoid using a verbose description. Here is an example of a description that is quite lengthy and, in addition, provides more information than is necessary:

> "Student Schedule—All the classes that a student will attend (including the days, times, and the faculty conducting the class) during the course of the school year. The data in this table is important because it will let the student know the name of the class and when and where

he's supposed to be. Also the student will know the duration of the class as well as the name of the teacher who is teaching the class."

The required information can be more clearly and succinctly conveyed as follows:

> "Student Schedule—Those classes that the student is scheduled to attend during this school year. The information provided by this table allows the student to manage his time efficiently and enables the school to figure class loads and student loads."

In this example, the first sentence provides the definition of the table, and the second sentence states why the table is important to the academic organization.

- *Do not include implementation-specific information in your table description, such as how or where the table is used.* Statements indicating how a table is specifically used or how it is physically accessed should not be part of the description. This information is more appropriately used during the database implementation process, which is separate from the database design process and beyond the scope of this book. Here is an example illustrating the error of including implementation-specific information:

> "Student Schedule—Those classes that the student is scheduled to attend during this school year. This information is used by the registrar and is accessed from the 'Student Admissions' menu in the Registration Program."

- *Do not make the table description for one table dependent on the table description of another table.* Each table description should be self-explanatory and independent from every other table description; it should be absolutely unnecessary to cross-reference one table description against another. Avoid using this type of statement:

  "Dependents—the spouse, children, or wards of a given employee. (See description of Employee table for further information.)"

  A better description for this field is as follows:

  "Dependents—the spouse, children, or wards of a given employee. This information allows us to make the appropriate tax deductions for the employee and is necessary for the employee benefits programs in which he or she is enrolled."

- *Do not use examples in a table description.* An example is a valuable communication tool that helps to convey a particular meaning or concept and is very helpful when used wisely. But an example depends on supplemental information to complete the idea it's supposed to convey. A well-defined description, on the other hand, does not depend on an example to convey its meaning. Think of the number of examples you would have to use in order to fully define what the table represents. Because a table description should be clear, succinct, and self-explanatory, it should be unnecessary to use an example.

Interviewing Users and Management

In order to define a good table description for each table, you'll enlist the help of users and management to establish the table's definition and importance. You'll conduct the interview with both groups at the same time; this is one of the few times you'll be able to do so. Your only objective here is to get a consensus regarding the description of each table. After your interviews are complete, take your notes and compose the descriptions yourself, making certain to follow the guidelines outlined above. Then, confer with both parties once more to make certain that the descriptions are acceptable and easily understood by all. When you're finished, the final table list is complete.

For example, say you're developing a database for a local software training organization. Your assistant, John, is conducting an interview with some of the people from the organization. Specifically, he's speaking to Mark from the administration department; Frits, the instructor coordinator; Sara, the vice-president of sales; and Caroline, the head of the organization. The dialog that follows is a partial transcript of John's interview. John is currently discussing the CLIENTS table.

> ❖ **Note** Unlike the interviews you conducted during the analysis and requirements review stages of the design process, it is no longer necessary to involve everyone in the organization. However, you should work with a representative group of users and management for the interviews you'll conduct throughout the remainder of the design process.

JOHN:　　Okay, let's talk about the CLIENTS table. How would you describe a client?

FRITS:　　A client is a student who comes in for one of our classes.

SARA: That's only partially true. A client can also be an organization that sends its employees to our classes. For example, many of the banks and insurance companies that send their employees to our classes are considered clients.

MARK: Yes, but some of their employees come in on their own, so they're clients as well. I guess the point is that a client can be an individual *or* a business of some sort.

JOHN: *(Makes a note of what Mark just said.)* Well said. Does everyone agree with Mark? *(Everyone nods in approval.)* Great. Now how would you explain to someone why client information is important to this organization?

CAROLINE: Without clients, we don't have a business!

FRITS: If we can keep track of the students who attend our classes, we can send them information regarding our new classes.

SARA: Keeping track of this information allows us to keep billing and contact information current. Training coordinators move on to other positions, and we have to know the name of the new person we'll be dealing with.

JOHN: Good point. Does anyone have anything further to add? No? Okay, does everyone agree with what was said?"

(Everyone once again nods in approval. Because no additional comments are made, John jots down some final notes and moves on to the next table.)

As you can see, conducting this interview is a fairly straightforward affair. Notice, however, that John attempts to get a consensus after he senses that there is nothing further to be said about the topic at hand.

He then makes note of any points that will help him compose the description, and then he moves on to his next topic.

After John has finished conducting the interview, he'll use his notes to develop a table description for each table on the final table list. John will have to interpret the responses and study them in order to develop a suitable table description. Based on the discussion of the CLIENTS table, John writes the following description:

> "Clients—those individuals who attend our classes and organizations that sponsor such individuals. The information provided by the data in the CLIENTS table allows our organization to further promote our classes and supports proper communications with our clients."

John will then write a description for each table on the final table list. He'll speak with Mark, Frits, Sara, and Caroline once more to make sure the descriptions are acceptable and that everyone understands them without any difficulty.

Associating Fields with Each Table

In Chapter 3 you learned that tables are composed of fields. During the next stage of the database design process you'll assign fields to each table on the *final table list*. The fields you use will be taken from your *preliminary field list*.

Assigning fields to a table is a relatively easy process: Determine which fields best represent characteristics of the table's subject and assign them to that table. Repeat this procedure for every table on the final table list. If you believe that a field or set of fields can be used to represent characteristics of more than one table, then assign them accordingly. You'll discover whether you've assigned the appropriate fields to each table later when you go through the process of refining the table structures.

> ❖ **Note** In the examples that follow, you'll note that I ask you to use sheets of paper for specific procedures. By using paper, you avoid the temptation of using an RDBMS program. I cannot over-emphasize or overstate the fact that you should not use the computer at all until the database design process is complete. Thus you will avoid the traps I discuss later in Chapter 14.

To begin this process, take a sheet of legal paper and lay it in front of you lengthwise from left to right. Write the name of each table (from the final table list) across the top of the paper, starting at the left-hand side; leave enough space between the table names to allow room for lengthy field names to be listed underneath. Repeat this procedure, using as many sheets as you need to account for every table on the list. Continuing with the example of a school database, Figure 7-10 shows the set of table structures currently under development.

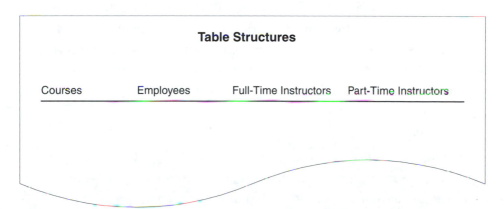

Figure 7-10. *Setting up a sheet for listing table structures.*

Table Structures

Courses	Employees	Part-Time Instructors	Students
Course Number	Employee Name	PT-Instructor Name	Student Name
Course Name	Employee Address	PT-Instructor Address	Student Address
Course Description	Employee Phone	PT-Instructor Phone	Student Phone
Instructor Name	SSN	PT-SSN	Phone Extension
Start Time	Date Hired	PT-Date Hired	Company Name
Days Held	Position	Pay Rate	Contact Name
		Status	Contact Phone

Figure 7-11. *Listing tables with their associated fields.*

Next assign fields from the preliminary field list to each table. Start with the first table and determine which fields best describe or define its subject. Then list these fields under the table name. After you've assigned the fields you believe to be appropriate for the table, move on to the next table and repeat the process. Continue in this manner until you've assigned fields to all of the tables. Figure 7-11 shows a partial set of table structures.

❖ **Reminder** Before you work through the remainder of the chapter, now is a good time to remember a principle I presented in the introduction: Focus on the concept or technique and its intended results, *not on the example used to illustrate it.* I bring this to your attention once again because you will certainly ask yourself why I have created an example in a particular manner. Maybe different or better approaches have occurred to you, and you might be absolutely correct. My sole reason for introducing the examples is to illustrate the concept or technique I'm trying to present. Therefore, study the way that I'm correcting the problems you see in a particular example so that you can use those techniques when you encounter similar problems in your database.

Refining the Fields

Now that you have assigned fields to each table, you'll refine the fields by improving the field names and resolving any problems that may exist with them. This step is preparation for the process of refining the table structures, which entails establishing that the appropriate fields have been assigned to the table and that the table is structurally sound.

Improving the Field Names

Earlier in this chapter, you used the set of guidelines for naming a table. Now you'll be introduced to another set of guidelines, which applies to field names. Fortunately, many of the guidelines are exactly the same as those governing table names, so you're already familiar with most of the concepts.

Guidelines for Creating Field Names

- *Create a unique, descriptive name that is meaningful to the entire organization.* There should be only one occurrence of a field name in the entire database. (There is only one exception: when a field is used to establish a relationship between two tables. This is explained in greater detail in Chapter 10.) Also the field name should be descriptive enough to convey the appropriate meaning to everyone who sees it.

- *Create a name that accurately, clearly, and unambiguously identifies the characteristic represented by the field.* "Phone Number" is a good example of an inaccurate, ambiguous field name. What kind of phone number does it represent? A home phone? An office phone? A cellular phone? The type of phone number should be identified in the field name, as here: "Home Phone."

- *Use the* minimum *number of words necessary to convey the meaning of the characteristic the field represents.* You want to avoid lengthy field names, but at the same time you also want to avoid using a single word as a field name if that word is inappropriate. For example, if you're trying to record the date a particular employee joined the organization, "Hired" is too short (and slightly vague) and "Date that the Employee Was Hired" is too long! In this case, a better name to represent the characteristic is "Date Hired."

- *Do not use acronyms, and be discriminating in the use of abbreviations.* As you know, acronyms are hard to decipher and easily misunderstood, so you shouldn't use them. On the other hand, you can use abbreviations in field names *so long as you're very careful.* If you use an abbreviation, you should make certain that it supplements or enhances the name in a positive manner, and that the abbreviation doesn't detract at all from the meaning of the field name.

When you were developing the preliminary field list (back in Chapter 6), you learned how to resolve "generic" field names such as "Address," "City," and "State." You added a word to each field name to make it more specific. This resulted in

names such as "Employee Address," "Customer Address," and
"Supplier Address." In field names that include a table name,
such as those mentioned above, you can abbreviate the
table name for the sake of brevity. The abbreviated part of the
field name should contain the first three or four letters of
the *table name* and the name of the characteristic that the
field represents. Thus you'll end up with names such as
"EmpAddress," "CustAddress," and "SuppAddress."

- *Do not use words that could confuse the meaning of the field
  name.* A problem can arise when a field name contains redundant words or synonyms, as illustrated in the name "Digital
  Identification Code Number." "Digital" and "Number" are
  redundant, so you'll use only one of the two words. In many
  organizations "Identification Code" and "Identification Number" are synonymous; use the name that is most meaningful
  within the organization, and be consistent in all related
  instances.

- *Do not use names that implicitly or explicitly identify more than
  one characteristic.* Some names can identify more than one
  characteristic. This is especially true of names that use the
  ampersand (&), the slash (\ ), the hyphen (-), and the
  words "and" and "or." Examples of this type of field name are
  "Phone/FAX," "ID Number or Code," and "Type & Description." If you find a field that represents more than one
  characteristic, you should determine what the separate characteristics are and make them into separate, unique fields.

- *Use the singular form of the name.* A table represents a collection of similar objects or events; therefore its name takes the
  plural form. A field, on the other hand, represents a single
  characteristic of that subject, so its name takes the singular
  form. When a field has a plural name, such as "Skills," for
  example, you imply that there may be many values for a single occurrence of that field.

Table Structures

Courses	Employees	Part-Time Instructors	Students
Course Number	EmpName	PTIName	Student Name
Course Name	EmpAddress	PTIAddress	Student Address
Course Description	EmpHome Phone	PTIHome Phone	Student Phone
Instructor Name	EmpSocial Security Number	PTISocial Security Number	Phone Extension
Start Time	Date Hired	PTIDate Hired	Company Name
Days Held	Position	Pay Rate	Contact Name
		Status	Contact Phone

Figure 7-12. *Revised field names.*

With these guidelines in mind, review each table and determine whether you can make improvements to any of the field names. When you're finished, you're ready to identify and resolve any problems with the fields. Figure 7-12 shows revisions to the field names of the table structures first shown in Figure 7-11.

In Figure 7-12 "Employee" is shortened to "Emp," "PT Instructor" is shortened to "PTI," and "SSN" is replaced by "Social Security Number." (Notice that in the original set of table structures in Figure 7-11, someone intuitively shortened "Part-Time" to "PT-.") For the sake of consistent abbreviations, "PT-" was replaced by "PTI." Remember that abbreviations can be very useful so long as they are meaningful and understood by everyone in the organization. If properly used abbreviations will do not detract from the meaning of the field name.

> ❖ **Note** Throughout the remainder of the chapter and the rest of
> the book, table names within the text are indicated using all cap-
> ital letters (such as EMPLOYEES) and field names within the
> text are indicted using small capital letters (such as EMPLOYEE
> ID NUMBER).

Using the Ideal Field to Resolve Anomalies

Although you've carefully identified the fields on your preliminary field
list, you may have created some fields that could prove problematic to
the table structure. Some problems that can arise from poorly defined
fields include duplicate data, redundant data, and difficulties in using
the data. Unless you know what to look for, it's hard to determine
whether any of the fields in a table is going to cause problems. The
best way to identify potentially troublesome fields is to determine
whether they are in accordance with the Elements of the *Ideal Field*.
Once you learn the Elements of the Ideal Field, you'll be able to spot
poorly designed fields easily.

Elements of the Ideal Field

- *It represents a characteristic of the subject of the table.* As you
  know, a table represents a specific subject, which can be an
  object or event. The Ideal Field defines or describes a particular aspect of that object or event.

- *It contains only a single value.* Two problems arise with fields
  that contain more than one value (commonly known as *multivalued fields*): data redundancy and difficulty in working with
  the data in the field. You'll encounter one problem or the
  other depending on how you use the field in the table.

- *It cannot be deconstructed into smaller components.* When a field has a value that comprises more than one piece of data (commonly known as a *multipart field*), it can be very difficult to work with the contents of the field.

- *It does not contain a calculated or concatenated value.* The values of the fields in a table should be mutually independent. In other words, a particular field should not have to depend on the values of other fields for its own value. A calculated field depends on the values of other fields for its own value. With a calculated field, it becomes the responsibility of the user or the database application program to update the calculated field whenever the values of the other related fields are modified. This places an undesirable burden on the user or the database program. That is why calculated fields are treated separately.

- *It is unique within the entire database structure.* In a properly designed database, the only fields that are duplicated are those used to establish relationships between tables. If fields other than these are duplicated in the database, the table will accumulate unnecessary redundant data, and there will be a high risk of inconsistent data existing between the duplicate fields.

- *It retains all of its characteristics if it appears in more than one table.* When a field is used to establish a relationship between two tables, it appears in both tables. The specifications established for the field will remain the same in each table. (This matter is discussed in greater detail in Chapters 9 and 10.)

Even though you now know the characteristics of the Ideal Field, you'll still find it difficult in many instances to identify problematic fields just by looking at their names. To illustrate this point, consider the

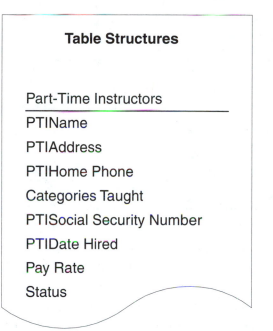

Table Structures

Part-Time Instructors

PTIName

PTIAddress

PTIHome Phone

Categories Taught

PTISocial Security Number

PTIDate Hired

Pay Rate

Status

Figure 7-13. *A table structure with fields to be constructed in accordance with the Ideal Field.*

table structure shown in Figure 7-13. Try to determine whether each field in this structure is in accordance with the elements of the ideal field and whether any field needs to be modified.

On the surface, each preliminary field seems to conform to the elements of the Ideal Field. However, after close examination you see that there are departures from the second and third elements of the Ideal Field. Three fields have anomalies that are going to cause problems unless they are resolved: PTINAME, PTIADDRESS, and CATEGORIES TAUGHT. If you are still doubtful, you can apply a simple test. The best way to confirm whether a field conforms with the Ideal Field is to "load" the table with sample data. This will quickly reveal anomalies, if such exist.

Part-Time Instructors

PTIName	PTIAddress	PTIHome Phone	Categories Taught	......
Kendra Bonnicksen	3131 Mockingbird Lane, Seattle, WA 98157	363-9948	DTP, OS, SS, WP	......
Timothy Ennis	7402 Kingman Drive, Redmond, WA 98115	527-4992	DB, OS, UT, WP	......
Shannon McLain	4141 Lake City Way, Seattle, WA 98136	336-5992	DB, PG, SS	......
Estela Pundt	970 Phoenix Avenue, Bellevue, WA 98046	322-6992	DTP, PG, WP	......

Figure 7-14. *Testing a table with sample data.*

You don't have to physically create a table to perform this test. Take a sheet of legal paper and lay it in front of you lengthwise from left to right. Write the name of each field across the top of the paper, starting from the left-hand side; leave enough space between the field names to allow room for the values you're going to place underneath them. Then enter records into the table by filling in each field with some sample data; be sure it represents the data you're actually going to enter into the database. You only need a few records for the test to work properly. Your sheet of paper should look similar to the one in Figure 7-14.

Now you can easily identify the fields that are going to be troublesome unless they are resolved. As you can see, PTINAME and PTIADDRESS are both multipart fields, and CATEGORIES TAUGHT is a multivalued field. You'll have to take care of these fields before you can refine the table structure.

Resolving Multipart Fields

Multipart fields are difficult to work with because they contain more than one item of data. It's hard to retrieve information from a multipart field, and it's hard to sort or group the records in the table by the field's value. The field PTIADDRESS illustrates these difficulties; using this field, you'd have a hard time retrieving data for the city of Seattle or sorting the records in the table by zip code.

Part-Time Instructors

PTIFirst Name	PTILast Name	PTIStreet Address	PTICity	PTIState	PTIZipcode	PTIHome Phone	Categories Taught
Kendra	Bonnicksen	3131 Mockingbird Lane	Seattle	WA	98157	363-9948	DTP, OS, SS, WP
Timothy	Ennis	7402 Kingman Drive	Redmond	WA	98115	527-4992	DB, OS, UT, WP
Shannon	McLain	4141 Lake City Way	Seattle	WA	98136	336-5992	DB, PG, SS
Estela	Pundt	970 Phoenix Avenue	Bellevue	WA	98046	322-6992	DTP, PG, WP

Figure 7-15. *Breaking down multipart fields.*

To resolve a multipart field, you need only identify the separate items making up the field and treat each one as an individual field. You can accomplish this by asking yourself a simple question: "How can the value of this field be broken down into smaller pieces?" Once you've answered this question and have broken the value down into separate items as much as possible, transform each item into a new field.

In Figure 7-14, the value of the field PTINAME represents two items: the first name and the last name of a part-time instructor. You'll resolve this field by creating two new fields: PTIFIRST NAME and PTI-LAST NAME. Meanwhile, the value of PTIADDRESS represents four items: the street address, city, state, and zip code of a part-time instructor. You'll transform these items into fields as well; they will appear in the table as PTISTREET ADDRESS, PTICITY, PTISTATE, and PTIZIPCODE. Your PART-TIME INSTRUCTORS table should now look like the one in Figure 7-15.

Resolving Multivalued Fields

Multivalued fields bring about the same set of problems as do multipart fields. Unlike a multipart field, whose value represents two or more *separate items*, a multivalued field represents two or more *occurrences* of the *same* value. This poses a problem if you try to enter more occurrences of the value than the field will allow. CATEGORIES TAUGHT exemplifies the problems with a multivalued field. Certainly, given that there are several categories listed in this field it would be difficult for you to retrieve information from the table for everyone who teaches just one category, for instance, the "WP" category. You'd also have a hard time sorting the records in the table by category. More important, you don't have room to enter more than four categories in the one field. What happens when one or more of your instructors teaches five categories? The only option you have at this point is to make the field larger every time you need to enter more values than it will currently allow.

To resolve a multivalued field, first remove the field from the table and use it as the basis for a new table. Next use a field (or set of fields) from the original table to link the original table with the new table; the connecting field(s) will appear in both tables. Then assign an appropriate name, type, and description to the new table and add the table to the final table list.

In Figure 7-15, CATEGORIES TAUGHT is a multivalued field because it contains multiple occurrences of the same value. To resolve the problem posed by this field, remove the Categories Taught field from the table and use it as the basis of a new table. Next use a field or set of fields from the PART-TIME INSTRUCTORS table to link that table together with the new table. Select PTIFIRST NAME and PTILAST NAME as the connecting fields and add them to the structure of the new table. Finally, give the table a proper name, compose a suitable description, and add it to the final table list. (Indicate the table's type as "Data.") The description that appears in the final table list for the new table might look something like this:

> "Part-Time Instructor Categories—the categories of software programs that an instructor is qualified to teach. The information this table provides allows us to make certain that there is an adequate number of instructors for each software category."

Part-Time Instructors

PTIFirst Name	PTILast Name	PTIStreet Address	PTICity	PTIState	PTIZipcode	PTIHome Phone
Kendra	Bonnicksen	3131 Mockingbird Lane	Seattle	WA	98157	363-9948
Timothy	Ennis	7402 Kingman Drive	Redmond	WA	98115	527-4992
Shannon	McLain	4141 Lake City Way	Seattle	WA	98136	336-5992
Estela	Pundt	970 Phoenix Avenue	Bellevue	WA	98046	322-6992

Part-Time Instructor Categories

PTIFirst Name	PTILast Name	Category Taught
Kendra	Bonnicksen	DTP
Kendra	Bonnicksen	OS
Kendra	Bonnicksen	SS
Kendra	Bonnicksen	WP
Timothy	Ennis	DB
Timothy	Ennis	OS
Timothy	Ennis	UT
Timothy	Ennis	WP

Figure 7-16. *Resolving a multivalued field.*

Your PART-TIME INSTRUCTORS table and the new PART-TIME INSTRUCTOR CATEGORIES table should look like what is shown in Figure 7-16.

You'll note that the new PART-TIME INSTRUCTOR CATEGORIES table is free from the problems typically associated with multivalued fields; CATEGORIES TAUGHT is now a single-value field. With this table it will be much easier for users to retrieve information for a particular instructor or category, and the records in the table can be sorted easily. Also note that the PTIFIRST NAME and PTILAST NAME fields retain their names in the new table. This condition is in accordance with the fifth element of the ideal field.

Resolving this anomaly did not come without a price. You've now introduced redundant data into the database. But this redundancy is acceptable because it *does* resolve the anomaly. Although a relational database will never be completely free of redundant data, your goal is to make certain that it has only an *absolute minimum* amount of redundant data.

Refining the Table Structures

Now that you've refined the fields and made certain that each field is sound, you can begin the process of refining the table structures. Your objective in this phase of the design process is to make sure that the appropriate fields have been assigned to each table and that each table's structure is properly defined. This process will also reveal whether any of the tables has anomalies that need to be resolved.

A Word about Redundant Data and Duplicate Fields

You've seen the term *redundant data* used quite often in this chapter. In many cases, redundant data was characterized as being unacceptable; in others it was characterized as being appropriate. To better understand how to determine when redundant data is acceptable, a definition of the term is in order.

Redundant data is a value that is repeated in a field as a result of the fields' use as a link between two tables, or is the result of some field or table anomaly. In the first instance, the redundant data is appropriate; by definition, fields used to link tables together contain redundant data. (You'll learn more about this in Chapter 10.) In the second instance, the redundant data is entirely unacceptable because it poses problems with data consistency and data integrity. Therefore you should always strive to keep redundant data to an absolute minimum level.

Duplicate fields are fields that appear in two or more tables for any of the following reasons: they are used to link a set of tables together, they indicate multiple occurrences of a particular type of value, or they are there as a result of a perceived need for supplemental information. The only instance in which duplicate fields are necessary is in the case of linking two tables together; using duplicate fields is the only way to associate records from the first table with records from the second table. In any other instance, duplicate fields are unnecessary and should be avoided primarily because they introduce needless, redundant data.

As you refine each table structure, you're going to assess whether a duplicate field should be retained in the table. If the reason for its existence in the table is valid, then it will remain in the table; otherwise, the field will be removed. In the sections that follow, you'll learn how to effectively deal with both redundant data and unnecessary duplicate fields.

Using the Ideal Table to Refine Table Structures

Despite your efforts to refine the fields in a table, the table structure itself may contain anomalies that can produce unnecessary redundant data and make working with the data in the table difficult. You can identify a potentially problematic table structure by determining whether it is in accordance with the characteristics of the *Ideal Table*. You'll refine your tables more effectively once you understand the aspects of an ideal table.

Elements of the Ideal Table

- *It represents a single subject, which can be an object or event.* As you learned in Chapter 3, an object is a person, place, or thing and an event is something that occurs at a specific point in time. This element validates the work you did previously during the analysis and interview stage of the database design process, as well as the work you just recently performed.

- *It has a Primary key.* Every table in the database must have a Primary key. The Primary key uniquely identifies each record in a table and has specific characteristics that help to implement and enforce various levels of data integrity. Primary keys are discussed in detail in Chapter 8.

- *It does not contain multipart fields.* You should have resolved this problem when you were refining the fields in each table. However, at this stage it's a good idea to review the fields once again to make certain that all multipart fields were found and resolved.

- *It does not contain multivalued fields.* Here is another problem you should have resolved while refining the fields in each table. Make absolutely sure that you've found and fixed all of these fields as well.

- *It does not contain calculated fields.* Although you believe your current table structures to be free of calculated fields, it's common that you may overlook some calculated fields during the field refinement process. Therefore, you'll want to ensure that you've removed every calculated field by reviewing the table structures once more.

- *It does not contain unnecessary duplicate fields.* (Note that this guideline does not apply to fields used to link a set of tables together, such as those used in the example in Figure 7-16.) There are two types of unnecessary duplicate fields: those that are used to indicate multiple occurrences of a particular type of value, and those that supply reference information. Both types of fields cause problems with retrieving information from the table and working with the data in the table. Figure 7-17 shows an example of these types of fields.

It's easy to see that trying to identify all the students who checked out an electric piano is going to be an unnecessarily difficult and tedious task. Also an undesirable burden is placed on the user or the database application program to ensure that the home phone numbers stored in this table always match their counterparts in the Students table.

- *It contains only an absolute* minimum *amount of redundant data.* Remember that a relational database will never be completely free of redundant data. But you can, and should, make certain that each table contains as little redundant data as possible.

This field duplicates the StudHome Phone field in the Students table.

Student Instruments

StudFirst Name	StudLast Name	Instrument 1	Instrument 2	Instrument 3	StudHome Phone
Angie	Beltran	Guitar	Tenor Sax		363-9948
Laura	Chow	Tenor Sax	Clarinet	Electric Piano	527-4992
Debbie	Canaday	Drum set	Bass Guitar		336-5992
Raul	Garcia	Guitar	Electric Piano	Snare Drum	322-6992

These duplicate fields represent three occurrences of the same *type* of value.

Figure 7-17. *Examples of unnecessary duplicate fields.*

Resolving Unnecessary Duplicate Fields

Before you make final modifications to the table structures, you must first purge the database of any unnecessary duplicate fields. Once you've resolved these fields, you can refine the tables so that they are in accordance with the Ideal Table.

Duplicate fields used for the purpose of providing reference information are unnecessary and easy to resolve: just remove these fields from the table. Many people believe that a table must contain every field that will appear on certain types of reports, so they duplicate particular fields throughout the database as they deem necessary. They assume that a given table will then be able to provide all the requisite information for the report. But they are mistaken, and their action is both unwise and undesirable. Tables constructed in this manner are poorly designed (which causes a number of problems), the reasons for which will become increasingly clear as the database design process unfolds. When a field is unnecessarily duplicated, the user or the database application program is forced to ensure that the values in all occurrences of the field are mutually consistent, and this process carries a high risk for error.

In Figure 7-17, STUDHOME PHONE is an example of a field that is unnecessarily duplicated. Since it already appears in the STUDENTS table, it need not appear in the STUDENT INSTRUMENTS table. It is removed from the STUDENT INSTRUMENTS table in order to resolve the unnecessary duplication problem. As you'll learn later in Chapter 12, you can work with fields from the STUDENTS table *and* the STUDENT INSTRUMENTS table at the same time by combining them in a *View* (virtual table). You can then use this View as the basis for compiling any reports you require.

Resolving a set of duplicate fields used to indicate multiple occurrences of the same type of value is a straightforward affair: remove the duplicate fields from the table, consolidate them into one field, and use the new field as a replacement for the fields you removed. The problems caused by the duplicate fields have been eliminated by removing them, and information can now be easily retrieved from the table. Although this procedure resolves the duplicate data problem, it does introduce redundant data into the database. However, this is another instance in which the redundant data is acceptable.

In Figure 7-17 INSTRUMENT 1, INSTRUMENT 2, and INSTRUMENT 3 are duplicate fields that represent multiple occurrences of the same type of value. Their purpose in the table is to allow the music department to keep track of the instruments checked out by any student. Along with the difficulties these fields pose in retrieving information about a particular instrument, the three fields also limit the number of instruments a student can check out. What happens if several students want to check out more than three instruments? A typical response to this problem is to add more "instrument" fields to the table structure or add redundant data to the table. But there is a much better and more preferable way to deal with this situation.

To resolve the remaining duplicate fields in the STUDENT INSTRUMENTS table, remove the INSTRUMENT 1, INSTRUMENT 2, and INSTRUMENT 3 fields from the table and consolidate them into one field called INSTRUMENT. Then use the new field as a replacement for the fields you removed from the table. When you're finished, you'll be able to enter any number of instruments for a particular student. You'll also be able to easily retrieve information such as how many students have checked out a guitar, how many instruments are currently checked out by a particular student, and the names of the students who have checked out an electric piano. Your table should then look similar to the one in Figure 7-18.

In some instances, a table contains more than one set of the type of duplicate fields just described. Fortunately, each set of duplicate fields is resolved in the same manner. Figure 7-19 shows such a table. In the SALES INVOICES table, the fields ITEM 1, ITEM 2, and ITEM 3 constitute

Student Instruments

StudFirst Name	StudLast Name	Instrument
Angie	Beltran	Guitar
Angie	Beltran	Tenor Sax
Laura	Chow	Clarinet
Laura	Chow	Electric Piano
Laura	Chow	Tenor Sax
Debbie	Canaday	Bass Guitar
Debbie	Canaday	Drum set
Raul	Garcia	Guitar

Figure 7-18. *An example of duplicate fields resolved.*

Sales Invoices

Invoice Number	Invoice Date	Item 1	Quantity 1	Item 2	Quantity 2	Item 3	Quantity 3
13000	06/15/96	Eraser, Chalk	3	Pencils	12	Rubber Bands	1
13001	06/15/96	Batteries, 9 Volt	6	Notebook Dividers	8	Printer Paper	2
13002	06/15/96	Floppy Disks, 3½"	22	Pencils	5	Notebook, 3"	1
13003	06/16/96	Batteries, 9 Volt	4	Floppy Disks, 3Ω"	12	Scissors	1

Figure 7-19. *An example of a table with multiple sets of duplicate fields.*

one set of duplicate fields, and the fields QUANTITY 1, QUANTITY 2, and QUANTITY 3 constitutes another set of duplicate fields.

Remove the field ITEM 1, ITEM 2, and ITEM 3 and consolidate them into one field called ITEM; use ITEM as a replacement for these three fields. Then remove the fields QUANTITY 1, QUANTITY 2, and QUANTITY 3 and consolidate them into one field called QUANTITY; use QUANTITY as a replacement for these three fields. Now you can enter as many items as you need for each "Sales Invoice." When you're done, your table should look like the one shown in Figure 7-20.

Sales Invoices

Invoice Number	Invoice Date	Item	Quantity
13000	06/15/96	Eraser, Chalk	3
13000	06/15/96	Pencils	12
13000	06/15/96	Rubber Bands	1
13001	06/15/96	Batteries, 9 Volt	6
13001	06/15/96	Notebook Dividers	8
13001	06/15/96	Printer Paper	2
13002	06/15/96	Floppy Disks, 3½"	22
13002	06/15/96	Pencils	5
13002	06/15/96	Notebook, 3"	1

Figure 7-20. *An example of multiple sets of duplicate fields resolved.*

Now that you're familiar with the Elements of the Ideal Table, refine the structures of your tables. If you are in doubt about a particular table, lay out its structure on a piece of paper and load it with data. Then you'll be able to resolve any anomalies revealed by the data.

Establishing Subset Tables

As you refine the structures of your tables, you may find that some of the fields in a particular table do not always contain values. Although no data or information retrieval problems will occur in a table where there are fields that contain no values, such a table might need some further refinement. Consider the structure of the inventory table in Figure 7-21.

In this scenario, the table contains data about various items in a person's office, such as office furniture, office equipment (computers, faxes, and so forth), and books. Clearly, the values of several fields in many of the records will be blank. For example, a book will not have a MANUFACTURER, MODEL, or WARRANTY EXPIRATION DATE. Similarly, a fax machine will not have an AUTHOR, PUBLISHER, or ISBN. The main problem with this table is that it contains fields that describe more specific

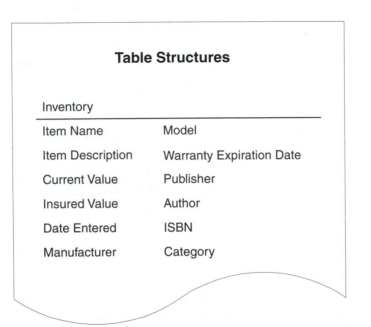

Table Structures

Inventory

Item Name	Model
Item Description	Warranty Expiration Date
Current Value	Publisher
Insured Value	Author
Date Entered	ISBN
Manufacturer	Category

Figure 7-21. *An example of a table structure for an office inventory table.*

versions of the subject represented by the table. In other words, the table actually represents *equipment* inventory as well as *books* inventory. Furthermore, both types of items share common characteristics, such as ITEM NAME, ITEM DESCRIPTION, and so forth.

To solve this problem, you'll create *subsets* of the main table. Each subset table contains only those fields that describe a specific version of the subject represented by the main table. A field from the main table is also included in order to connect the main table together with the subset table. Do not copy fields to the subset table that represent characteristics that are common to both the main table and the subset table; these fields must remain in the main table.

Create the first subset table by removing the MANUFACTURER, MODEL, and WARRANTY EXPIRATION DATE fields from the INVENTORY table and using them as the basis for a new table called EQUIPMENT. Remove

Table Structures

Inventory	Equipment	Books
Item Name	Item Name	Item Name
Item Description	Manufacturer	Publisher
Current Value	Model	Author
Insured Value	Warranty Expiration Date	ISBN
Date Entered		Category

Figure 7-22. *The new subset tables.*

the PUBLISHER, AUTHOR, ISBN, and CATEGORY fields from the INVENTORY table and use them as the basis for a new subset table called BOOKS. Now, add ITEM NAME to both tables; this field will link each subset table to the main table. After you've created the subset tables, compose a suitable description for each subset table and add the subset tables to the final table list. Indicate "Subset" under the Type column on the list. Figure 7-22 shows the new tables.

Further investigation of your table structures may reveal that you've previously created subset tables without knowing it. It's common to inadvertently create tables that have *almost* identical structures; the table structures usually contain only a few unique fields. If you study the two table structures in Figure 7-23 closely, you'll discover that they represent different versions of the *same* subject. The figure shows a partial field list of two such table structures.

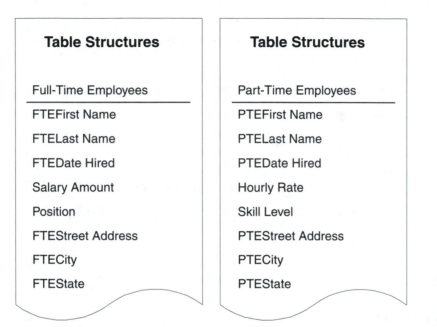

Figure 7-23. *An example of previously unidentified subset tables.*

In Figure 7-23, both tables represent "employees," but each represents a specific type of employee. Notice, however, that there are generic fields common to both tables: first name, last name, date hired, street address, city, and state. It's really unnecessary to duplicate all these fields, so you'll need to refine the table structures.

Refine Previously Unidentified Subset Tables

When you identify subset tables such as these, you can refine them by following these steps:

- Remove all the fields that the subset tables have in common and place them into a new table; this becomes your main table.

- Identify the subject represented by the new main table; give the table an appropriate name.

- Make certain that the subset tables define a specific version of the subject represented by the main table. If necessary modify the subset table names.

- Compose a suitable description for the main table and add that table to the final table list. Indicate the table type as "Data."

Figure 7-24 shows the results of using these steps on the FULL-TIME EMPLOYEES table and the PART-TIME EMPLOYEES table.

At this point, all of your table structures should be in pretty good shape. However, you'll need to refine them even further as you learn about Primary keys, Foreign keys, relationships, and business rules.

Table Structures

Employees	Full-Time Employees	Part-Time Employees
EmpFirst Name	EmpFirst Name	EmpFirst Name
EmpLast Name	EmpLast Name	EmpLast Name
Date Hired	Salary Amount	Hourly Rate
EmpStreet Address	Position	Skill Level
EmpCity		
EmpState		

Figure 7-24. *An example of refined subset tables.*

CASE STUDY

You're now going to define the *preliminary table list* for Mike's Bikes.
As you know, the first thing you need to do is review the preliminary
field list to determine what subjects you can infer from the fields on
the list. A *partial* sample of the list you're working with is shown in
Figure 7-25.

After carefully reviewing the entire preliminary field list, you determine
that the following tables are suggested by the fields on the list: CUS-
TOMERS, EMPLOYEES, INVOICES, PRODUCTS, and VENDORS.
These items constitute the first version of your *preliminary table list*.

Next create a *second* version of the preliminary table list by merging the
first version of the list with the *list of subjects* you created during the
analysis process. Keep the following steps in mind as you merge the two
lists together:

Preliminary Field List
as of 07/05/96

Birth Date	Office Phone
Employee Name	Product Name
Employee Address	Category
Employee City	Unit Price
Customer Name	Invoice Number
Customer Address	Invoice Date

Figure 7-25. *A preliminary field list for Mike's Bikes.*

1. *Resolve items that are duplicated on both lists.* Remember that a single item can appear on both lists, yet represent *different* subjects. If you identify any such items, use the appropriate techniques to resolve this problem.

2. *Resolve items that represent the* same *subject but have* different *names.* You want to make certain that a particular subject is represented by only *one* table.

3. *Combine the remaining items together into one list.* The combined list becomes the *second* version of the preliminary table list.

After following these steps, your preliminary table list should look similar to the one shown in Figure 7-26. Note that CUSTOMERS, EMPLOYEES, and PRODUCTS are crossed out on the list of subjects; they represent the same subjects as their counterparts on the preliminary table list. SALES has no counterpart on the preliminary table list, but it represents the *same* subject as INVOICES. However, INVOICES is most meaningful to Mike and his staff, so it is used instead of SALES on the preliminary table list. A similar situation exists between SUPPLIERS and VENDORS; Mike selects VENDORS as the name to appear on the preliminary table list, so Suppliers is crossed out.

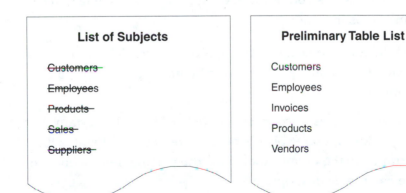

List of Subjects	Preliminary Table List
~~Customers~~	Customers
~~Employees~~	Employees
~~Products~~	Invoices
~~Sales~~	Products
~~Suppliers~~	Vendors

Figure 7-26. *The second version of the preliminary table list.*

> ❖ **Reminder** The selection of the name that best represents the subject of the table is arbitrary. The rule of thumb is to use the name that is *most* meaningful to everyone in the organization.

Now you'll work toward the second version of the preliminary table list. Use the mission objectives you created at the beginning of the database design process to determine whether you have overlooked any subjects during the previous two procedures. Identify each subject represented in the mission objectives using the subject identification technique. Once you've identified as many subjects as possible, you can use the steps from the previous procedure to cross-check these subjects against the subjects listed on the preliminary table list. After your review of the items is complete, and you have resolved any duplicate items, you have the second version of the preliminary table list.

As it turns out, *all* of the subjects identified from the mission objectives for Mike's Bikes already appear on the preliminary table list. Therefore, your cross-checking is easily completed, and you now have the second version of the preliminary table list.

Once the preliminary table list is complete, you're ready to transform it into a *final table list*. As you begin to create the final table list, keep the following steps in mind:

1. *Refine the table names.* Use the appropriate guidelines to ensure that each table name is clear, unambiguous, descriptive, and meaningful.

2. *Compose a suitable description for each table.* Make certain that the table description explicitly defines the table and states its importance to the organization. Use the pertinent guidelines to create each table description.

Final Table List

Name	Type	Description
Customers	Data	The people who purchase the products we have to offer. Keeping track of our customers allows us to promote our business and obtain valuable feedback in assessing the quality of our customer service.
Employees	Data	The people who work for our company in various capacities. This information is important for tax purposes, health benefits, and work-related issues.

Figure 7-27. *A partial listing of the final table list for Mike's Bikes.*

3. *Indicate the table's type.* Remember that a table can be classified in one of four ways—*data, linking, subset,* or *validation*. At this point, all of your tables are *data* tables.

Figure 7-27 shows a *partial* example of the final table list for Mike's Bikes.

The next order of business is to associate fields from the preliminary field list with each table in the final table list. Make certain you select the fields that best represent characteristics of each table's subject; each field should define or describe a particular aspect of the subject. Figure 7-28 shows a *partial* example of the table structures for Mike's Bikes.

Table Structures

Customers	Employees	Invoices	Products
Customer First Name	Employee Name	Invoice Number	Product Name
Customer Last Name	Employee Address	Invoice Date	Product Description
Customer Phone	Employee Phone	Employee Name	Category
Customer Address	SSN	Customer Last Name	Wholesale Price
Status	Date Hired	Customer First Name	Retail Price
	Position	Customer Phone	Quantity

Figure 7-28. *A partial listing of the table structures for Mike's Bikes.*

Now prepare the fields for the process of refining the table structures. Remember to use the following steps as you work with each field:

1. *Improve the field names.* Use the appropriate guidelines to ensure that each field name is as clear, unambiguous, and descriptive as possible.

2. *Determine whether each field is in accordance with the Elements of the* Ideal Field. Make certain to check for multipart and multivalued fields; these types of fields can cause the most problems.

As you review the fields, you may decide to abbreviate some of the field names in the CUSTOMERS, EMPLOYEES, and INVOICES tables, shortening "CUSTOMER" to "CUST" and "EMPLOYEE" to "EMP." You may also decide that the field QUANTITY (in the PRODUCTS table) does not completely describe the characteristic it represents, so you change it to QUANTITY ON HAND. The Phone fields in the CUSTOMERS and EMPLOYEES tables suffer the same problem, so you change them to CUSTHOME

PHONE and EMPHOME PHONE. Furthermore, you've changed SSN to SOCIAL SECURITY NUMBER so that this field is more quickly and easily identified.

Further investigation of the fields reveals that almost all of them conform with the characteristics of the ideal field. The only exceptions are the Address fields in the CUSTOMERS and EMPLOYEES tables, and the EMPLOYEE NAME fields in the EMPLOYEES and INVOICES tables. After ascertaining that each Address field can be broken down into four individual items—street address, city, state, and zip code—you transform these items into fields and add them to each table. Similarly, you notice that the EMPLOYEE NAME field represents two items—first name and last name—and you make the appropriate adjustments to each table.

The result of all the changes you've made to the fields is shown in Figure 7-29.

Table Structures

Customers	Employees	Invoices	Products
CustFirst Name	EmpFirst Name	Invoice Number	Product Name
CustLast Name	EmpLast Name	Invoice Date	Product Description
CustHome Phone	EmpHome Phone	EmpFirst Name	Category
CustStreet Address	Social Security Number	EmpLast Name	Wholesale Price
CustCity	EmpStreet Address	CustFirst Name	Retail Price
CustState	EmpCity	CustLast Name	Quantity On Hand
CustZipcode	EmpState	CustHome Phone	

Figure 7-29. *Refinements to the fields in the table structures.*

Your final task is to refine the table structures. Make certain that you have assigned the appropriate fields to each table and that you have properly defined each table. Remember to follow these steps as you work with each table:

1. *Resolve unnecessary duplicate fields.* If you create any new tables, be sure to properly identify them and add them to the final table list.

2. *Determine whether each table is in accordance with the elements of the* Ideal Table. Make certain you resolve all the anomalies you identify in any of the fields.

3. *Establish subset tables as appropriate.* Make certain you properly identify these tables and add them to the final table list as well.

As you complete your review of the tables, you determine that all of them conform to the Ideal Table with the exception of the INVOICES table. The only problem with the INVOICES table is that it contains an unnecessary duplicate field: CustHome Phone. This field is dispensable because it provides only reference information. Therefore, remove it from the table.

While you were working with the PRODUCTS table, you noticed that it may contain fields that can be removed and placed instead in a subset table. So you review the table once again. Figure 7-30 shows the PRODUCTS table structure. (This is an expanded version of the table structure shown in Figure 7-29.)

Your assumption proves correct. You determine that there are fields that describe a "service," and a service can be construed as being a different type of product. A service is similar to a product in that it has a name, description, and category. But it's different inasmuch as it has a type, materials charge, and service charge. To avoid unnecessarily duplicating any fields, you create a subset table called SERVICES and make the appropriate modifications to the PRODUCTS table; you've

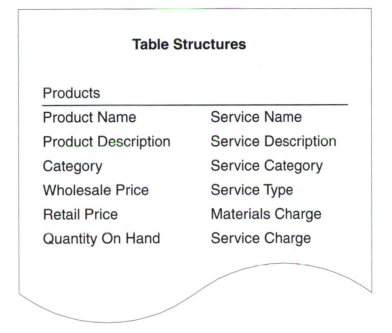

Figure 7-30. *The Products table structure (expanded version).*

used the PRODUCT NAME field to connect the two tables. Then you add the suitable listing for the SERVICES table to the final table list. Figure 7-31 shows the new PRODUCTS table and the new SERVICES subset table.

Summary

We opened the chapter with a discussion of the *preliminary table list*. This list constitutes the initial table structures for the new database. You learned how to develop this list using the preliminary field list, the list of subjects, and the mission objectives, all of which you compiled during the analysis phase of the database design process.

Figure 7-31. *The new PRODUCTS and SERVICES tables.*

Next we discussed the procedure for transforming the preliminary table list into a *final table list*, which contains the name, type, and description of each table in the database. You learned a set of guidelines for creating table names, as well as a set of guidelines for composing table descriptions. We worked on creating table names that are unambiguous, descriptive, and meaningful, and descriptions that explicitly define tables as well as stating their importance to the organization. You also learned that enlisting the help of users and management is crucial to the process of developing well-defined table descriptions. Table descriptions must be suitable and easily understood by everyone in the organization.

We then discussed the process of associating fields with each table on the final table list. Fields from the preliminary field list that best represent the characteristics of a particular table's subject are assigned to that table to build a table structure.

The process of refining the fields was the next subject of discussion. You learned a set of guidelines for creating field names that will help you make your field names clear, descriptive, and meaningful. You also learned to identify the elements of the Ideal Field. Now you know that you can resolve anomalies in a field by determining whether it conforms to the elements of the Ideal Field. We then discussed the procedures for resolving *multipart fields* and *multivalued fields*. You discovered that breaking down multipart fields results in creating new fields; whereas breaking down multivalued fields yields new tables.

The chapter closes with a discussion of the process used to refine table structures. You learned to identify the elements of the *Ideal Table*, and you now know that you can ferret out a problem in table structure by determining whether a table is in accordance with these elements. Another technique you learned is how to resolve unnecessary duplicate fields. You're now aware of the fact that some duplicate fields are mistakenly used to supply supplemental information; whereas others represent different occurrences of the same type of value. You learned how to resolve these problems.

The entire discussion ends on the topic of *subset tables*. As you now know, a subset table is connected to some particular table in the database, and the subset table describes a specific version of the subject represented by the main table. You also know that you can explicitly create subset tables. In fact, you may have unknowingly created subset tables earlier in the database design process, so you need to look for subset tables you have not previously identified. Once you have identified subset tables you need to refine them and add them to the final table list.

8

Keys

*A fact in itself is nothing. It is valuable
only for the idea attached to it, or for
the proof which it furnishes.*
—CLAUDE BERNARD

Topics Covered in This Chapter

- Why Keys Are Important

- Establishing Keys for Each Table

- Reviewing the Initial Table Structures

- Case Study

- Summary

By now you've identified all the subjects that will be tracked in the
database. You've also assigned fields to each table, thus defining its
structure. Furthermore, you've put the structures through a screening
process to control their makeup and quality. In this next stage of the
database design process you'll begin the task of assigning *keys* to each
table. As you'll soon learn, there are different types of keys, and each
plays a particular role within the database structure. All but one key is
assigned during this stage; the remaining key is assigned when you
are in the process of establishing relationships between tables.

Why Keys Are Important

Keys are crucial to a table structure for the following reasons:

- *They ensure that each record in a table can be properly identified.* Remember that a table represents a single subject that is an object (person, place, or thing) or event (something that occurs at a specific point in time). You can expand on this definition by recognizing that the single subject represents a *collection* of similar objects or events. Each record in the table represents a unique instance within the collection. You must have some means of accurately identifying a single instance, and a key is the device that allows you to do so.

- *They help establish and enforce various types of integrity.* Keys are used as a major component of table-level integrity and relationship-level integrity. This means, for example, that you can ensure that a table has distinct records and that the fields used to link a pair of tables always contain matching values.

- *They are used to establish table relationships.* As you'll learn in Chapter 10, you will use keys to form a connection between a pair of tables.

You should always make certain that you have defined the appropriate keys for each table. When the keys are appropriate, you guarantee that the table structures are sound, redundant data within each table is minimal, and the relationships between tables are solid.

Establishing Keys for Each Table

Your next task is to establish keys for each table in the database. The function of a key within a table is determined by the key *type*. There are four main types of keys: *Candidate*, *Primary*, *Foreign*, and *Non-*

keys. All but the Foreign key is covered in this chapter. Foreign keys are discussed in detail in Chapter 10.

Candidate Keys

The first type of key you'll establish for a table is the *Candidate* key. Each table must have at least *one* Candidate key. It is from the pool of available Candidate keys that a Primary key for the table is drawn. Simply put, a Candidate key is a field or set of fields that uniquely identifies a single instance of the subject represented by the table. In order for a field to qualify as a Candidate key, it must conform to *all* of the following elements:

Elements of a Candidate Key

- *It must uniquely identify each record in the table.* Remember that a record represents a single instance of the subject represented by the table. This element ensures that you have a means of accurately identifying or referencing each record from other tables in the database as well as avoiding duplicates of a particular record within one table.

- *It must contain unique values.* By choosing a field that contains a value unique to each record you create a means of ensuring that there are no duplicates of a particular record. However, in the case of a Candidate key that comprises two or more fields, the value of each field doesn't have to be unique—it's the *combination* of the values that must be unique.

- *It cannot be null.* If the value of a Candidate key field is null, there's absolutely no way to identify the record it represents. Remember that a null value represents the *absence* of a value.

- *It cannot be a multipart field.* You've seen the problems with multipart fields, so you know that using a multipart field for an identifier is a bad idea.

- *It comprises a minimum number of fields necessary to define uniqueness.* You can use a combination of fields (viewed as a single unit) to serve as a Candidate key so long as each field contributes to defining a unique value. But keep in mind that overly complex Candidate keys can be difficult to work with and difficult to understand. So try to use as few fields as possible.

- *Its value is not optional in whole or in part.* The value of a Candidate key cannot be optional. A value must exist in order to conform to the previous elements. This caveat also applies to the values of two or more fields that together constitute a Candidate key.

- *Its must directly identify the value of each field in the table.* A Candidate key value identifies a particular record within the table. Therefore, you can infer that the Candidate key value identifies the value of each field for that record. (This will be explained in more detail later in this chapter.)

- *Its value can only be modified in rare or extreme cases.* Unless you have an absolute and compelling reason to do so, you should never change the value of a Candidate key. It can be difficult for a field to conform with the previous elements if its value can be changed arbitrarily.

Establishing Candidate keys for a table is quite simple: look for a field or set of fields that conforms to all the elements of a Candidate key. It's quite possible that you can define more than one Candidate key for a given table. In many cases it's a good idea to load a table with sample data (as you did in the previous chapter) as a means of accurately identifying fields that qualify as Candidate keys.

See if you can determine the Candidate keys for the table in Figure 8-1. Remember that a field must conform to *all* the elements of a Candidate key in order to be considered.

Employees

Social Security Number	EmpFirst Name	EmpLast Name	EmpStreet Address	EmpCity	EmpState	EmpZipcode	EmpHome Phone
456-91-9938	Kendra	Bonnicksen	1204 Bryant Road	Seattle	WA	98157	363-9948
386-11-2231	Katherine	Erlich	101 C Street, Apt. 32	Bellevue	WA	98046	322-6992
501-48-0039	Timothy	Ennis	7402 Kingman Drive	Redmond	WA	98115	527-4992
116-93-1299	Shannon	McLain	4141 Lake City Way	Seattle	WA	98136	336-5992
478-02-1129	Susan	McLain	2100 Mineola Avenue	Seattle	WA	98115	572-9948
655-92-5583	Estela	Pundt	101 C Street, Apt. 32	Bellevue	WA	98046	322-6992
601-22-1734	Timothy	Sherman	66 NE 120th	Bothell	WA	98216	522-3232

Figure 8-1. *Identify the Candidate keys for the EMPLOYEES table.*

As you visually scan the table, you see a possible five Candidate keys: SOCIAL SECURITY NUMBER, EMPLAST NAME, EMPFIRST NAME *and* EMPLAST NAME, EMPZIPCODE, and EMPHOME PHONE. However, further investigation will reveal which of these are true Candidate keys. Remember that if a field (or set of fields) fails to conform to even *one* characteristic of a Candidate key, it is automatically disqualified.

Upon close examination, you can draw the following conclusions:

- *SOCIAL SECURITY NUMBER qualifies.* This field conforms to every element of the Candidate key.

- *EMPLAST NAME is disqualified because of duplicate values.* As you've learned, the values of a candidate key must be unique. In this case there can be more than one occurrence of a particular last name.

- *EMPFIRST NAME* and *EMPLAST NAME qualify.* If the values of both fields are viewed as a unit, they will supply a unique value to identify a particular record. Although there may be multiple occurrences of a last name, it is unlikely that the combination of a particular first name and last name will be duplicated.

- *EMPZIPCODE is disqualified because it will contain duplicate values.* The values in EMPZIPCODE cannot be unique because many people live in the same zip code area.

- *EMPHOME PHONE is disqualified because it could contain duplicate values.* This would be a likely candidate were it not for the fact that more than one individual from the same family can be employed in the organization, and people who share a residence can have the same phone number, as illustrated in the example.

You can confidently state that the EMPLOYEES table has two Candidate keys: SOCIAL SECURITY NUMBER and the combination of EMPFIRST NAME and EMPLAST NAME.

To identify Candidate keys in your table structures, write the letters "CK" next to the name of each field you identify as a Candidate key. If you have a Candidate key composed of two or more fields, it's termed a *Composite Candidate key*. Use "CCK" next to the names of the fields that make up the Composite Candidate key. If you have more than one Composite Candidate key, use "CCK1," "CCK2," and so forth, to distinguish one from another. Now use the appropriate letters to identify the Candidate keys for the EMPLOYEES table. Your structure should look similar to the one shown in Figure 8-2.

Now consider the table shown in Figure 8-3 and try to identify as many Candidate keys as you can.

At first glance, you may believe that there are four possible Candidate keys for the PARTS table: PART NAME; MODEL NUMBER; the combination of PART NAME and MODEL NUMBER; and the combination of MANUFAC-TURER and PART NAME. However, after investigating this theory you come up with the following results:

- *PART NAME is disqualified because it could contain duplicate values.* In this case, a part name can be used more than once because each occurrence of a part name is distinguished by its model number.

Table Structures

Employees

Social Security Number	*CK*
EmpFirst Name	*CCK*
EmpLast Name	*CCK*
EmpStreet Address	
EmpCity	
EmpState	
EmpZipcode	
EmpHome Phone	

Figure 8-2. *Marking Candidate keys in the EMPLOYEES table structure.*

Parts

Part Name	Model Number	Manufacturer Name	Retail Price
Shimka XT Cranks	XT-113	Shimka Incorporated	199.95
Faust Brake Levers	BL / 45	Faust USA	53.79
MiniMite Pump		MiniMite	35.00
Hobo Fanny Pack		Hobo Bike Company	59.00
Diablo Bike Pedals	Mtn-A26	Diablo Sports	129.50
Shimka Truing Stand	SP-100		37.95
Faust Brake Levers	BL / 60	Faust USA	79.95

Figure 8-3. *Identifying Candidate keys for the PARTS table.*

- *MODEL NUMBER is disqualified because there can be null values.* A Candidate key value must exist for each record in the table. As you can see, some parts do not have a model number.

- *PART NAME* and *MODEL NUMBER are disqualified because there can be null values in each field.* The fact that Model Number can contain null values instantly disqualifies this combination of fields.

- *MANUFACTURER* and *PART NAME are disqualified because the values for these fields seem to be optional.* As you know, a Candidate key value cannot be optional in whole or in part. In this instance, you can infer that entering the manufacturer name is optional if this information already appears in the part name. Therefore, this combination cannot be designated a Candidate key.

It's evident that for the PARTS table you don't have a single field or set of fields that qualifies as a Candidate key. This is a problem because each table must have at least *one* Candidate key. Fortunately, there is a solution to this problem.

Artificial Candidate Keys

If none of the fields in a table, either singularly or as a set, qualifies as a Candidate key, you can use an *Artificial* Candidate key. (Here, "artificial" is used in the sense that a Candidate key does not "naturally" occur in the table; you have to manufacture one.) You establish an Artificial Candidate key by creating a new field that conforms to the elements of a Candidate key and then adding that field to the table. The new field becomes the "official" Candidate key for the table; it is not necessary to document the fact that it is an Artificial Candidate key. In Figure 8-4, we make PART NUMBER the Artificial Candidate key that has been assigned for the PARTS table.

Once you've established an Artificial Candidate key for your table, mark that field name with a "CK" in the table structure, just as you did for the EMPLOYEES table in the previous example.

Parts

Part Number	Part Name	Model Number	Manufacturer Name	Retail Price
41000	Shimka XT Cranks	XT-113	Shimka Incorporated	199.95
41001	Faust Brake Levers	BL / 45	Faust USA	53.79
41002	MiniMite Pump		MiniMite	35.00
41003	Hobo Fanny Pack		Hobo Bike Company	59.00
41004	Diablo Bike Pedals	Mtn-A26	Diablo Sports	129.50
41005	Shimka Truing Stand	SP-100		37.95
41006	Faust Brake Levers	BL / 60	Faust USA	79.95

Figure 8-4. *The PARTS table with the Artificial Candidate key* PART NUMBER.

There is one other instance in which you may choose to create an Artificial Candidate key: when the new field you add would be a stronger, and thus more appropriate, Candidate key than any of those fields that currently exist in a particular table. Let's take another EMPLOYEES table to use as an example of such an instance. Say that the only Candidate key for this table is the combination of the fields EMPFIRST NAME and EMPLAST NAME. Although this combination may be a valid Candidate key, using a single field Candidate key might be more efficient and might identify the subject of the table more easily. For example, users may be accustomed to using a number rather than a name as a means of identifying an employee. Therefore, you can decide to create a new field named EMPLOYEE ID and use it as an Artificial Candidate key. This is an absolutely acceptable practice—do this without hesitation or reservation if you can see that it's appropriate.

You'll want to review the Candidate keys you have selected to make absolutely certain that the fields they include are in complete accordance with the elements of a Candidate key. You may discover that one of the fields is not a Candidate key after all. If you identify such a field, remove the "CK" designator from its name in the table structure. So long as each table has more than one Candidate key, you won't have any problems if you need to delete a Candidate key. But if you discover that the only Candidate key for a table *is not* a Candidate key at all, you'll have to establish an Artificial Candidate key for that table. After you've defined the new Candidate key, mark its name with a "CK" in the table structure.

Primary Keys

Once you have listed all the Candidate keys that seem proper for each of your tables, the next operation is to establish a Primary key for each table. A Primary key must conform to the exact same elements as the Candidate key, and it is the most important key assigned to the table: It is the key that officially identifies the table throughout the database structure. The Primary key is used to enforce table-level integrity, to help establish relationships with other tables, and to accurately identify and refer to a particular record within the table. Establishing a Primary key involves two steps: reviewing the Candidate keys for the table and then selecting one of them to serve as the Primary key.

Assuming that there is no other marginal preference, here are a couple of guidelines you can use to select an appropriate Primary key:

- *If you have a "simple" (single field) Candidate key and a Composite Candidate key, choose the "simple" Candidate key.* It's *always* best to use a Candidate key that contains the least number of fields.

- *Choose the Candidate key that uses a field that incorporates part of the table name within its name.* For example, a Candidate key comprising SALES INVOICE NUMBER is the good choice for the SALES INVOICES table.

So select a Candidate key that you want to use as the Primary key. The choice is largely arbitrary—choose the one that you believe is the most meaningful to everyone in the organization in terms of being the one

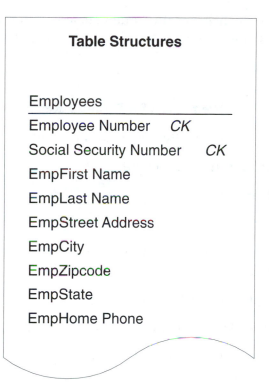

Figure 8-5. *Selecting a Candidate key to become the Primary key of the EMPLOYEES table.*

that identifies the subject of the table. Consider, for instance, the EMPLOYEES table shown in Figure 8-5.

In this particular EMPLOYEES table, the Candidate keys are EMPLOYEE NUMBER and SOCIAL SECURITY NUMBER. Either one of these fields could serve as the Primary key. You might decide to choose the EMPLOYEE NUMBER field if everyone in the organization is used to identifying an employee by this number, in tax forms and employee benefits programs, for instance.

The Candidate key you choose becomes the Primary key of the table and is governed by the elements of a Primary key. These elements are exactly the same as those for the Candidate key, and they should be enforced to the letter. For the sake of clarity, here are the elements of a Primary key:

Elements of a Primary Key

- It must uniquely identify each record in the table.

- It must contain unique values.

- It cannot be null.

- It cannot be a multipart field.

- It should contain the minimum number of fields necessary to define uniqueness.

- It is not optional in whole or in part.

- It must directly identify the value of each field in the table.

- Its value can only be modified in rare or extreme cases.

Before you make your selection of a Primary key final, you must subject it to one more test. The test involves the Primary key element:

- It must directly identify the value of each field in the table.

This is the final check you can perform to verify that you have a sound Primary key. In order for a Primary key to accurately identify an instance of the subject represented by the table, it must also identify the values of each of the fields in the table. If the Primary key fails to do this, you know you have one of two possible problems: it's not a good Primary key, or there are inappropriate fields in the table.

To solve this quandary pose the following question to determine whether the Primary key conforms to this element:

"Does the Primary key of this table *directly* determine the current value of each field in the table?"

To answer this question, you should look for fields that are *indirectly* determined by the Primary key. If you find such a field, you should remove it because it's very likely that this field is unnecessary within the table structure. Consider the partial table structure shown in Figure 8-6.

Select a record to work with and pose the question about whether the Primary key determines the current value of each field in the record. Say you're working with the Primary key value "13002." Does the current Primary key value *directly* determine the value of

INVOICE DATE? Yes, it does. This is the date that the invoice was created.

CUSTFIRST NAME? Yes, it does. This is the first name of the particular customer who made this purchase.

CUSTLAST NAME? Yes, it does. This is the last name of the particular customer who made this purchase.

EMPFIRST NAME? Yes, it does. This is the first name of the particular employee who serviced the customer for this sale.

EMPLAST NAME? Yes, it does. This is the last name of the particular employee who serviced the customer for this sale.

Sales Invoices

Invoice Number	Invoice Date	CustFirst Name	CustLast Name	EmpFirst Name	EmpLast Name	EmpHome Phone
13000	06/15/96	Frank	Lerum	Estela	Pundt	363-9948
13001	06/15/96	Gregory	Piercy	Katherine	Erlich	322-6992
13002	06/15/96	Caroline	Coie	Kendra	Bonnicksen	527-4992
13003	06/16/96	David	Cunningham	Kendra	Bonnicksen	336-5992
13004	06/16/96	Caroline	Coie	Shannon	McLain	572-9948
13005	06/17/96	Frank	Lerum	Estela	Pundt	322-6992

Figure 8-6. *Looking for fields indirectly identified by the Primary key.*

EMPHOME PHONE? No, it doesn't. It *indirectly* determines EMPHOME PHONE through EMPFIRST NAME and EMPLAST NAME. The value in EMPHOME PHONE is directly determined by the *current value* of EMPFIRST NAME and EMPLAST NAME. If the values of these two fields change, so will the value of EMPHOME PHONE. This field should be removed from the table for two reasons: its current value is not directly determined by the Primary key, and (as you have probably already ascertained) it is an unnecessary field.

After you've removed any unnecessary fields that you identified using this test, you have a sound Primary key if that key determines the values of all the other fields in the table. Now you can designate this as *the* Primary key for the table. Remove the "CK" next to the field name in the table structure and replace it with a "PK." (If the Primary key is made up of two or more fields, it is termed a *Composite Primary key* and is identified by the letters "CPK.") Figure 8-7 shows *part* of the SALES INVOICE table structure with INVOICE NUMBER designated as the Primary key.

As you create a Primary key for each table in the database, keep these two rules in mind:

Rules for Establishing a Primary Key

- *Each table must have one—and only one—Primary key.* Because the Primary key *must* conform to each of the elements that govern it, only one Primary key is needed for a particular table.

- *Each Primary key within the database should be unique—no two tables should have the* same *Primary key unless one of them is a* subset *table.* You learned at the beginning of this section that the Primary key identifies a table throughout the database structure. Therefore, each table must have its own

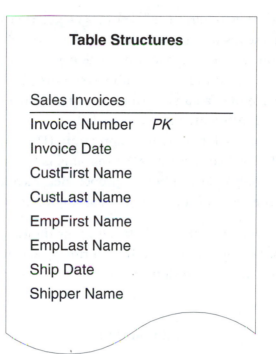

Figure 8-7. *The SALES INVOICES table with its Primary key.*

unique Primary key in order to avoid any confusion or ambiguity concerning each table's identity. A subset table is excluded from this rule because it represents a more specific version of a particular table's subject—both tables *must* share the same Primary key.

Later in the database design process, you'll learn how to use the Primary key to help establish a relationship between a pair of tables.

Alternate Keys

Once you've selected a Candidate key to serve as the Primary key for a particular table, the remaining Candidate keys (if any) are now renamed

Alternate keys. They retain their usefulness since they can be used as an alternative means of uniquely identifying a particular record within the table. If you choose to use an Alternate key in this manner, you should write "AK" next to it on the table structure. Otherwise, you can remove its designation as an Alternate key and return it to the status of a normal field. Alternate keys are typically used once the database has been implemented in an RDBMS program. (The implementation and use of Alternate keys in RDBMS programs is beyond the scope of this work—our only objective here is proper identification. This is in keeping with the focus of the book: the logical design of the database.)

Figure 8-8 shows *part* of the final structure for the EMPLOYEES table with the proper designation for both the Primary key and the Alternate key. (This structure was previously used in Figure 8-5.)

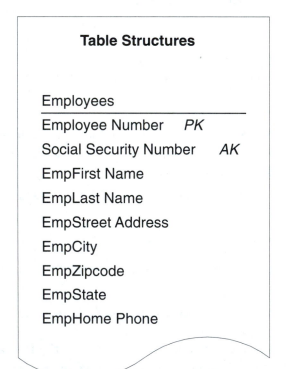

Table Structures

Employees
Employee Number	*PK*
Social Security Number	*AK*
EmpFirst Name	
EmpLast Name	
EmpStreet Address	
EmpCity	
EmpZipcode	
EmpState	
EmpHome Phone	

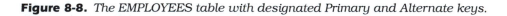

Figure 8-8. *The EMPLOYEES table with designated Primary and Alternate keys.*

Non-keys

A *Non*-key is a field that does not serve as a *Candidate*, *Primary*, *Alternate*, or *Foreign* key. Its sole purpose is to represent a characteristic of the table's subject, and its value is determined by the Primary key. There is no particular designation for a Non-key, so you won't write anything next to a Non-key field on the table structure.

Table-Level Integrity

Table-level integrity is established by making certain that

- there are no duplicate records in a table;

- every record in a table is identified by a Primary key value;

- every Primary key value is unique; and

- Primary key values are not null.

You began establishing table-level integrity by defining a Primary key for each table. You further ensured the enforcement of this integrity by making absolutely certain that each Primary key fully conformed to the elements of a Primary key.

In the following chapter, you'll further establish the integrity of the table as you establish *Field Specifications* for the fields in each table.

Reviewing the Initial Table Structures

Now that the fundamental table definitions are complete, you'll need to conduct interviews with users and management to review the work you've done so far. This set of interviews is straightforward and should be relatively easy to conduct.

During these interviews, you will

- *ensure that the appropriate subjects are represented in the database.* Although it's highly unlikely that an important subject will be missing at this stage of the database design process, it can happen. If this is the case, identify the subject, use the proper techniques to transform it into a table, and develop it to the same degree as the rest of your tables.

- *make certain that the table names and table descriptions are suitable and meaningful to everyone.* If a name or description appears to be confusing or ambiguous to several people in the organization, work with them to clarify the name or description as much as possible. It's common for some table names and descriptions to improve during the interview process.

- *make certain that the field names are suitable and meaningful to everyone.* Selecting field names typically generates a great deal of discussion, especially when there is an existing database in place. There will be people who are used to referring to a particular field by a certain name because "that's what it's called on my screen." If you've changed the name of the field—you have good reasons for doing so—you'll have to be diplomatic and explain that the field was renamed in order to conform with the standards imposed by the new database. You can also tell them that the field can appear with the more familiar name once the database is implemented in an RDBMS program. What you've said is true; many RDBMSs allow you to use one name for the physical definition of the field and another name when the field is displayed on the screen or on a report. The capacity to change field names once the program is implemented doesn't change the need to observe the rules we are discussing for the field-naming process.

- *verify that all the appropriate fields are assigned to each table.* This is your best opportunity to make certain that all of the *necessary* characteristics pertaining to the subject of the table are in place. It's common at this stage to identify one or two characteristics of a subject that were unintentionally over-looked earlier in the design process. If you identify such a characteristic, use the appropriate techniques to transform it into a field and follow all the necessary steps to add it to the table.

When the interviews are complete, you're ready to begin the next phase of the database design process: establishing *Field Specifications*.

CASE STUDY

It's now time to establish keys for each table in the Mike's Bikes database. As you know, your first order of business is to establish Candidate keys for each table. Let's say you decide to start with the CUSTOMERS table shown in Figure 8-9.

As you review each field, you try to determine whether it conforms to the elements of a Candidate key. You identify three possible Candidate keys: STATUS, CUSTHOME PHONE, and the combination of CUSTFIRST NAME and CUSTLAST NAME. But you're not quite sure whether any of these will completely conform to the elements of a Candidate keys, so you load the table with sample data, as shown in Figure 8-10.

Keep this in mind as you review each field: if a field violates even one of the elements of a Candidate key, this is grounds for immediate dis-qualification. A field must be in complete accordance with *all* the elements in order to qualify as a Candidate key.

Upon completing your review, you draw these conclusions:

- *STATUS is disqualified because of the probability that there will be duplicate values.* As business grows, Mike is going to have many "Valued" customers.

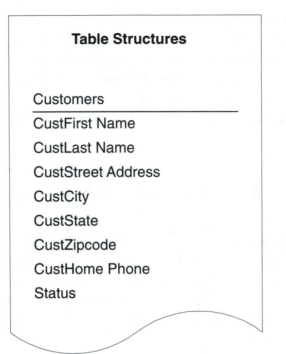

Figure 8-9. *The CUSTOMERS table structure in the Mike's Bikes database.*

Customers

CustFirst Name	CustLast Name	CustStreet Address	CustCity	CustState	CustZipcode	CustHome Phone	Status
Bridget	Berlin	2121 NE 35th	Bellevue	WA	98004	422-4982	Valued
Phillip	Bradley	101 9th Avenue	Kent	WA	98126	322-1178	
Kel	Brigan	7525 Taxco Lane	Redmond	WA	98225	363-9360	Valued
Barbara	Carmichael	7525 Taxco Lane	Redmond	WA	98225	363-9360	Preferred
Daniel	Chavez	750 Pike Street	Bothell	WA	98001	441-3987	Valued
Daniel	Chavez	301 N Main	Seattle	WA	98115	365-7199	
Sandi	Cooper	115 Pine Place	Seattle	WA	98026	332-0499	Preferred

Figure 8-10. *Identifying Candidate keys in the CUSTOMERS table.*

- *CustHome Phone is disqualified because of the likelihood that there will be duplicate values.* The sample data reveals two customers can live in the same residence and have the same phone number.

- *CustFirst Name and CustLast Name is disqualified because of the possibility that there will be duplicate values.* The sample data reveals the fact that the combination of first name and last name can represent more than one distinct customer.

As a result of these findings, you decide to establish an Artificial Candidate key for this table. You then create a field called Customer ID, confirm that it conforms to the requirements for a Candidate key, and add the new field to the table structure with the appropriate designation. Figure 8-11 shows the CUSTOMERS table with the new Candidate key.

Now you'll repeat this procedure for each table in the database. Remember to make certain that every table has at least *one* Candidate key.

The next order of business it to establish a Primary key for each table. As you know, the Primary key for a particular table is selected from the table's pool of available Candidate keys. Here are a few points to keep in mind in choosing a Primary key when a table has more than one Candidate key:

- Select the Candidate key that is most meaningful to everyone in the organization.

- Select the Candidate key that best identifies the subject of the table.

- Choose a "simple" (single field) Candidate key over a Composite Candidate key.

- If possible, pick a Candidate key that has the table name incorporated into its own name.

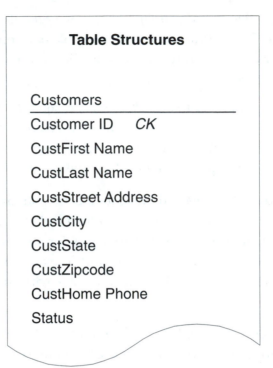

Figure 8-11. *The CUSTOMERS table with the new Artificial Candidate key, CUSTOMER ID.*

You begin by working with the EMPLOYEES table. In reviewing the Candidate keys, you decide that EMPLOYEE ID is a much better choice for the Primary key than SOCIAL SECURITY NUMBER, so you select it as the Primary key. Your decision is based on the fact that Mike's employees are used to identifying themselves by ID number. Therefore it does make sense to use EMPLOYEE ID as the Primary key.

Now you perform one final test on your selection before you make this Candidate key your final choice as *the* Primary key of the table: you determine whether the Primary key identifies the value of each field in the table. As you know, you'll use the following steps to make the test:

1. Load the table with sample data.

2. Look for fields that are indirectly identified by the Primary key and remove them from the table.

3. Select a record to work with, pick a field, and ask yourself if the current value of the Primary key directly determines the current value of the field.

You know that if your chosen Primary key doesn't pass the test, you'll have to select another Candidate key and start over again. However, EMPLOYEE ID does pass the test, so you'll use it as the official Primary key for the EMPLOYEES table. Be sure to place the letters "PK" next to the EMPLOYEE ID field in the table structure. You would then repeat this process with the rest of the tables in Mike's new database until every table has a Primary key.

Remember to keep these rules in mind as you establish Primary keys for each table:

*   Each table must have one—and only one—Primary key.

*   Each Primary key within the database should be unique—no two tables should have the same Primary key (unless one of them is a subset table).

There is, in fact, a subset table in Mike's database: the SERVICES table. You created this table during the previous stage of the design process (in Chapter 7). As you know, the SERVICES subset table represents a more specific version of the subject represented by the PRODUCTS table. Currently, the PRODUCTS table and the SERVICES subset table are connected to one another by the PRODUCT NAME field. You now know, however, that a subset table *must* have the same Primary key as the table to which it is connected. Therefore, you'll establish the same Primary key for the SERVICES subset table that you established for the PRODUCTS table: the PRODUCT NUMBER field. Figure 8-12 shows the PRODUCTS table and the SERVICES subset table with their Primary keys.

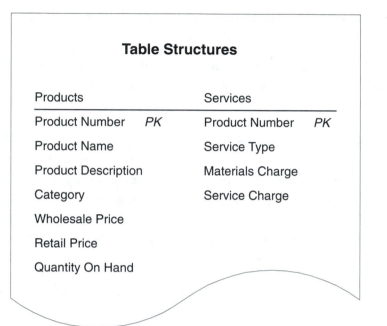

Figure 8-12. *Establishing the Primary key for a subset table.*

The last order of business is conducting interviews with Mike and his staff. During the interviews, you'll review all the work you've performed on the tables in the database. As you conduct the interviews,

- make certain that the appropriate subjects are represented in the database;

- make certain that the table names and descriptions are suitable and meaningful to everyone;

- make certain that the field names are suitable and meaningful to everyone; and

- verify that all the appropriate fields are assigned to each table.

By the end of the interview, everyone agrees that the tables are in good form and that all the subjects with which they are concerned are represented in the database. Only one minor point came up during the discussions: Mike wants to add a CALL PRIORITY field to the VENDORS table. There are instances in which more than one vendor supplies a particular product, and Mike wants a way to indicate which vendor should be called first if that product is unexpectedly out of stock. So you add the new field to the VENDORS table and bring the interview to a close.

Summary

The chapter opens with a discussion on the importance of *keys*. You learned that there are different types of keys, and each type plays a different role within the database. Based on the type of key, a record can be identified, various types of integrity can be established, and relationships between tables can be established. You now know that you can guarantee sound table structure by making certain that the appropriate keys are established for each table.

We then discussed the process of establishing keys for each table. We began by identifying the four main types of keys: *Candidate*, *Primary*, *Foreign*, and *Non-keys*. First, we looked at the process of establishing Candidate keys for each table. You learned about the *elements of a Candidate key* and how to make certain that a field (or set of fields) has these elements. Then you learned that an Artificial Candidate key is used when none of the fields in a table can be used as a Candidate key, or when a new field would make a stronger Candidate key than any of the potential Candidate keys you could select from among the fields.

The chapter continues with a discussion of *Primary keys*. You learned that a Primary key is established from an existing Candidate key and that it is governed by specific elements. Then, we covered a set of guidelines you can use to determine which Candidate key to use as a Primary key. We then looked at a way to ensure that the chosen Primary key truly identifies a particular record and its values. If a Primary key fails this test, you know that you must select another Candidate key and start the process over again. You also know that each table must have a single and unique Primary key.

Next you learned that any Candidate keys that remain after you have settled on a Primary key are then termed *Alternate keys*. They should be the same elements as Candidate keys and are used mainly when the database is implemented in an RDBMS. You also learned that any field not designated as a Candidate, Primary, Alternate, or Foreign key is a *Non-key* field—it represents a characteristic of the table's subject and its value is identified by the Primary key. We then discussed *table-level integrity* and how it is established through the use of Primary keys and enforced by the elements of a Primary key.

The chapter closes with some guidance on conducting further *interviews* with users and management. You now know that these interviews are used as a means of reviewing the work you have performed on the tables. Use these interviews with the people in the organization to verify and validate the current database structure.

9

Field Specifications

*It has long been an axiom of mine
that the little things are infinitely the
most important.*
—SHERLOCK HOLMES,
THE ADVENTURES OF SHERLOCK HOLMES

Topics Covered in This Chapter

Why Field Specifications Are Important

Field-Level Integrity

Anatomy of a Field Specification

Defining Field Specifications for Each Field in the Database

Case Study

Summary

Fields are the bedrock of the database. They represent characteristics of the subjects that are important to the organization. They store the data that is retrieved and then presented as information—information that is vital to the organization's daily operations, success, and future growth. They are the most overlooked, underutilized, and most often neglected assets of the organization! Frequently little or no time is spent ensuring the structural and logical integrity of the fields in the database.

Much is said and written about data integrity, but little is *done* about it. Many people believe that as long as they keep an eye on their data-entry personnel and they have a "foolproof" database application program, there's really not much to worry about. This lack of concern and action on behalf of data integrity commonly stems from an incorrect belief that it takes too much time to establish. It's important to note, however, that the people who don't have time for establishing data integrity usually spend a large amount of time fixing their improperly designed databases—typically up to three times more time than it would have taken them to design the database properly in the first place!

In this chapter, you'll learn how to establish data integrity by defining *Field Specifications* for each field in the database. The elements of a Field Specification are covered in detail first, followed by a discussion on conducting interviews with users and management; these interviews are used as a means to enlist help in defining the specifications for the fields.

Why Field Specifications Are Important

Contrary to popular belief, the time it takes to establish Field Specifications for each field in the database is an *investment* toward building consistent data and quality information—you *are not* wasting any time whatsoever by performing this process. In fact, you'll waste *more* time in the end if you only partially perform this process or neglect it entirely. Shirking this duty means you're bound to encounter (and suffer from) inconsistent and erroneous data, as well as inaccurate information.

There are several reasons why Field Specifications are crucial:

- *Field-level integrity is established and enforced as a result of defining Field Specifications.* The consistency and validity of the data can be guaranteed once the specifications are set.

- *Defining Field Specifications for each field enhances overall data integrity.* Remember there are four categories of *overall* data integrity, one of which is field-level integrity. Field-level integrity enhances (to some extent) the table-level integrity you established in the previous stage of the design process.

- *Defining Field Specifications compels you to acquire a complete understanding of the nature and purpose of the data in the database.* Understanding the data means that you can judge whether the data is truly necessary and important to the organization, and you can learn how to use it to your best advantage.

- *Field Specifications are valuable when you implement the database in an RDBMS program.* When you implement your database in an RDBMS, you can use these specifications as a guide for creating the fields and setting their fundamental properties. When an application is created for the database, you (or the application programmer) will know what type of data-entry and data-validation procedures are required because these procedures will need to be based on elements within these specifications.

Keep in mind that the levels of consistency, quality, and accuracy of the data in the database and information retrieved from it are in direct proportion to the degree of completion of the Field Specifications. If your organization depends heavily on the information you retrieve from the database, it is paramount that you establish each field specification as completely as possible.

Field-Level Integrity

A field has *field-level integrity* after a full set of Field Specifications has been defined for the field. Field Specifications help to warrant that

- the identity and purpose of each field is clear, and that all of the tables in which it appears are properly identified;

- field definitions are consistent throughout the database;

- the values of the field are consistent and valid; and

- the types of modifications, comparisons, and operations that can be applied to the values in the field are clearly identified.

The integrity established through Field Specifications, in addition to the integrity resulting from a field's conformance to the Elements of the Ideal Field, guarantees that a field structure is sound and optimally designed. In fact, if you adhere to the Elements of the Ideal Field, defining Field Specifications is a relatively easy task.

If you've had any lingering doubt about a particular field's conformance to the Elements of the Ideal Field, now is a good time to review that field once more. If you determine that it is *not* in conformance, use the appropriate techniques to resolve the problem and make the proper adjustments to the table. Otherwise, you can begin the process of defining Field Specifications for each field in the database. The Elements of the Ideal Field are repeated here for convenience:

Elements of the Ideal Field

- It represents a characteristic of the subject of the table.

- It contains only a single value.

- It cannot be broken down into smaller components.

- It does not contain a calculated or concatenated value.

- It is unique within the entire database structure.

- It retains all of its characteristics if it appears in more than one table.

Anatomy of a Field Specification

Field Specifications comprise a number of elements that are used to define every attribute of a field. These elements are divided into three categories: *General Elements*, *Physical Elements*, and *Logical Elements*. There is a fourth separate category: *Specification Information*. Grouping the elements in this manner makes them easier to find. It also allows you to focus on a specific aspect of the field as you're defining the Field Specification.

The items found within each category are

- *General Elements:* Field Name, Parent Table, Label, Shared By, Alias(es), Description

- *Physical Elements*: Data Type, Character Support, Length, Decimal Places, Input Mask, Display Format

- *Logical Elements*: Type of Key, Uniqueness, Required Value, Null Support, Edit Rule, Comparisons Allowed, Operations Allowed, Values Entered By, Default Value, Range of Values

- *Specification Information:* Specification Type, Based on Existing Specification, Source Specification

Figure 9-1 shows an example of a Field Specifications worksheet that lists the Elements and items of a Field Specification. Each of the elements and items of the worksheet are covered in detail in the following pages. A *setting* is the entry or option you select for a particular element or item. For the remainder of the book, this worksheet is used whenever we are working on the Field Specifications of a particular field.

Field Specifications

General Elements

Field Name:

Label:

Parent Table:

Shared By:

Alias(es):

Description:

Physical Elements

Data Type:

Character Support:

☐ Letters (A-Z) ☐ Extended (. , / $ # %)

☐ Numbers (0-9) ☐ Special (© ® ™ ∑)

Length:

Decimal Places:

Input Mask:

Display Format:

Logical Elements

Type of Key: ☐ Non ☐ Primary

☐ Foreign ☐ Alternate

Uniqueness: ☐ Non-Unique ☐ Unique

Required Value: ☐ No ☐ Yes

Null Support: ☐ Nulls Allowed ☐ No Nulls

Edit Rule: ☐ Enter Now, Edits Allowed

☐ Enter Now, Edits Not Allowed

☐ Enter Later, Edits Allowed

☐ Enter Later, Edits Not Allowed

Comparisons Allowed:

☐ Same Field | ☐ = ☐ > ☐ >=

☐ Other Fields | ☐ ≠ ☐ < ☐ <=

Operations Allowed:

☐ Same Field | ☐ + ☐ x

☐ Other Fields | ☐ - ☐ ÷

Values Entered By: ☐ User ☐ System

Default Value:

Range of Values:

Specification Information

Specification Type: ☐ Unique ☐ Generic ☐ Replica

Based on Existing Specification: ☐ No ☐ Yes

Source Specification:

Figure 9-1. *Field specifications worksheet.*

General Elements

Items under the General Elements category represent the most fundamental attributes of the field. They provide information on the purpose of the field, the name of the table(s) in which the field appears, and the pseudonyms the field may assume under certain circumstances.

Field Name

The *field name* is the unique identifier for the field itself. It is the set of *absolute minimal* words used to identify a particular field throughout the database. You created and refined field names earlier in the database design process (back in Chapter 7). There's no need to refine the field names any further here; you'll just enter each field name in the appropriate location on the Field Specifications worksheet.

Label

A *label* is an alternate name for the field that may be used to identify the field in an RDBMS program. For example, a label for a field named QUANTITY ON HAND might be *QTY ON HAND*. A label is typically a shorter form of the Field Name, used to conserve space on a data-entry screen, to allow more fields to fit on a particular report, or because many of the people in the organization are accustomed to seeing this particular name used for this particular field.

Avoid the temptation of using the label as the "legal" field name. The field should have a precise and accurate name. Shortening the "legal" name will greatly increase the chances of the field being incorrectly identified or misinterpreted. As you already know, you want to avoid such a situation at all costs.

Labels are typically used during the implementation and application development processes. However, it's also common that some fields will incorporate a label because it is more easily identified by the people in the organization. Make sure to maintain the distinction between the label and the "legal" field name.

Parent Table

A field represents a characteristic of a particular table's subject. The table that represents this subject is referred to as the *parent table* of the field, and it is the only table in which the field will appear. (A field can appear in another table under the following circumstances: when the field is used to connect the parent table to a *subset* table, and when the field is used to help establish a *relationship* between the parent table and another table.)

Shared By

This element is used to list the names of other tables that share this field. The only table names that should appear here are those that use this field as a connection to its parent table. For example, the parent table of an EMPLOYEE ID NUMBER field is the EMPLOYEES table. But the field is shared by a PART-TIME EMPLOYEES subset table. In this instance, EMPLOYEE ID NUMBER is used to connect the subset table (PART-TIME EMPLOYEES) to the parent table (EMPLOYEES).

Alias(es)

An *alias* is a name that a field assumes under very *rare* circumstances. One instance when a field would use an alias is when there *must* be two occurrences of the field in the *same* table. For example, say the organization is accustomed to identifying everyone by the field EMPLOYEE ID. Now, consider the SUBSIDIARIES table structure in Figure 9-2 (this is a *partial* structure only).

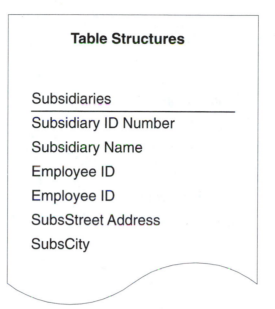

Figure 9-2. *A table requiring two occurrences of the same field.*

In this instance, each subsidiary has a president and a vice-president. Both of these individuals *must* be represented in the table because of their positions within the subsidiary organization. Although each employee is normally identified by an EMPLOYEE ID—and assuming that proper database design procedures are being followed—there can only be *one* occurrence of this field in the SUBSIDIARIES table. Yet the requirement is that *both* employees must be represented in the table. The only solution is to use an alias, such as VICE-PRESIDENT ID, for the second occurrence of EMPLOYEE ID. Once the alias is in place, employees can be properly represented in the table—the president is identified by EMPLOYEE ID, and the vice-president is identified by VICE-PRESIDENT ID. (For the sake of further clarity, you could use PRESIDENT ID as an alias for the first occurrence of EMPLOYEE ID.) The revised table structure is shown in Figure 9-3.

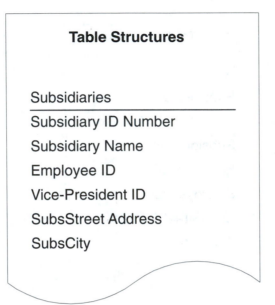

Table Structures

Subsidiaries
_____

Subsidiary ID Number

Subsidiary Name

Employee ID

Vice-President ID

SubsStreet Address

SubsCity

Figure 9-3. *VICE-PRESIDENT ID used as an alias for the second occurrence of EMPLOYEE ID.*

Although the use of an alias is an acceptable practice under these circumstances, you should avoid using aliases casually, because they can become difficult to manage and maintain, and they can eventually conceal or disguise the true meaning of the original fields. This can lead to a misunderstanding of what the data actually represents. This will become even clearer when you begin to establish table relationships.

Description

In the *description* you provide a complete interpretation of the field. The single most important benefit derived from composing a field description is that it forces you (and everyone in the organization) to think carefully about the nature of the data that will be stored in the field. If you find it difficult to compose a suitable description, this may be a signal that the field needs some further refinement.

Earlier in the database design process you learned a set of guidelines to use in composing a description for a table. Similarly, there is a set of guidelines that governs how a description for a field should be written.

Guidelines for Composing a Field Description

- *Use a statement that accurately identifies the field and clearly states its purpose.* The description should supplement the field name in terms of defining what the field represents. It should also state the field's role within the table or its relationship to the table's subject. Here's an example of such a description:

  "CustCity—the metropolitan area in which a customer resides or conducts business. This is an integral component of a customer's complete address."

- *Write a statement that is clear and succinct.* The description should be free of confusing sentences or ambiguous phrases. Although the description should be as complete as possible, use the minimum number of words necessary to convey the required information. As you've seen with table descriptions, verbose statements can be difficult to read and understand.

- *Refrain from restating or rephrasing the field name.* Neither of these practices does anything to illuminate the identity or purpose of the field. Remember that the purpose of a description is to provide a complete interpretation of the field. Therefore, a statement such as the following constitutes a poor description:

  "CustLast Name—the last name of a customer."

Here's a better way to phrase this description:

> "CustLast Name—the surname of a customer, whether original or by marriage, that we use in all formal communications and correspondence with that customer."

- *Avoid using technical jargon, acronyms, or abbreviations.* Although these types of terms and phrases may be understood by some people within the organization, very likely many will not understand their meaning. Remember that the description must be as clear as possible to *everyone* who reads it. For example, avoid using a statement such as this one:

> "Employee ID—a unique number used to identify an employee within the organization. It is a component of the SSP."

Here there is no inherent way to determine the meaning of the acronym "SSP." A simple resolution to this problem would be to spell out the complete term. On the other hand, it would be better to restate the purpose of the field.

- *Do not include implementation-specific information.* There's no reason to include the fact that a particular field appears on a particular data-entry screen or is used within a particular piece of programming code. It would be more appropriate to share this type of information during the implementation phase of the overall database development process.

- *Do not make this description statement dependent on the description of another field.* Each description should be as complete as possible and independent of every other description in the database. Otherwise, there could be some confusion

General Elements

Field Name: Label:	Employee ID Number Employee #	Parent Table:	Employees
Shared By:	Part-Time Employees, Customers	Alias(es):	
Description:	A unique number used to identify each employee within our organization. It is assigned during the first day of Employee Orientation and remains with the employee throughout the duration of his or her employment.		

Figure 9-4. *The General Elements category for an* EMPLOYEE ID NUMBER *field.*

and misunderstanding about the field. You want to avoid using a statement such as this one:

"Item Reorder Level—minimum number of items that must exist for a particular product. (See description for 'Quantity On Hand')."

- *Do not use examples.* As you learned in Chapter 7, the problem with examples is that they depend on supplemental information to convey their full meaning. Therefore, it is best to avoid them completely in order to ensure that the description is as clear and succinct as possible.

Figure 9-4 shows the General Elements section of a Field Specifications worksheet for an EMPLOYEE ID NUMBER field.

Physical Elements

The *Physical Elements* category pertain to the structure of a field. These elements are stated in general terms because they are not implemented in the exact same manner by all RDBMS programs. By establishing these elements during this phase of the design process you can ensure consistent field definitions throughout the database and reduce the time it will take to implement the field structures in an RDBMS program.

Data Type

In the Data Type setting you indicate the nature of the data that is stored in the field. The most common types of data are

- *Alphanumeric—stores any combination of letters, numbers, extended characters, or special characters.* Extended characters include symbols such as the period, the comma, the dollar sign, the percentage sign, and the exclamation mark. Special characters include items such as the copyright symbol, the trademark symbol, and the symbol for pi.

- *Numeric—stores numbers only; both whole numbers and real numbers are permitted.* Numbers with leading zeroes (such as 0000234) are not permitted, because they are not genuine numbers.

- *Date—stores any valid date.* The range of dates that can be represented by this field is determined by the RDBMS being used to implement the database.

- *Time—stores any valid time.* The manner in which a particular time is entered (twelve- or twenty-four-hour time, available formats) and stored by this field is determined by the RDBMS being used to implement the database.

Character Support

This element is used to indicate the characters that are permitted to be entered into the field. Controlling the characters that can be entered into a field helps to prevent the insertion of meaningless data; as a result *field-level integrity* is enhanced. You can choose to include or exclude any of the following types of characters:

- *Letters*—all letters of the alphabet *including* letters such as "é" and "ñ."

- *Numbers*—0 through 9.

- *Extended characters*—any character (other than letters and numbers) that can be entered from the keyboard, such as the comma, period, exclamation point, and percent sign. Note that a sample of these characters is provided on the Field Specifications worksheet as a reminder of the types of characters that belong to this category.

- *Special characters*—any character that must be entered by some means other than the keyboard, such as through a special software program. Characters under this category include the copyright symbol, the trademark symbol, and the symbol for pi. A sample of these characters is provided on the Field Specifications sheet as well.

For example, say you're working with a CUSTSTATE field, and its data type is alphanumeric. By definition, numbers are allowed in an alphanumeric field. However, entering a number into this field would render the value meaningless—there are no state names or abbreviations that contain a number. Therefore, you want to make certain that only letters can be entered into this field. (The issue of a *valid* combination of letters will be addressed in the Logical Elements section.)

Length

The total number of characters that can be entered into a particular field is indicated by this element. The maximum number of characters you allow for a field will depend on the RDBMS program you use to implement the database. Although the length element can be applied to any data type, you should be aware of the fact that some RDBMS programs do not allow you to specify a length for a numeric field. In this instance, it's common that the length of a numeric field will be determined by the *type* of number it stores, such as an integer, a long integer, or a real number.

Decimal Places

The number of digits to the *right* of the decimal point is indicated by this element. The number of decimal places determines the amount of precision a number should have. For example, many businesses require four digits of precision to the right of the decimal point for all currency values.

Input Mask

This element is used to indicate the manner in which the data should be entered into the field. Controlling the way the data is entered results in consistent entries within the field. For example, there are many ways to enter a date, such as "01/01/96," "01-01-96," and "01-Jan-1996." To prevent confusion over the meaning of the date sequence, it's best to have a consistent manner in which dates are entered. Using an *input mask* will ensure that values are correctly entered into a field.

Be as generic as possible when you designate an input mask; the implementation of this element will depend greatly on the RDBMS being used. You can provide the desired latitude by indicating the input mask in a generic manner. In the case of the date field, you could use "mm/dd/yy" as the input mask. This mask provides the following information: it tells you the sequence of the date (month, day, year), that elements of the date should be separated by slashes, and that each element should be represented by no more than two numbers.

Display Format

This element allows you to indicate how the value of the field should be presented. Through the use of a display format you can present the value in a more meaningful fashion than the manner in which it was entered. For example, you may want to enter a date as "mm/dd/yy," but it is much more meaningful when it is displayed as "January 1, 1996."

Be as generic as possible when designating a display format, just as you were with the input mask—its implementation is also dependent on the RDBMS program. If necessary, use a complete sentence to indicate the required display format. Say you're working with a COMPANY NAME field. You might use a statement such as

"Each word should start with a capital letter."

Figure 9-5 shows the physical elements section of a Field Specification worksheet for an EMPLOYEE ID NUMBER field.

Logical Elements

This category of elements pertains to the values of the field. These elements indicate whether the values should be unique, when they should be entered, whether they can be edited, the types of comparisons and

Physical Elements		
Data Type: Numeric	**Length:**	4
Character Support:	**Decimal Places:**	0
☐ Letters (A-Z) ☐ Extended (., / $ # %)	**Input Mask:**	####
☒ Numbers (0-9) ☐ Special (© ® ™ Σ)	**Display Format:**	0000

Figure 9-5. *The Physical Elements category for an* EMPLOYEE ID NUMBER *field.*

operations that can be performed on the values, and the range of acceptable values that can be entered into the field. Setting these elements in particular helps to establish and enforce a large part of field-level integrity.

Type of Key

In the Type of Key element you indicate the role of the values within the field. As you know, the values in a Primary key field uniquely identify each record within the table. You also know that the values in a Non-key field define or describe a characteristic of the table's subject. In Chapter 10, you'll learn about Foreign keys and when to designate a field as a Foreign key on the Field Specifications worksheet.

Uniqueness

This element determines whether the values of a field should be unique. In the case of a Primary key field, this element will be set to "Unique." Otherwise, this element is commonly set to "Non-Unique." You should think very carefully about the values that will be entered into the field and determine whether they ought to be unique. You'll have to base your decision on how the data is going to be used. Consider the DEPARTMENTS table structure shown in Figure 9-6.

In this example, the EMPLOYEE ID field is used to identify the person who is the manager of a particular department. Assuming that a person is only allowed to manage one department at any given time, there should be no duplicate EMPLOYEE ID numbers in this field. Therefore, the Uniqueness element in the Field Specifications worksheet for this field is set to "Unique."

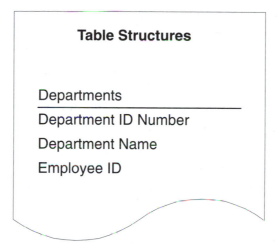

Figure 9-6. *Should the values of* EMPLOYEE ID *be unique?*

Required Value

Whether a user must enter a value into a given field is indicated by this element. The Required Value item is typically set to "No" for most of the fields in a table. However, in the case of a Primary key field, it *must* be set to "Yes." This is in compliance with the Elements of a Primary key—the value of a Primary key field cannot be missing. You may also need to set Required Value to "Yes" for a field such as CUSTZIP-CODE, because a zip code is required for accurate Post Office handling.

Null Support

As you learned in Chapter 3, "Null" represents a missing or unknown value. The Null Support element indicates whether null values should be allowed in the field. Obviously, Null Support is set to "No Nulls" for a Primary key field *and* an Alternate key field. (Remember that Alternate keys are governed by the same elements as a Primary keys.) Null

Support must be set to "No Nulls" whenever the Required Value element of the field is set to "Yes."

Null Support can be set to "Nulls Allowed" for a field such as CUST-COUNTY, because a customer may not know the name of the county in which he or she lives. Therefore, the value for the field may be *currently* unknown; in other words, you can allow the customer to provide the required piece of data at a later time. However, in most cases, Null Support is set to "No Nulls" because you want to make certain that an appropriate value is entered for each field in the table.

Remember that a Null does not represent a "blank"; it represents a *missing* or *unknown* value. A common mistake is to use a "blank" to represent a *meaningful* value. It is typically used to represent values such as "None," "Not Applicable," "No Response," and "Not Wanted." If these values are applicable for a particular field, make sure you include "None," "Not Applicable," and so forth, in the range of values for the field. Above all, *do not* use blanks, and do use Nulls judiciously!

Edit Rule

This element indicates at what point in time a value must be entered into the field and whether that value can be modified. There are four settings for Edit Rule, and only *one* may be chosen at a time:

- *Enter Now, Edits Allowed.* A value *must* be entered for this field when a new record is created for the parent table. The value can then be edited at any time.

- *Enter Later, Edits Allowed.* Entering a value for this field when a new record is created for its parent table is *optional*. This does not imply in any way that the field's value can be Null; you must enter a value for this field *at some point* in the near future. After the value is entered, it can then be edited at any time.

- *Enter Now, Edits Not Allowed.* A value *must* be entered for this field when a new record is created for the parent table. The value *cannot* be altered at all at any time.

- *Enter Later, Edits Not Allowed.* Entering a value for this field when a new record is created for its parent table is *optional.* This does not imply in any way that the field's value can be Null; you must enter a value for this field *at some point* in the near future. Once the value has been entered, however, it *cannot* be altered at all at any time.

Comparisons Allowed

The types of comparisons that can be made to a particular value of this field are indicated by the Comparisons Allowed element. There are six types of comparisons: equal to (=), not equal to (≠), greater than (>), less than (<), greater than or equal to (>=), and less than or equal to (<=). This element also indicates whether a value in this field can be compared to another value within the same field or compared to a value of another field in the table (or in the entire database); the settings are "Same Field" and "Other Fields," respectively.

Controlling the types of comparisons made to the values of the field allows you to avoid introducing meaningless comparisons. For example, say that you are working with an EMPLOYEE ID field that has a numeric data type. Although using a "greater than or equal to" comparison is generally acceptable on a numeric field, it is not appropriate in this instance. There is no reason for you to make a comparison such as this one:

"Is an Employee ID in the Employees table greater than or equal to an Employee ID in the Part-Time Employees table?"

Similarly, it is pointless to make the following type of comparison from one field to other fields within the table or database:

"Is an Employee ID in the Employees table greater than or equal to a Quantity On Hand in the Products table?"

But it is both suitable and *reasonable* to use the following comparison to determine whether an employee's status is part-time or full-time:

"Is an Employee ID in the Employees table *equal to* an Employee ID in the Part-Time Employees table?"

In some instances, it is perfectly suitable to compare a particular value of one field to the value of another field. Consider a DATE SHIPPED field. It makes sense to use the following type of comparison:

"Is the current value of Date Shipped greater than or equal to the current value of Date Ordered?"

You certainly don't want the value of DATE SHIPPED to be earlier than the value of DATE ORDERED. Therefore, you can set the Comparisons Allowed element to indicate which comparisons are appropriate for this field.

It's very likely that you'll review the Comparisons Allowed element later in the design process when you establish table relationships and define business rules.

Operations Allowed

This element indicates the types of operations that can be performed on the values in the field. Four types of operations are allowed: addition (+), subtraction (–), multiplication (×), and division (÷). (Obviously, any combination of these operations is allowable as well.) You can also indicate whether the operations can be performed against other values within the same field or values from other fields.

To avoid meaningless operations you can limit the types of operations that can be performed on the values of the field. To continue with the EMPLOYEE ID field example, there is no reason to perform any mathematical operations on a pair of EMPLOYEE IDs, nor is there any reason to perform such operations using values in this field in conjunction with values in another numeric field. But in the case of the DATE SHIPPED field, it *is* suitable to perform some of these operations using values from this field and other appropriate fields in the database. For example, you might need to subtract DATE ORDERED from DATE SHIPPED to determine the time that elapsed between ordering and shipping.

The settings for the Operations Allowed item are likely to change once you begin to establish Business Rules later in the database design process.

Values Entered By

This element indicates how values are entered into a field. Either the user will enter each value manually or the values will be entered automatically by the database application, also known simply as the "system." When this element is set to "System," this means that the person developing the database application program will have to provide some means of automatically generating the values for a particular field within the database application itself.

Default Value

A *default value* is a value that is used when an entry is required but not yet available, and when Nulls are not allowed. You should use default values very judiciously—only use a default value if it is *meaningful.* For example, "WA" is a meaningful default value for a CUSTSTATE field if the vast majority of your customers live in the state of Washington. But "01/01/96" is not a good default value for a DATE HIRED field because it's a completely arbitrary value that has no real meaning. In this instance, it's best to leave the field Null and enter the proper value at a later time.

Range of Values

The *Range of Values* element lets you determine every possible value that can be entered into a field. It can be represented in various ways, such as with a lower and upper limit (1000 to 9999) or with a specific list of values ("WA," "OR," "ID," "MT"). A range of values can be established under three categories:

- *General—the complete collection of every possible value for this field.* For example, the general range of values for a CUST-STATE field might include all valid abbreviations for every state in the United States.

- *Integrity specific—the collection of values that is based on the field's role in establishing a table relationship.* (This will be discussed in complete detail in Chapter 10.)

- *Business specific—the collection of values that is the result of a particular business requirement.* Organizations commonly have requirements of some sort that limit the range of values for a field. If the organization only conducts its business in the Pacific Northwest, for example, the states that can be entered into the CUSTSTATE field are limited to "WA," "OR," "ID," and "MT." (This topic will be discussed in more detail in Chapter 11.)

You're only concerned with the general range of values during this stage of the database design process. You'll revisit the Range of Values

---

Logical Elements

Type of Key:	☐ Non	☒ Primary
	☐ Foreign	☐ Alternate
Uniqueness:	☐ Non-Unique	☒ Unique
Required Value:	☐ No	☒ Yes
Null Support:	☐ Nulls Allowed	☒ No Nulls
Edit Rule:	☐ Enter Now, Edits Allowed	
	☒ Enter Now, Edits Not Allowed	
	☐ Enter Later, Edits Allowed	
	☐ Enter Later, Edits Not Allowed	

Comparisons Allowed:

☒ Same Field　　☒ =　☐ >　☐ >=
☐ Other Fields　☐ ≠　☐ <　☐ <=

Operations Allowed:

☐ Same Field　　☐ +　☐ x
☐ Other Fields　☐ -　☐ ÷

Values Entered By: ☒ User　☐ System
Default Value:
Range of Values: 1000 - 9999

Figure 9-7. *The Logical Elements category for an* EMPLOYEE ID NUMBER *field.*

element of the Field Specifications later when you establish table relationships and Business Rules.

There are two values that you *do not* want to set within any category of the Range of Values elements: "Other" and "Miscellaneous." Both can cause innumerable problems; they are nonspecific, so in this context they are meaningless. Some form of explanation is needed whenever these values are used, and they are an indication of mental laziness, since they represent a group of values that should be appropriately stored in a suitable table. The presence of these values indicates a need to review the purpose of the field and its values for possible refinement. You can eliminate many problems by refraining from using "Other" and "Miscellaneous."

Figure 9-7 shows the third section of a Field Specifications worksheet for an EMPLOYEE ID NUMBER field.

Specification Information

The elements under this category pertain to the nature of the field specification as a whole. The information specified here is helpful in creating and maintaining consistent Field Specifications.

Specification Type

A Field Specification falls into one of the following three categories:

- *Unique.* This specification is used only for the field indicated by the Field Name element in the General Elements category. The settings for all of the elements will pertain directly to this field.

- *Generic.* This specification is used as the basis for other Field Specifications. Establishing a generic field specification ensures consistent definitions for fields containing values that have the same *general* meaning. You could, for example, create a generic Field Specification for "State" and then use it as the basis for all "State" fields, such as CUSTSTATE, EMPSTATE, and VENDSTATE. In this instance, the values of all three fields have the same meaning—they represent a state within the United States—yet there is enough of an obvious distinction to require that they remain separate fields.

  The only requirements for creating a generic Field Specification are that you use a nonspecific field name and that the settings for all of the elements be as broad and general as possible. Consider the generic Field Specification for "State" shown in Figure 9-8.

  Note that there are no settings for various elements within the specification. You will set them in any new Field Specifications you create that are based on this Generic Field Specification. This permits you to thoroughly customize the settings for a particular field. You can also change the predefined settings of other elements as necessary. For example, the Range of Values element is commonly changed in order to refine it for a particular field.

Field Specifications

General Elements

Field Name: State   **Parent Table:**
Label:

Shared By: **Alias(es):**

Description: A state or territory within the United States in which a person, organization, or institution resides or conducts business.

Physical Elements

Data Type: Alphanumeric   **Length:** 2

Character Support: **Decimal Places:** Not Applicable

[X] Letters (A-Z)   [ ] Extended (. , / $ # %)   **Input Mask:** AA

[ ] Numbers (0-9)   [ ] Special (© ® ™ ∑)   **Display Format:** Capitalized letters

Logical Elements

Type of Key: [X] Non   [ ] Primary   **Comparisons Allowed:**

            [ ] Foreign   [ ] Alternate   [ ] Same Field | [ ] =   [ ] >   [ ] >=

Uniqueness: [X] Non-Unique   [ ] Unique   [ ] Other Fields | [ ] ≠   [ ] <   [ ] <=

Required Value: [ ] No   [X] Yes   **Operations Allowed:**

Null Support: [ ] Nulls Allowed [X] No Nulls   [ ] Same Field | [ ] +   [ ] x

Edit Rule: [X] Enter Now, Edits Allowed   [ ] Other Fields | [ ] -   [ ] ÷

            [ ] Enter Now, Edits Not Allowed   **Values Entered By:** [X] User   [ ] System

            [ ] Enter Later, Edits Allowed   **Default Value:**

            [ ] Enter Later, Edits Not Allowed   **Range of Values:** All recognized state abbreviations.

Specification Information

Specification Type: [ ] Unique   [X] Generic   [ ] Replica

Based on Existing Specification: [X] No   [ ] Yes

Source Specification:

Figure 9-8. *The generic Field Specification for "State."*

- *Replica.* This specification draws a majority of the settings for its elements from a particular generic field specification. Those elements that are not predefined by the generic Field Specification are then set specifically for the field. Figure 9-9 shows a replica field specification for an EMPSTATE field. The specification is based on the generic Field Specification for "State."

In this example, some of the elements that were not predefined have been set (such as Parent Table and Default Value), and some of the settings for the predefined elements have been modified (such as Description and Range of Values).

Based on Existing Specification

This element indicates whether any of the elements in this specification have drawn their settings from another field specification. Whenever Specification Type is set to "Replica," the Based on Existing Specification element is set to "Yes." (As you'll see in Chapter 10, there are specific instances in which a specification must be based on a "unique" Field Specification.) Otherwise, this element is commonly set to "No."

Source Specification

This element indicates the name of the generic Field Specification upon which the current specification is based. (Under the circumstances defined in Chapter 10, a unique field specification name can appear here as well.)

Figure 9-10 shows the Specification Information category of a Field Specifications worksheet for an EMPLOYEE ID NUMBER field.

Field Specifications

General Elements

Field Name: EmpState   **Parent Table:** Employees
Label:

Shared By: **Alias(es):**

Description: The state in which an employee resides or conducts business on our behalf. This data is a component of the Employee's overall mailing address.

Physical Elements

Data Type: Alphanumeric   **Length:** 2
Character Support: **Decimal Places:** Not Applicable
                                                  Input Mask: AA
[X] Letters (A-Z)   [ ] Extended (. , / $ # %) **Display Format:** Capitalized letters
[ ] Numbers (0-9)   [ ] Special (© ® ™ Σ)

Logical Elements

Type of Key:	[X] Non	[ ] Primary	**Comparisons Allowed:**			
	[ ] Foreign	[ ] Alternate	[ ] Same Field	[ ] =	[ ] >	[ ] >=
Uniqueness:	[X] Non-Unique	[ ] Unique	[ ] Other Fields	[ ] ≠	[ ] <	[ ] <=
Required Value:	[ ] No	[X] Yes	**Operations Allowed:**			
Null Support:	[ ] Nulls Allowed	[X] No Nulls	[ ] Same Field	[ ] +	[ ] x	
Edit Rule:	[X] Enter Now, Edits Allowed		[ ] Other Fields	[ ] -	[ ] ÷	
	[ ] Enter Now, Edits Not Allowed		**Values Entered By:**	[X] User	[ ] System	
	[ ] Enter Later, Edits Allowed		**Default Value:**	WA		
	[ ] Enter Later, Edits Not Allowed		**Range of Values:**	CA, ID, MT, OR, WA		

Specification Information

Specification Type: [ ] Unique   [ ] Generic   [X] Replica
Based on Existing Specification: [ ] No   [X] Yes
Source Specification: State

Figure 9-9. *Replica Field Specifications for the* EMPSTATE *field.*

┌─ **Specification Information** ───┐

Specification Type: [X] Unique   [ ] Generic   [ ] Replica
Based on Existing Specification: [X] No   [ ] Yes
Source Specification:

└───┘

Figure 9-10. *The Specification Information category for an* EMPLOYEE ID NUMBER *field.*

Defining Field Specifications for Each Field in the Database

Now that you have all the necessary fields assigned to each table, and you understand the choices to be made in establishing Field Specifications, you can begin the process of establishing Field Specifications for each field in the database. Although this process will take some time, remember that you are working diligently to establish field-level integrity. You're investing your time and effort to make certain that the data is consistent, valid, and as free from errors as possible. The result will be information that is always timely and accurate.

In order to make the specifications as complete and accurate as possible, enlist the help of both users and management to help you define them. They can provide insights into the data, and they can be of special assistance in refining the Logical Elements category of the specification. Although you don't have to speak with *everyone* within the organization, you want to assemble and meet with a representative number of people who are very familiar with the data and how it is used. Because this process is going to take some time, make certain you schedule as many meetings as are necessary to complete the interviewing process. Above all, *do not* rush through this phase! Take as much time as you need and be as thorough as you can.

The best approach to this task is to establish as many of the specifications as you can (as completely as you can), and then work with the participants to complete the rest. Begin by reviewing each field in the database and establishing its Field Specifications. Use your best judgment to define the settings for each element in the worksheet. Don't worry if your settings are slightly incorrect or if you have difficulty providing settings for some of the elements—you will be reviewing them with the participants anyway. When you've established specifications for all the fields you're familiar with, begin meeting with the participants to work on the specifications for the remaining fields.

Your first order of business during the *initial* meeting is to explain the General, Physical, and Logical Elements of the specification. Make certain that everyone understands each element; the more the participants understand a Field Specification, the better prepared they will be to help you establish Field Specifications. (In subsequent meetings, just review the elements to make certain that everyone remembers what they represent.)

Next review all of the specifications you've created. Ask the participants whether the settings for the elements are suitable and correct. In some cases, the participants will reveal new information about a field that will affect that field's specifications. For example, a participant may remember (prompted by some topic in the discussion) that there is a specific set of values that has always been used for a particular field. Therefore, you can set the Range of Values item of that field's specification to reflect this new information. Make sure that each part of the Field Specification is examined, and when there are no suggestions for refinement, move on to the next specification. Repeat this process for all of the specifications you've already established.

Now work with the participants on the specifications you were unable to establish or complete. Try to work with the people who are *most* familiar with the field under discussion, because they are likely to know what settings should be used for the Logical Elements category. Once you've identified the appropriate settings, mark them on the

Field Specifications sheet and move on to the next field. After you've established specifications for every field in the database, the entire process is complete.

The design of the new database is now close to completion. In the next chapter, you'll learn how to establish *relationships* between the tables. These relationships provide the mechanism needed to create views, which allow you to view and work with data from multiple tables simultaneously.

CASE STUDY

Now that you have all the appropriate fields assigned to the tables in the Mike's Bikes database, it's time to establish Field Specifications for each field. Before you meet with Mike and his staff, you establish as many Field Specifications as you can. None of the tables are unusual in any way, and the fields are pretty straightforward, so you have little difficulty in establishing the specifications. Figure 9-11 shows the field specifications for the PRODUCT DESCRIPTION field in the PRODUCTS table.

Now you meet with Mike and his staff to discuss the Field Specifications you've established. No one seems to have problems with any of the specifications; they confirm that all the settings for the elements seem suitable and correct. However, you have a question concerning the CATEGORY field in the PRODUCTS table: What is the appropriate setting for the Range of Values item? The response to your question is mixed; no one seems to know the complete list of categories that can be entered into the field. So you decide to indicate a general range of values for now. Figure 9-12 shows the revised Logical Elements category of the Field Specifications for the CATEGORY field.

You'll revisit this field (and element) again when you establish Business Rules for the database. With this problem solved, your meeting—as well as the process of establishing Field Specifications—is complete.

Field Specifications

General Elements

Field Name:	Product Description	**Parent Table:**	Products
Label:	Description		

Shared By: **Alias(es):**

Description: A statement which provides pertinent details about the product. This information is useful to our sales and promotion efforts and is provided to our customers by means of various promotional materials.

Physical Elements

Data Type:	Alphanumeric	**Length:**	180
Character Support:		**Decimal Places:**	Not Applicable
[X] Letters (A-Z) [X] Extended (. , / $ # %)		**Input Mask:**	Not Applicable
[X] Numbers (0-9) [X] Special (© ® ™ Σ)		**Display Format:**	Not Applicable

Logical Elements

Type of Key: [X] Non   [ ] Primary
                   [ ] Foreign   [ ] Alternate
Uniqueness: [ ] Non-Unique [X] Unique
Required Value: [ ] No   [X] Yes
Null Support: [ ] Nulls Allowed [X] No Nulls
Edit Rule: [X] Enter Now, Edits Allowed
                   [ ] Enter Now, Edits Not Allowed
                   [ ] Enter Later, Edits Allowed
                   [ ] Enter Later, Edits Not Allowed

Comparisons Allowed:
[ ] Same Field | [ ] =   [ ] >   [ ] >=
[ ] Other Fields | [ ] ≠   [ ] <   [ ] <=

Operations Allowed:
[ ] Same Field | [ ] +   [ ] x
[ ] Other Fields | [ ] -   [ ] ÷

Values Entered By: [X] User   [ ] System
Default Value: Not Applicable
Range of Values: Not Applicable

Specification Information

Specification Type: [X] Unique   [ ] Generic   [ ] Replica
Based on Existing Specification: [X] No   [ ] Yes
Source Specification:

Figure 9-11. *Field specifications for the PRODUCT DESCRIPTION field.*

Logical Elements

Type of Key:	[X] Non	[ ] Primary	**Comparisons Allowed:**			
	[ ] Foreign	[ ] Alternate	[ ] Same Field	[ ] =	[ ] >	[ ] >=
Uniqueness:	[X] Non-Unique	[ ] Unique	[ ] Other Fields	[ ] ≠	[ ] <	[ ] <=
Required Value:	[ ] No	[X] Yes	**Operations Allowed:**			
Null Support:	[ ] Nulls Allowed	[X] No Nulls	[ ] Same Field	[ ] +	[ ] x	
Edit Rule:	[X] Enter Now, Edits Allowed		[ ] Other Fields	[ ] -	[ ] ÷	
	[ ] Enter Now, Edits Not Allowed		**Values Entered By:**	[X] User	[ ] System	
	[ ] Enter Later, Edits Allowed		**Default Value:**	Not Applicable		
	[ ] Enter Later, Edits Not Allowed		**Range of Values:**	Any valid internal or external product category.		

Figure 9-12. *The Logical Elements category for the* CATEGORY *field in the PRODUCTS table.*

Summary

The chapter opens with an explanation of the reasons that Field Specifications are important. You now know the benefits derived from establishing Field Specifications. You learned that establishing field specifications results in *field-level integrity* and enhances overall data integrity. You also learned that defining these specifications compels you to completely understand the nature and purpose of the data in the database. With this level of understanding you can leverage the data to your best advantage.

Next we discussed the anatomy of a Field Specification. You are now familiar with the four categories of elements within a Field Specification as well as the Field Specification worksheet used to record them. We then discussed each category and its elements in detail. You learned that *General Elements* category represents the most basic attributes of the field. Among these elements is the Description item, and you have now had some experience with the set of guidelines used to compose a good field description. We looked at the *Physical Elements* category next, and you learned that it pertains to the structure of the field. The *Logical Elements* category was discussed next, and you now know that it pertains to the values of a field. You learned about elements such as the Type of Key, Edit Rule, and Range of Values. The discussion ends with a look at *Specification Information.* You saw that the elements of Specification Information pertain to the specification itself and are helpful in creating and maintaining consistency.

The chapter ends with a discussion on defining Field Specifications for each field. Here you learned that the best way to ensure complete and accurate specifications is to enlist the help of users and management. First you should establish as many specifications as you can, and then you should work with the staff on the remaining specifications. You also learned that you can work with staff to refine the specifications you initially established.

Table Relationships

*There is no substitute for the comfort
supplied by the utterly
taken-for-granted relationship.*
—IRIS MURDOCH

Topics Covered in This Chapter

As you learned in Chapter 3, a *relationship* is a connection between a pair of tables. A relationship exists when the tables are connected by a Primary key and a Foreign key, or are linked together by a *linking* table; the manner in which the tables are connected depends on the *type* of relationship that exists between them.

A relationship is a crucial part of the database because

- *it establishes a connection between a pair of tables that are logically related to each other in some form or manner.* The logical relationship exists between the data contained in the tables.

For example, a logical relationship exists between the data in a CUSTOMERS table and the data in an ORDERS table. Because a customer places an order for a specific piece of merchandise, a record in the CUSTOMERS table (representing the customer) is related to a record in the ORDERS table (representing a particular order).

- *it helps to further refine table structures and minimize redundant data.* These benefits come about as a result of the manner in which the tables are connected. The process used to establish the relationship modifies the table structures in a manner that makes them more efficient.

- *it is the mechanism that allows data from multiple tables to be drawn together simultaneously.* In Chapter 12 you'll learn that fields from related tables can be combined into a View, which allows you to view (and, in some cases, modify) the data as if it were in a single table.

- Relationship-level integrity *is established when a relationship is properly defined.* Establishing relationship-level integrity guarantees that the relationships are reliable and sound. And, as you know, relationship-level integrity is a component of overall data integrity.

In order to take advantage of the many benefits provided by a relational database, you must make certain that you establish each relationship carefully and properly. Failure to do so can make working with multiple tables at the same time difficult, and it can also make inserting, updating, and deleting records in related tables difficult. These types of problems are discussed later as the design process unfolds.

Types of Relationships

Before you begin to establish relationships between tables in the database, you must learn what *types of relationships* can exist between a pair of tables. Two tables that are related to each other have a specific type of relationship. Knowing how to properly identify each type of relationship is invaluable for designing a successful database.

As you learned in Chapter 3, there are three possible types of relationships that can exist between a pair of tables: *one-to-one*, *one-to-many*, and *many-to-many*.

❖ **Note** A "generic" example of each type of relationship follows. It's a good idea to learn how to visualize a relationship generically *first*—that way you can learn to identify more clearly the type of relationship that exists between a pair of tables. It also causes you to be more objective when you are determining a relationship between a pair of tables.

Each discussion also includes an example of how the relationship is diagrammed. Any special instructions pertaining to the diagramming process are included in the discussion. Symbols used in the diagrams will be explained as necessary. This method of presentation allows you to see how the symbols are used in the context of the diagram and keeps you from having to memorize them all at once.

The first symbols you will use to diagram table relationships are shown in Figure 10-1.

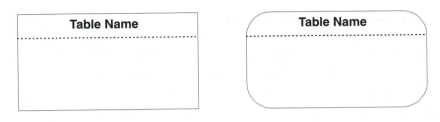

Data Table   Subset Table

Figure 10-1. *Diagramming symbols for a data table and a subset table.*

One-to-One Relationships

A pair of tables are defined as bearing a *one-to-one relationship* if a single record in the first table is related to one and *only* one record in the second table, *and* a single record in the second table is related to one and *only* one record in the first table. Figure 10-2 shows a generic example of a one-to-one relationship.

In Figure 10-2, a single record in TABLE A is related to only one record in TABLE B, and a single record in TABLE B is related to only one record in TABLE A. A one-to-one relationship usually (but not always) involves a subset table. For the sake of example, assume that TABLE B is the subset table. Figure 10-3 shows how to diagram a one-to-one relationship.

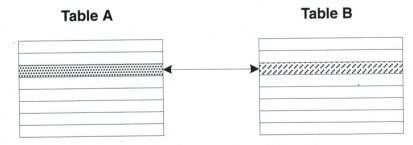

Figure 10-2. *A generic example of a one-to-one relationship.*

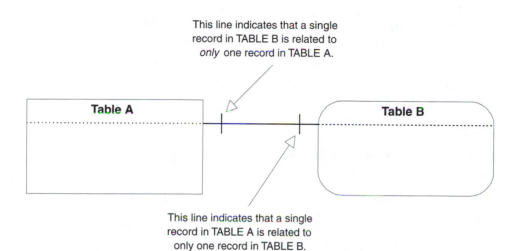

This line indicates that a single
record in TABLE B is related to
only one record in TABLE A.

This line indicates that a single
record in TABLE A is related to
only one record in TABLE B.

Figure 10-3. *A diagram of a one-to-one relationship.*

In a relationship diagram, the type of relationship is indicated by the type of line drawn between the tables. Later in this chapter, you'll learn how to indicate the characteristics of the relationship on the diagram as well.

One-to-Many Relationships

A one-to-many relationship is defined as one in which a single record in the first table can be related to one or more records in the second table, *but* a single record in the second table can be related to only one record in the first table. Two diagrams are needed to illustrate this type of relationship.

Say you're working with two tables, TABLE A and TABLE B. A one-to-many relationship exists between these tables because a single record in TABLE A can be related to one or more (but not necessarily all) records in TABLE B, *and* a single record in the TABLE B can be related to *only* one record in TABLE A.

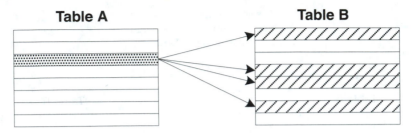

Figure 10-4. *A one-to-many relationship from the viewpoint of TABLE A.*

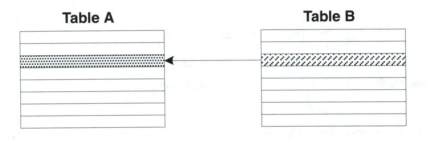

Figure 10-5. *A one-to-many relationship from the viewpoint of TABLE B.*

This is the most common relationship found between a pair of tables, and it is the easiest to identify. Figure 10-6 shows how to diagram a one-to-many relationship.

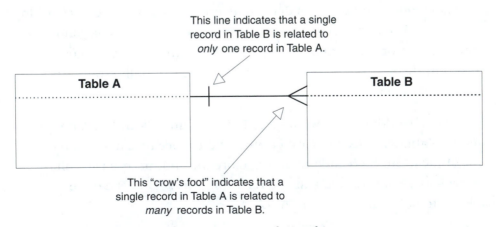

Figure 10-6. *A diagram of a one-to-many relationship.*

Many-to-Many Relationships

A many-to-many relationship exists between a pair of tables if a single record in the first table can be related to one or more records in the second table, *and* a single record in the second table can be related to one or more records in the first table.

Assume once again that you're working with TABLE A and TABLE B. A many-to-many relationship exists between these tables because a single record in TABLE A can be related to one or more records (but not necessarily all) in TABLE B, *and* a single record in TABLE B can be related to one or more (but not necessarily all) records in TABLE A.

Figure 10-9 shows how to diagram a many-to-many relationship.

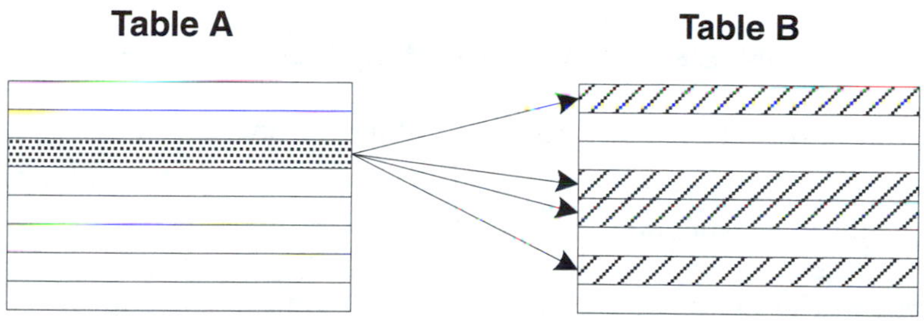

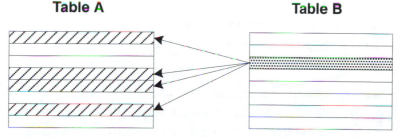

Figure 10-7. *A many-to-many relationship from the viewpoint of TABLE A.*

Figure 10-8. *A many-to-many relationship from the viewpoint of TABLE B.*

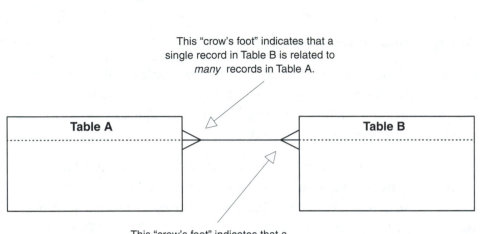

This "crow's foot" indicates that a
single record in Table B is related to
many records in Table A.

Table A

Table B

This "crow's foot" indicates that a
single record in Table A is related to
many records in Table B.

Figure 10-9. *A diagram of a many-to-many relationship.*

Problems with Many-to-Many Relationships

Before you can use the data from the tables involved in a many-to-many relationship you must resolve a few problems. If the relationship is not properly established,

- *one of the tables involved in the relationship will contain a large amount of redundant data.* You would have to introduce duplicate fields into one of the tables (which, as you know, results in producing redundant data) to establish this relationship, *unless* you know the proper procedure.

- *both tables will contain some amount of duplicate data because of the redundancies.* If you introduce duplicate fields into one of the tables, you get duplicate data in both tables.

- *it will be difficult to insert, update, and delete data in the participating tables.* When you introduce duplicate fields, the same data (in the duplicate fields) has to be maintained in *both* tables, rather than in one table.

In order to illustrate these problems, consider the table structures in Figure 10-10. There is a many-to-many relationship between the STUDENTS table and the CLASSES table—one *student* can attend many *classes*, and one *class* can be associated with many *students*.

Currently there is no actual connection between the two tables. Unless you know how to properly establish a many-to-many relationship, you would probably be inclined to add the CLASS ID, CLASS NAME, and INSTRUCTOR ID fields from the CLASSES table to the STUDENTS table in order to identify the classes in which a student is currently enrolled. But you will see the problems that arise from such modifications if you "load" the revised STUDENTS table with sample data. Figure 10-11 shows the "amalgamated" version of this table loaded with sample data.

Table Structures

Students	Classes
Student ID *PK*	Class ID *PK*
StudFirst Name	Class Name
StudLast Name	Class Description
StudStreet Address	Instructor ID
StudCity	Category
StudState	
StudZipcode	
StudHome Phone	

Figure 10-10. *Establishing a many-to-many relationship between the STUDENTS and CLASSES tables.*

Students

Student ID	Student First Name	Student Last Name	Class ID	Class Name	Instructor ID	...
60003	Zachary	Erlich	900001	Intro. to Political Science	220087	...
60003	Zachary	Erlich	900002	Advanced Music Theory	220039	...
60003	Zachary	Erlich	900003	American History	220148	...
60003	Zachary	Erlich	900013	Computers in Business	220121	...
60928	Susan	McLain	900001	Introduction to Poli. Sci.	220087	...
60928	Susan	McLain	900002	Adv. Music Theory	220039	...
60928	Susan	McLain	900008	Introduction to Biology	220117	...
60866	Gregory	Piercy	900100	Intro. to Database Design	220120	...
60765	Joe	Rosales	900013	Computers in Business	220121	...
60765	Joe	Rosales	900022	Advanced Calculus	220101	...
60765	Joe	Rosales	900024	Introduction to Physics	220075	...

Figure 10-11. *The revised STUDENTS table containing sample data.*

The problems with an improperly established many-to-many relationship are well-illustrated in Figure 10-11:

- *There are unnecessary duplicate fields.* It is very likely that the CLASS NAME and INSTRUCTOR ID fields are not appropriate in the STUDENTS table—the CLASS ID field identifies the class sufficiently, and it can be used effectively to identify the classes a student is taking.

- *There is a large amount of redundant data.* Even if the CLASS NAME and INSTRUCTOR ID fields are removed from the STUDENTS table, the presence of the CLASS ID field still produces a lot of redundant data.

- *It is difficult to insert a new record.* If someone tries to enter a record in the STUDENTS table for a new class (instead of entering it in the CLASSES table) without also entering student data, the fields pertaining to the student would be Null—including the Primary key of the STUDENTS table. As you know, this would automatically violate the Elements of a Primary key; a Primary key *cannot* be Null.

- *It is difficult to modify the value of a duplicate field.* It would be difficult to modify a value in the CLASS NAME field for two reasons: you have to be sure to make the modification in *both* tables, and you have to scan the values of the CLASS NAME field carefully in order to make certain that you make the modification to *all* the appropriate values. It's very common for values in a field such as this to be entered in several ways, thus making any modification to the values more difficult. For example, note the difficulty you would have if it were necessary to modify the name of the "Advanced Music Theory" class or the "Introduction to Political Science" class.

- *It is difficult to delete a record.* This is especially true if the only data about a new class has been recorded in the particular student record you want to delete. Note the record for Gregory Piercy, for example. If Greg decides not to attend any classes this year and you delete his record, you will lose the data for the "Intro. to Database Design" class. That might not create a serious problem—*unless* someone neglected to enter the data about this class into the CLASSES table as well. Once you deleted Greg's record, that would mean you'd have to reenter all of the data for the class in the CLASSES table.

Fortunately, you will not have to worry about these problems: you're going to learn the *proper* way to establish a many-to-many relationship.

❖ **Reminder** Before you begin to work through the examples in the remainder of the chapter, now is a good time to remember a principle I presented in the introduction: "Focus on the concept or technique and its intended results, *not on the example used to illustrate it.*" There are, without a doubt, any number of ways that the tables in these examples (and in the case study as well) can be related, depending on each table's role within a given database. The manner in which the examples are used here is not important; what is important is that you learn the proper techniques to identify and establish relationships between tables. Once you learn the techniques, you can identify and establish relationships for any pair of tables within any context you may encounter.

Establishing relationships always involves a three-step procedure: identifying the relationships that currently exist between the tables in the database, establishing each relationship in the appropriate manner, and then setting the proper characteristics for each relationship. When the relationships are in place, the tables are ready to be incorporated into V*iews*. You'll learn how to define and use a View later, in Chapter 12.

Identifying Existing Relationships

When you were composing the table descriptions earlier in the database design process (back in Chapter 7, to be exact), you assembled a representative group of users and management to help you with that task. These people were also designated to represent the organization to help with decision making for the remainder of the database design process. At this stage you'll arrange for further meetings with this group to help you identify table relationships.

These people can provide valuable input because they can be expected to have a good perspective of how various subjects (or tables) are related. Although their perceptions of the manner in which these subjects are related may not always be complete or accurate, their contributions will still be useful in identifying most of the relationships.

Relationships that are harder to identify can usually be clarified by "loading" given tables with some sample data; the sample data commonly reveals the type of relationship two tables should have.

In the first step of the procedure, you'll *identify* the relationships that currently exist between the tables. Begin this step by taking a particular table—you can choose a table at random because you'll repeat this process for every table anyway—and determine whether it has a relationship with any of the remaining tables. For example, assume you're working with these tables:

BUILDINGS   ROOMS

CLASSES   STAFF

FACULTY   STUDENTS

Say you've decided to start with the CLASSES table. Make up a two-column list, writing "Classes" in the first column and writing the names of the remaining tables in the second column, as shown in Figure 10-12.

Now determine whether the CLASSES table bears a relationship with any of the other tables in the list by using the process of elimination.

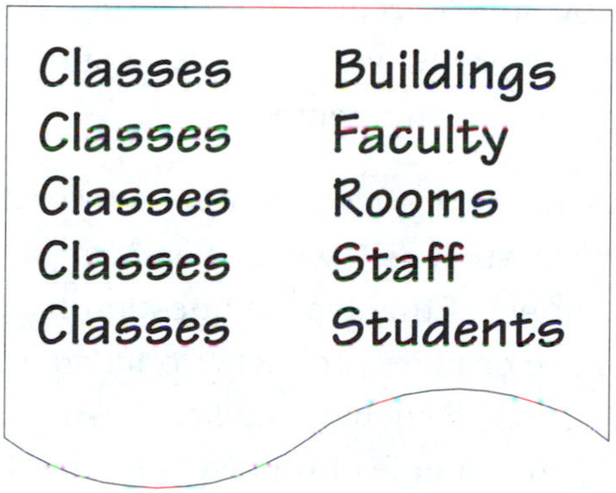

Classes   Buildings
Classes   Faculty
Classes   Rooms
Classes   Staff
Classes   Students

Figure 10-12. *Setting up the tables to determine relationships.*

You're only looking for *direct* relationships; There must be a specific connection between tables participating in a direct relationship. Tables that are indirectly related will be *implicitly* connected through a third table. (You don't have to worry about indirect relationships yet.)

Eliminate a pair of tables on the list by asking the participants questions about the records in each table. You want to determine the relationship between a single record in one table to one or more records in the other table, and vice versa. (Remember that each record represents a single instance of the subject represented by the table.) There are two types of questions you can ask:

- *Associative*. General in nature, this type of question can be generically stated as follows: "Can a single record in (name of first table) be associated with one or more records in (name of second table)?" For the example in Figure 10-12, you might use an associative question such as

    "Can a single record in CLASSES be associated with one or more records in BUILDINGS?"

- *Contextual*. This type of question contrasts a single instance of the subject represented by the first table against multiple instances of the subject represented by the second table. There are two categories within this type of question: ownership oriented and action oriented.

    Ownership-oriented questions are characterized by the use of words or phrases such as "owns," "has," "is part of," and "contains." (An example of this type of question is "Can a single order *contain* one or more products?") *Action-oriented* questions use action verbs such as "make," "visit," "place," "teach," and "attend." (An example of this type of question is "Does a single flight instructor *teach* one or more types of classes?")

Use the type of question you believe to be the most appropriate for the pair of tables you're working with. After you've chosen the type of question you want to use, pose the question twice—once from the perspective of the first table, and then again from the perspective of the second table. The answers to both of these questions will identify the type of relationship that exists between the tables.

Continuing with the example, assume that this is your first question:

"Is a single class held in one or more buildings?"

The answer to this question will reveal the type of relationship that exists between these tables *from the perspective of the CLASSES table*. If the answer is

"A single class is held in only one building."

then a one-to-one relationship exists between these tables. If the answer is

"A single class may be held in more than one building."

then there exists a one-to-many relationship between the two tables.

Assume you are told that a single class is held in only one building. You now follow up with this question:

"Is a single building used to conduct one or more classes?"

The answer to this question reveals the type of relationship *from the perspective of the BUILDINGS table*. If the answer is yes, then a one-to-many relationship exists between these tables; if no, it's a one-to-one relationship.

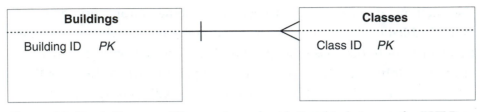

Figure 10-13. *A diagram of the one-to-many relationship between the BUILD-INGS and CLASSES tables.*

Often relationships will differ from one perspective to the other. When *both* a one-to-one and a one-to-many relationship are identified for a particular pair of tables, the one-to-many becomes the "official" relationship for these tables, because it accurately represents the relationship from *both* perspectives.

Now diagram the relationship as shown in Figure 10-13 and cross out this pair of tables on the list.

Although you began asking about relationships from the perspective of the CLASSES table, the relationship you discovered is diagrammed from the perspective of the BUILDINGS table. Always diagram one-to-many relationships from left to right—your diagrams will be consistent, and they'll be easier to read in the long run. Also note that each table's Primary key has been added to the diagram. From now on, make certain that each time you diagram a table you include its Primary key. (As you'll see in the following step, the Primary key is useful when you are *establishing* relationships.)

Continue this procedure of identifying relationships for each pair of tables on the list. Keep in mind that some pairs of tables will have a direct relationship; others will not. You want to identify only direct relationships. After you've crossed out each pair of tables on the list, select another table, create a new list, and repeat this process. When you've finished identifying all the appropriate relationships, move on to the next step.

Establishing Each Relationship

This step involves defining a connection between the tables for each relationship. The manner in which you define the connection is determined by the type of relationship that exists between the tables.

One-to-One and One-to-Many Relationships

One-to-one and one-to-many relationships are established by using a Primary key and a Foreign key to connect the tables within the relationship. You'll learn the definition of a Foreign key in just a moment.

The One-to-One Relationship

In this type of relationship, one of the tables is referred to as the "main" table and assumes a dominant role in the relationship; the other table is referred to as the "subordinate" table and assumes a subordinate role in the relationship. In some instances, you can arbitrarily decide what role each table is to play within the relationship. In the case where one of the tables is a *subset* table, the subset table is *usually* assigned the subordinate role. But there are instances in which a subset table can assume the dominant role within the relationship. As you can see, this type of one-to-one relationship exists between the STAFF and FACULTY tables shown in Figure 10-14.

You establish a one-to-one relationship by taking a copy of the Primary key from the main table and inserting it into the subordinate table, where it becomes a Foreign key. The name "Foreign key" comes from the fact that the subordinate table has its own Primary key, and since the field being added is the Primary key of a different table, it is "foreign" to the subordinate table. As long as you can visualize this process generically, you'll be able to establish a one-to-one relationship properly for any pair of tables involved in this type of relationship.

Staff	**Faculty**
Staff ID *PK*	Staff ID *PK*
StaffFirst Name	Title
StaffLast Name	Status
StaffStreet Address	Tenured
StaffCity	Salary
StaffState	
StaffZipcode	
StaffPhone Number	
Position	
Hourly Rate	
Date Hired	

Figure 10-14. *A diagram of the one-to-one relationship between the STAFF and FACULTY tables.*

As you can see in Figure 10-14, the Primary key of the main table (STAFF) already exists in the subordinate table (FACULTY). That is because FACULTY is already a properly defined subset table. (You learned how to define a subset table properly in Chapter 7, and you established its Primary key in Chapter 8.)

Next consider the one-to-one relationship between the two tables shown in Figure 10-15.

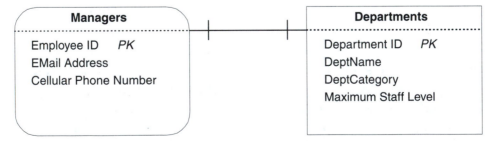

Managers	**Departments**
Employee ID *PK*	Department ID *PK*
EMail Address	DeptName
Cellular Phone Number	DeptCategory
	Maximum Staff Level

Figure 10-15. *The one-to-one relationship between the MANAGERS and DEPARTMENTS tables.*

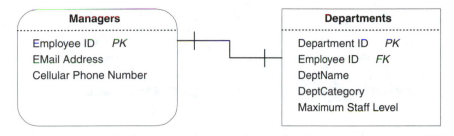

Figure 10-16. *Establishing a one-to-one relationship between the MANAGERS and DEPARTMENTS tables.*

In this example, MANAGERS is a subset table of EMPLOYEES, but it has a direct relationship to DEPARTMENTS. A single manager is associated with only one department, and a single department is associated with only one manager; MANAGERS is the main table, and DEPARTMENTS is the subordinate table. (This is a good example of an instance in which a subset table is in the dominant position within a relationship.) To establish the relationship between these tables, take a copy of the Primary key from the main table (MANGERS) and insert it into the subordinate table (DEPARTMENTS). Then identify the new Foreign key (Employee ID) by placing the letters "FK" next to its name. The result of these steps is shown in Figure 10-16.

Note that the relationship diagram now shows both the Primary key and the Foreign key, and that each end of the connecting line points specifically to them, making it easier to identify the relationship and the fields used to establish the connection.

The One-to-Many Relationship

The technique used to establish a one-to-many relationship is similar to the one used to establish a one-to-one relationship. In this case, you take a copy of the Primary key from the table on the "one" side of the relationship and insert it into the table on the "many" side, where

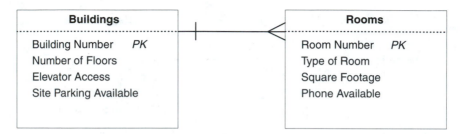

Figure 10-17. *A diagram of the one-to-many relationship between the BUILD-INGS and ROOMS tables.*

that field becomes a Foreign key. For example, consider the one-to-many relationship between the BUILDINGS table and the ROOMS table shown in Figure 10-17.

In this example, a single building can contain one or more rooms, but a single room is contained within only one building. You establish this relationship by taking a copy of the Primary key from the table on the "One" side (BUILDINGS) and inserting it into the table on the "Many" side (ROOMS), where it becomes a Foreign key. Now diagram the relationship, making the proper adjustments as you did with the diagram for the one-to-one relationship. Your diagram should look like the one shown in Figure 10-18.

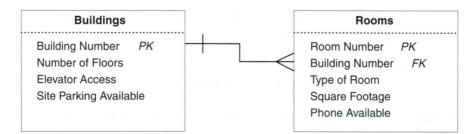

Figure 10-18. *Establishing a one-to-many relationship between the BUILDINGS and ROOMS tables.*

When you diagram a one-to-many relationship, make certain that the connection point on the "One" side points to the Primary key, and that the connection point on the "Many" side points to the Foreign key. (Note that the *middle* line of the "crow's-foot" is the significant connection point—it should point directly to the Foreign key.) Setting up your diagram this way makes it easier to identify the relationship and the fields used to establish the connection.

The Many-to-Many Relationship

A many-to-many relationship is established using a *linking* table. You create the linking table by taking a copy of the Primary key from each table involved in the relationship and using those Primary keys to create the new linking table. Next you give the linking table a meaningful name, one that represents the nature of the relationship between the two tables. Then add the linking table to the *final table list* and make the proper entries for "Table Type" and "Table Description." Figure 10-19 shows a diagram of a many-to-many relationship that has been established for the STUDENTS and CLASSES tables. (Note the new diagram symbol used to represent a linking table.)

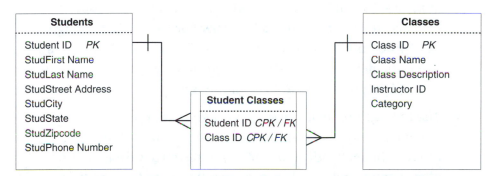

Figure 10-19. *The many-to-many relationship established between the STUDENTS and CLASSES tables.*

There are several points to note about the results of creating this linking table:

- *The many-to-many relationship has been dissolved.* There is no longer a *direct* relationship between the STUDENTS and CLASSES tables. It has been replaced by *two* direct one-to-many relationships: one between STUDENTS and STUDENT CLASSES and another between CLASSES and STUDENT CLASSES. In the first relationship, a single record in STUDENTS can be associated with one or more records in STUDENT CLASSES, but a single record in STUDENT CLASSES table can be associated with only one record in STUDENTS. In the second relationship, a single record in the CLASSES table can be associated with one or more records in STUDENT CLASSES table, but a single record in STUDENT CLASSES can be associated with only one record in CLASSES.

- *The STUDENT CLASSES linking table is assigned a Composite Primary key, composed of two fields: STUDENT ID and CLASS ID.* Except in rare instances, a linking table always contains a Composite Primary key.

- *The STUDENT CLASSES linking table contains two Foreign keys.* Each of the two fields in the linking table is a copy of a Primary key from another table. Therefore, each is a Foreign key by definition and is treated as such *individually*. It is only when the fields are treated as a unit that they are referred to as the Composite Primary key of the table.

- *The linking table helps to keep redundant data to an absolute minimum.* There is no superfluous data in this table at all. In fact, the main advantage of this table structure is that it allows you to enter as few or as many classes for a single student as is necessary. Later in the database design process, you'll learn how to create Views to draw the data from these tables together in order to present it as meaningful information.

- *The name of the linking table reflects the purpose of the relationship it helps establish.* The data stored in the STUDENT CLASSES table represents a *student* and the *classes* in which he or she is enrolled.

As you work with many-to-many relationships, there will be instances in which you will need to *add* fields to the linking table in order to reduce data redundancy and further refine the table structures. For example, consider the many-to-many relationship between the ORDERS and PRODUCTS tables shown in Figure 10-20.

As you can see, this relationship is improperly established—the fields PRODUCT NUMBER, QUOTED PRICE, and QUANTITY ORDERED were inserted into the ORDERS table in order to associate various products with a particular order. But the presence of these fields in the ORDERS table produces a large amount of redundant data, as shown in Figure 10-21.

There is so much redundant data largely because only one PRODUCT NUMBER can be entered into each record. Therefore, if a customer orders eight items, *eight records* will have to be entered in this table for

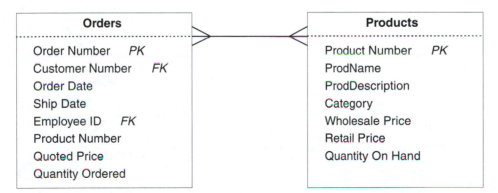

Figure 10-20. *The many-to-many relationship between the ORDERS and PRODUCTS tables.*

Orders

Order Number	Customer Number	Order Date	..	Product Number	Quantity Ordered	Quoted Price
1000	9001	05/16/96	...	410001	4	8.95
1000	9001	05/16/96	...	410004	12	3.75
1000	9001	05/16/96	...	410005	6	5.99
1000	9001	05/16/96	...	410007	5	6.50
1000	9001	05/16/96	...	410011	5	6.50
1000	9001	05/16/96	...	410015	11	4.45
1000	9001	05/16/96	...	410021	2	31.50
1000	9001	05/16/96	...	410029	8	5.00
1001	9012	05/16/96	...	410011	5	6.50
1001	9012	05/16/96	...	410015	3	4.00
1001	9012	05/16/96	...	410022	12	6.35

Figure 10-21. *The problematic ORDERS table, which results from an improperly established many-to-many relationship.*

this one order—one record for every item the customer orders. You can completely avoid this problem by properly establishing the relationship between the ORDERS and PRODUCTS tables with a linking table. Figure 10-22 shows a diagram of this relationship as it should be established.

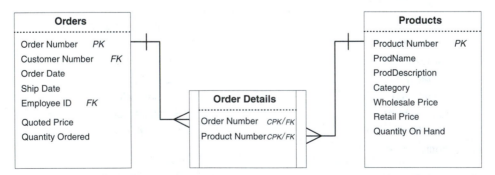

Figure 10-22. *A properly established many-to-many relationship between the ORDERS and PRODUCTS tables.*

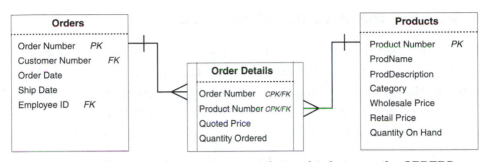

Figure 10-23. *The revised many-to-many relationship between the ORDERS and PRODUCTS tables.*

Although this arrangement eliminates the redundant data, there is still one minor problem: QUOTED PRICE and QUANTITY ORDERED are no longer appropriate in the ORDERS table. First and foremost, their values are not directly determined by the Primary key of the ORDERS table. Second, they bear no relationship to any of the remaining fields in the table. They do, however, relate to a particular PRODUCT NUMBER that appears within a given order. Therefore, the QUOTED PRICE and QUANTITY ORDERED fields should be removed from the ORDERS table and placed in the ORDER DETAILS linking table. Figure 10-23 shows the revised diagram of this relationship.

Whenever you establish many-to-many relationships between tables, check each table within the relationship to determine whether there are any fields that should be transferred to the linking table. When in doubt, load all the tables with sample data; you should be able to see immediately which fields should be transferred to the linking table.

With all these techniques in mind, establish each of the relationships you identified in the previous step. Make certain you create a diagram for each relationship—you'll add new information to each diagram as the design process further unfolds.

Reviewing the Structure of Each Table

Once you've established the relationships between tables, review all of the table structures. As you established each relationship, you made modifications to the existing table structures and created several new table structures. (Remember the linking tables?) Therefore, you want to make certain that each table conforms to the Elements of the Ideal Table:

Elements of the Ideal Table

- It represents a single subject, which can be an object or event.

- It has a Primary key.

- It does not contain multipart fields.

- It does not contain multivalued fields.

- It does not contain calculated fields.

- It does not contain unnecessary duplicate fields.

- It contains only an absolute minimum amount of redundant data.

If you determine that a table is not in conformance with the Elements of the Ideal Table, identify the problem and make the necessary modifications. Then take the table through the appropriate stages of the database design process until you reach the stage we're at now. As long as you've been following proper procedures thus far, you shouldn't encounter any problems with the tables.

Refining All Foreign keys

As you've seen, a Primary key from one particular table becomes a Foreign key in another table when that field is used to establish a relationship between those two tables. A Foreign key must conform to a set of elements, just as all the other keys you've worked with so far.

Elements of a Foreign Key

- *It has the same name as the Primary key from which it was copied.* This rule should be adhered to *unless* there is an absolutely compelling reason not to do so. (Such a reason is shown in the example under "Alias" in Chapter 9.)

- *It uses a replica of the Field Specifications for the Primary key from which it was copied.* This is in accordance with the sixth element of the Elements of the Ideal Field, as you learned in Chapter 7. There are, however, a few settings in the Logical Elements category of the Field Specifications that will be slightly different for the Foreign key than for its parent Primary key. Figure 10-24 shows the Logical Elements for an EMPLOYEE ID field used as a Primary key in the EMPLOYEES table, and Figure 10-25 shows the Logical Elements for the same EMPLOYEE ID field when it is used as a Foreign key in the ORDERS table.

Logical Elements

Type of Key:	☐ Non	☒ Primary	**Comparisons Allowed:**			
	☐ Foreign	☐ Alternate	☒ Same Field	☒ =	☐ >	☐ >=
Uniqueness:	☐ Non-Unique	☒ Unique	☐ Other Fields	☐ ≠	☐ <	☐ <=
Required Value:	☐ No	☒ Yes	**Operations Allowed:**			
Null Support:	☐ Nulls Allowed	☒ No Nulls	☐ Same Field	☐ +	☐ x	
Edit Rule:	☐ Enter Now, Edits Allowed		☐ Other Fields	☐ -	☐ ÷	
	☒ Enter Now, Edits Not Allowed		**Values Entered By:**	☒ User	☐ System	
	☐ Enter Later, Edits Allowed		**Default Value:**			
	☐ Enter Later, Edits Not Allowed		**Range of Values:**	1000 - 9999		

Figure 10-24. *The Logical Elements category for the EMPLOYEE ID field when it is being used as a Primary key in the EMPLOYEES table.*

```
┌─ Logical Elements ──────────────────────────────────────────────────────────────┐
│                                                                                  │
│  Type of Key:      ☐ Non         ☐ Primary      Comparisons Allowed:             │
│                    ☒ Foreign     ☐ Alternate    ☒ Same Field   ☒ =  ☐ >  ☐ >=    │
│  Uniqueness:       ☒ Non-Unique  ☐ Unique       ☐ Other Fields ☐ ≠  ☐ <  ☐ <=    │
│  Required Value:   ☐ No          ☒ Yes          Operations Allowed:              │
│  Null Support:     ☐ Nulls Allowed ☒ No Nulls   ☐ Same Field   ☐ +  ☐ x          │
│  Edit Rule:        ☒ Enter Now, Edits Allowed   ☐ Other Fields ☐ -  ☐ ÷          │
│                    ☐ Enter Now, Edits Not Allowed  Values Entered By:  ☒ User  ☐ System │
│                    ☐ Enter Later, Edits Allowed    Default Value:                │
│                    ☐ Enter Later, Edits Not Allowed  Range of Values:  Any existing Employee ID │
│                                                                        in the Employees table.  │
└──────────────────────────────────────────────────────────────────────────────────┘
```

Figure 10-25. *The Logical Elements category for the EMPLOYEE ID field when it is being used as a Foreign key in the ORDERS table.*

As you can see in Figure 10-25, three minor changes have been made to these elements. The Type of Key setting is indicated as "Foreign" because the EMPLOYEE ID field is being used as a Foreign key in this instance. The Uniqueness setting is designated as "Non-Unique" because you want to be able to associate a single employee with *many* orders; if you marked this as "Unique," you'd only be able to enter an employee into the ORDERS table one time, which would greatly limit his or her sales potential! The Edit Rule setting is designated as "Enter Now, Edits Allowed" because there will be times when the wrong employee is credited for an order and you'll need to be able to change the value to reflect the correct employee for the order.

The setting in the Specification Information category of the field specification is also different for a Foreign key as compared with that of the Primary key from which it was created. Figure 10-26 shows the Specification Information for the EMPLOYEE ID field used as a Foreign key in the ORDERS table.

Specification Information

Specification Type:	☐ Unique		☐ Generic		☒ Replica	
Based on Existing Specification:	☐ No		☒ Yes			
Source Specification:	Employee ID from the Employees table					

Figure 10-26. *Specification Information for the EMPLOYEE ID field when it is being used as a Foreign key in the ORDERS table.*

A Foreign key uses a replica field specification because its specification is based on an existing Primary key's unique specification. Make certain you include the name of the *Primary* key's parent table in the Source Specification item, as shown in Figure 10-26. This makes it easy to compare the Primary key's specifications and the Foreign key's specifications as the need arises.

- *It draws its values from the Primary key to which it refers.* A Foreign key's range of values is limited to existing values of the Primary key to which it refers. For example, you *cannot* enter an invalid Employee ID into the ORDERS table. Any Employee ID you enter into the ORDERS table must first exist as an Employee ID in the EMPLOYEES table. This ensures consistency in the values of both fields in both tables.

Review the Foreign keys in each table to make certain that they conform to the Elements of a Foreign key. If they are not in accordance with these elements, make the appropriate modifications. But if you've followed proper procedure up to this point, it should be a rare instance when you would have to make any changes.

Establishing Relationship Characteristics

The final step in this procedure is to establish the characteristics of each relationship. These characteristics indicate what will occur when a record is deleted, the type of participation each table bears within the relationship, and to what degree each table participates in the relationship.

Establishing a Deletion Rule for Each Relationship

Now you must establish a deletion rule for the relationship. This rule defines what will happen if a user places a request to delete a record in the main table of a one-to-one relationship or in the "one" side of a one-to-many relationship. Defining a deletion rule for a relationship helps to guard against "orphaned" records, which are records that exist in a subordinate table of a one-to-one relationship but have no related records in a main table, or records that exist in the "many" side of a one-to-many relationship that have no related records in the "one" side.

Two options are available for the deletion rule:

- *Restrict.* The requested record cannot be deleted if there are related records in the subordinate table of a one-to-one relationship or the "many" side of a one-to-many relationship. Related records must be deleted before the requested record can be deleted.

- *Cascade.* The requested record will be deleted *as well as* all related records in the subordinate table of a one-to-one relationship or the "many" side of a one-to-many relationship.

Use a *restrict* deletion rule as a matter of course; use a cascade deletion rule very judiciously. The best way to determine whether a cascade deletion rule is appropriate for a set of related tables is to study the relationship diagram for those tables. Consider the diagram shown in Figure 10-27.

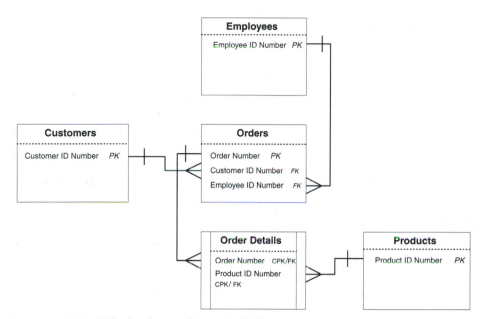

Figure 10-27. *Which relationships should have a cascade deletion rule?*

Select a pair of related tables and pose the following question:

> "If a record in [name of main or 'one' table] is deleted, should
> related records in [name of subordinate or 'many' table] be
> deleted as well?"

Here the question is framed so that you can understand the premise
behind it. When you pose this question against a particular pair of
tables, such as the CUSTOMERS and ORDERS tables, just "fill in the
blanks." The question now becomes:

> "If a record in the CUSTOMERS table is deleted, should related
> records in the ORDERS table be deleted as well?"

If the answer to this question is no, you must use a restrict deletion rule
for this relationship; otherwise, the cascade deletion rule is appropriate.

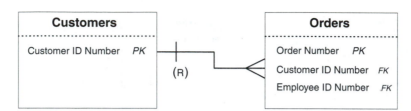

Figure 10-28. *Indicating the deletion rule for a relationship.*

The answer to this question greatly depends on how the data is being used within the database. If you cannot easily provide an answer, make note of the relationship and continue with the next table relationship. You'll revisit these relationships when you establish Business Rules for the database later in Chapter 11.

After you've identified the type of deletion rule you want to use for a relationship, add it to the relationship diagram. Restrict deletion rules are indicated by an "(R)" and cascade deletion rules by a "(C)." Place the designation *under* the connection line of the main table or the table on the "one" side of the relationship as shown in Figure 10-28.

You probably noticed that the deletion rule only applies to a record in the main table or the "one" side of the relationship. There is no need to worry about deleting records in the subordinate table or the "many" side of the relationship because there can be no adverse affects as a result of doing so.

Identifying the Type of Participation for Each Table

Each table participates within a relationship in a particular manner. A table's *type of participation* determines whether a record must exist in that table before a record can be entered into the other table. There are two types of participation:

- *Mandatory.* There must be *at least* one record in this table before you can enter any records into the other table.

- *Optional.* There is no requirement for *any* records to exist in this table before you can enter any records into the other table.

The type of participation for most tables is usually determined later when you're defining Business Rules. However, it's common to establish the type of participation for tables in relationships where the type of participation for each table is obvious, is a result of common sense, or is in accordance with some particular set of standards. Consider the one-to-many relationship between the EMPLOYEES and CUSTOMERS tables shown in Figure 10-29.

Say that in this instance, a particular employee must be assigned to each customer. This employee acts as the customer's "account representative" and takes care of all transactions and communications between the organization and that customer. Although each customer *must* be associated with a particular employee, not every employee is required to be associated with even a single customer. Remember that many of the people represented in the EMPLOYEES table perform some other function within the organization and may never come into contact with a customer at all.

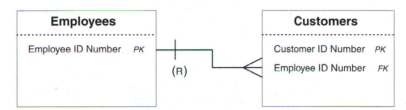

Figure 10-29. *What should the type of participation be for each table in this relationship?*

This scenario does not describe or define any special circumstances; it is the way the organization conducts its business. Therefore, you can infer that

- *the type of participation for the EMPLOYEES table should be designated as "Mandatory."* The EMPLOYEES table must have *at least* one record because each customer is required to be associated with a particular employee.

- *the type of participation for the CUSTOMERS table should be designated as "Optional."* It is unnecessary for any records to exist in the CUSTOMERS table before you can enter an employee into the EMPLOYEES table.

Once you've determined the type of participation for each table within the relationship, modify the relationship diagram to reflect this new information. A mandatory type of participation is symbolized by a vertical line; an optional type of relationship is symbolized by a circle. Figure 10-30 shows the relationship diagram for the EMPLOYEES and CUSTOMERS tables and illustrates the use of these two symbols.

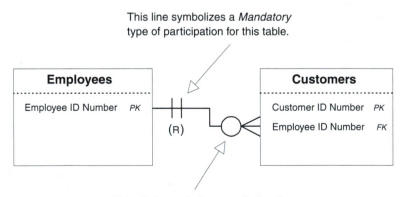

Figure 10-30. *The type of participation indicated for the relationship between the EMPLOYEES and CUSTOMERS tables.*

Identifying the Degree of Participation for Each Table

Now you must determine the degree to which each table will participate within the relationship. This is a simple matter of identifying the
total number of records in one table that can be related to a single
record in the other table. The factors used in determining the *degree* of
participation—obvious circumstances, common sense, or conformance
to some set of standards—are the same as those used to determine the
type of participation. Therefore you will identify the degree of participation for some tables now and leave the remaining tables to be revisited
when you define Business Rules for the database.

The degree of participation is symbolized by two numbers, separated
by a comma, and enclosed in parentheses, such as "(1,8)." The numbers in this symbol represent the lower and upper boundaries, respectively, of the total number of records in one table that can be related to
a single record in the other table. In this instance, a single record in
one table can be related to a minimum of one record and a maximum
of eight records in the other table.

When you add this symbol to a relationship diagram, place it *over* the
connection line of the appropriate table. Figure 10-31 illustrates the
proper use of this symbol within a relationship diagram. This particular diagram indicates the degree of participation for the relationship
between the EMPLOYEES and CUSTOMERS tables.

In this example, the diagram indicates that a customer must be
related to *at least* one employee, but *no more* than one. It also indicates that an employee is not required to be associated with a
customer. On the other hand, an employee cannot be associated with
more than ten customers.

Figure 10-32 shows an example of an *unlimited* degree of participation,
which is represented by the letter *N* inside the parenthesis. In this

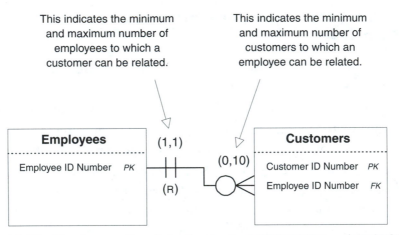

Figure 10-31. *The degree of participation for the EMPLOYEES and CUSTOMERS tables.*

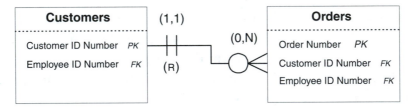

Figure 10-32. *An example of an unlimited degree of participation.*

instance, a customer can exist within the CUSTOMERS table *without* being associated with an order in the ORDERS table. On the other hand, a particular customer can be associated with an unlimited number of records in the ORDERS table. You certainly wouldn't want to limit the amount of purchases a customer can place.

Now that you know how to define the characteristics of a relationship, execute this step for every relationship you've established thus far. As you identify these characteristics, revise the diagram for each relationship to reflect the new information.

Verifying Table Relationships with Users and Management

The very last order of business is to verify the relationships. This is a relatively easy task that can be performed using the following checklist:

1. Make sure that each relationship between a pair of tables has been properly identified.

2. Make certain that each relationship has been properly established.

3. Make certain that each Foreign key is in conformance to the Elements of a Foreign key.

4. Make sure that the proper deletion rule has been established for each relationship.

5. Make certain that the proper type of participation has been identified for each table within the relationship.

6. Make certain that the appropriate degree of participation has been established for each table within the relationship.

If all the relationships check out and everyone agrees to this assessment, you can be confident that the relationships are sound and are ready to be used to create Views.

Relationship-Level Integrity

Relationship-level integrity is a direct result of properly establishing a table relationship and defining its characteristics in the proper manner. In establishing relationship-level integrity, you have

- *made certain that the connection between two tables in a relationship is sound.* You have accomplished this by using a Primary key and a Foreign key to establish a one-to-one and one-to-many relationship, and a linking table to establish a many-to-many relationship.

- *ensured your ability to insert new records into each table in a meaningful manner.* You have made this possible by properly identifying the type of participation for each table within the relationship.

- *ensured your ability to delete an existing record without creating adverse affects.* This is guaranteed by the deletion rule defined for the relationship.

- *established a meaningful limit to the number of records that can be interrelated within the relationship.* You have made this possible by properly identifying the degree of participation for each table within the relationship.

As you know, relationship-level integrity is the third component of overall data integrity. (The first is table-level integrity and the second is field-level integrity.) In the next chapter, you'll establish the final component of overall data integrity by learning how to establish Business Rules for the database.

CASE STUDY

It's now time to identify the relationships that exist for the tables that appear on the final table list for Mike's Bikes. Your assistant, Zachary, is working on this part of the design process. The tables Zachary is working with are

CUSTOMERS   PRODUCTS
EMPLOYEES   VENDORS
INVOICES

The first order of business is to identify the relationships that currently exist between the tables. Because there are few tables in this database, Zachary elects to meet with only Mike; Zachary figures that Mike should be familiar enough with the tables to help him identify the relationships.

Zachary and Mike have easily determined that the following tables bear a one-to-many relationship:

- *CUSTOMERS and INVOICES.* A single customer can be associated with one or more invoices, but a single invoice is associated with only one customer.

- *EMPLOYEES and INVOICES.* A single employee can be associated with one or more invoices, but a single invoice is associated with only one employee.

They've also determined that these two tables have a many-to-many relationship:

- *INVOICES and PRODUCTS.* A single invoice can be associated with one or more products, *and* a single product can be associated with one or more invoices.

Zachary diagrams the relationships and then sets them aside for the moment. He's not quite sure about a particular relationship, so he discusses it with Mike.

ZACHARY: I wanted to ask you about the relationship between the PRODUCTS and VENDORS tables. Can a single product be associated with one or more vendors?

MIKE: Yes, in a manner of speaking. What I mean is, a single type of product—such as a bike lock—can be associated with one or more vendors. However, each lock is given its own product number and treated as a distinct item, regardless of the vendor who supplies it. Now, if the true meaning of your question is 'Can a single *record* in the Products table be associated with one or more records in the Vendors table?' then the answer is no because each record in the Products table contains a reference to *only one* vendor in the VENDORS table.

ZACHARY: I thought as much. In that case, there's a one-to-many relationship between the VENDORS and PRODUCTS tables. I automatically figured that a single vendor could be associated with many products in the PRODUCTS table.

Zachary now diagrams the one-to-many relationship between the VENDORS and PRODUCTS tables and continues with the next step. He establishes the one-to-many relationships by taking a copy of the Primary key from the "one" side of the relationship and inserting it into the "many" side as a Foreign key, and then he revises the relationship diagrams accordingly. One of the diagrams is shown in Figure 10-33.

Zachary then establishes the many-to-many relationship between the INVOICES and PRODUCTS tables by creating a new linking table called INVOICE PRODUCTS, with the Composite Primary key made up of the INVOICE NUMBER and PRODUCT NUMBER keys. The relationship diagram for these tables is shown in Figure 10-34.

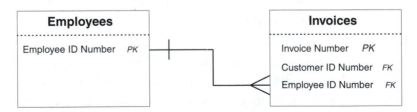

Figure 10-33. *The one-to-many relationship diagram for the EMPLOYEES and INVOICES tables.*

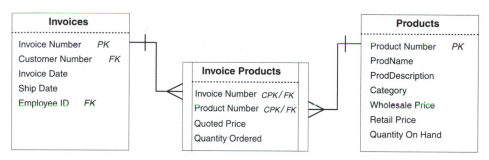

Figure 10-34. *A many-to-many relationship diagram for the INVOICES and PRODUCTS tables.*

Now Zachary reviews each table structure to ensure that it conforms to the Elements of the Ideal Table; fortunately, all the table structures are sound. Next he refines the Foreign keys in each table by making certain that each one conforms to the Elements of a Foreign key. He then modifies the Logical Elements and Specification Information categories of each Foreign key's Field Specifications sheet as warranted. The modifications he has made for one of the Foreign keys is shown in Figure 10-35.

Next Zachary establishes the appropriate relationship characteristics for each table in a relationship. He defines a deletion rule for each relationship and then identifies both the type of participation and the degree of participation for each table within the relationship. Zachary finishes this step by adding this new information to the relationship diagram. One of the finished diagrams is shown in Figure 10-36.

Finally, Zachary reviews and verifies all of the table relationships with Mike. He checks each relationship against his final checklist and marks it as "Completed."

Logical Elements

Type of Key:	☐ Non	☐ Primary	**Comparisons Allowed:**
	☒ Foreign	☐ Alternate	☒ Same Field　☒ =　☐ >　☐ >=
Uniqueness:	☒ Non-Unique	☐ Unique	☐ Other Fields　☐ ≠　☐ <　☐ <=
Required Value:	☐ No	☒ Yes	**Operations Allowed:**
Null Support:	☐ Nulls Allowed	☒ No Nulls	☐ Same Field　☐ +　☐ x
Edit Rule:	☒ Enter Now, Edits Allowed		☐ Other Fields　☐ -　☐ ÷
	☐ Enter Now, Edits Not Allowed		**Values Entered By:**　☒ User　☐ System
	☐ Enter Later, Edits Allowed		**Default Value:**
	☐ Enter Later, Edits Not Allowed		**Range of Values:**　Any existing Customer ID in the Customers table.

Specification Information

Specification Type:	☐ Unique	☐ Generic	☒ Replica
Based on Existing Specification:	☐ No	☒ Yes	
Source Specification:	Customer ID from the Customers table.		

Figure 10-35. *A partial listing of field specifications for the CUSTOMER ID Foreign key field in the INVOICES table.*

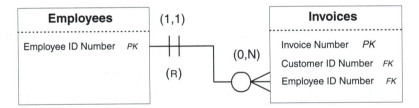

Figure 10-36. *An example of a completed relationship diagram.*

Summary

We opened this chapter with a discussion of the three types of relationships that can exist between a particular pair of tables—*one-to-one*, *one-to-many*, and *many-to-many*. You now know that the one-to-many is the most common relationship that occurs between a pair of tables, and that the many-to-many relationship gives rise to problems that must be resolved.

Next we discussed how to identify the relationships that exist between tables in a database. We looked at the types of questions that can be used to help accomplish this task: *associative* and *contextual*.

The chapter continued with a discussion of how relationships are *established*. You learned that one-to-one and one-to-many relationships are established by using Primary keys and *Foreign* keys, and that many-to-many relationships are established using *linking tables*. You also learned that you must review all of the table structures to ensure that they still conform to the Elements of the Ideal Table. Foreign keys must be refined as well, and you must make certain that they are in accordance with the Elements of a Foreign key.

We then discussed relationship characteristics. You now know how to define a *deletion rule* for the relationship, and that the two settings for a deletion rule are *Restrict* and *Cascade*. Next you learned how to identify the *type of participation* and *degree of participation* for each table within a relationship. As you now know, a table's type of participation can be set at either *Mandatory* or *Optional*. You also know that the degree of participation gauges the total number of records in one table that can be associated with a single record in the other table. Finally, you learned that you must verify the relationships with users and management, and that you can use a checklist to accomplish this task.

The chapter closed with a look at relationship-level integrity. You learned that this type of integrity is established by properly defining a relationship and its characteristics. Once relationships are properly established, they are ready to be used in Views.

11

Business Rules

You are remembered
for the rules you break.
—GENERAL DOUGLAS MACARTHUR

Topics Covered in This Chapter

What Are Business Rules?

Defining and Establishing Business Rules

Validation Tables

Reviewing the Business Rule Specification Sheets

Case Study

Summary

Throughout the database design process, you've performed tasks that helped to establish various levels of data integrity. Thus far, you've established table-level integrity, field-level integrity, and relationship-level integrity. In doing so, you've ensured that the table and field structures are sound, that data entered into the fields will be consistent and basically valid, and that the relationships between the tables are meaningful and properly established. In this chapter you'll learn how to establish the final component of overall data integrity: *Business Rules.*

What Are Business Rules?

A *Business Rule* is statement that imposes some form of constraint on elements within a field specification for a particular field or on characteristics of a relationship between a specific pair of tables. A Business Rule is based on the way the organization perceives and uses its data; this perception is derived from the manner in which the organization functions or conducts its business.

An important element of any design process is making choices. In database design, one category of choice is which data to record, since obviously we cannot record all data. What data will be recorded clearly will be driven by the way the organization uses its data. A hospital may wish to record times of events to the second; whereas a warehouse only needs to record a date. To guide these and other choices during the database design process and later, during the use of the database, the designer needs a formal statement of the organization's Business Rules. These rules influence the selection of data, the construction of relationships, and the structure of the reports that the database can produce, as well as issues of security and confidentiality. No "one-size-fits-all" set of Business Rules can be drawn up. Instead each organization needs its own specific list of Business Rules.

The following statement is an example of a typical Business Rule:

"A SHIP DATE cannot be prior to an ORDER DATE for any given order."

This statement, or Business Rule, imposes a constraint on the *Range of Values* element of the field specifications for a SHIP DATE field. The organization imposes this constraint in order to ensure that the value of SHIP DATE is meaningful within the context of a "Sales Order." Without this constraint, any date—including one prior to the ORDER DATE— could be entered into the field, thus rendering the value in the SHIP

DATE field meaningless. The Business Rule ensures the meaningfulness of the SHIP DATE field.

Because Business Rules depend on the manner in which an organization perceives and uses its data, several organizations might use Business Rules cast in the same words, yet apply them for completely *different* reasons.

For example, say that the Music Department at "Bel Air High School" is known far and wide for the quality of musicianship it develops in its student musicians. This quality is attained by encouraging the students to focus their musical studies and restrict themselves to learning no more that two instruments. In another part of town, the Music Department at "Lake City High School" (a private school) also imbues its student musicians with a high quality of musicianship by helping the students focus their musical studies. But the students at this school are restricted to learning no more than two instruments due to school policy; the school's inventory of musical instruments is very limited.

Coincidentally, both schools are in the process of designing their own database. In each case, the database will be used to support the daily operations and administrative functions of the school. It so happens that each database contains the tables shown in Figure 11-1. Furthermore, both schools are at the same stage of the database design process and are currently establishing Business Rules. As it turns out, each school happens to be using the following Business Rule in their respective databases:

> "A student cannot have more than two instruments checked out at the same time."

This Business Rule applies to the *degree of participation* between the STUDENTS table and STUDENT INSTRUMENTS table shown in Figure 11-1.

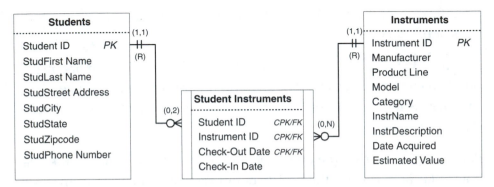

Figure 11-1. *Reviewing the degree of participation between the STUDENTS and STUDENT INSTRUMENTS tables.*

(Both of these tables appear in each database.) In this instance, a single record in the STUDENTS table cannot be associated with more than two records in the STUDENT INSTRUMENTS table where the value of CHECK-IN DATE for each record is Null.

As you should see, this Business Rule applies to both schools. Yet each school requires this constraint for a different reason. "Bel Air High School" requires the constraint because of the manner in which its music program has been established; whereas "Lake City High School" requires the constraint because of the physical limitations of its instrument inventory. This unusual but quite possible example of two identical Business Rules shows that future revisions of the data would result in contrasting changes in the respective Business Rules. The idea, then, is to define and establish the proper set of Business Rules that pertain to the way an organization functions or conducts its business.

This example illustrates another concern. The constraint imposed by certain Business Rules, such as this one, cannot be established within the logical design of the database. For instance, there is no clear way to indicate that the values in CHECK-IN DATE must be tested in order to determine whether a student can check out another instrument. Therefore, the constraint must be addressed and established *outside* of the logical design of the database. How do you determine whether a constraint can be properly represented within this process? You make this determination by identifying the *type* of Business Rule you're defining.

Types of Business Rules

There are two major types of Business Rules: *database-oriented* and *application-oriented*. Both types of Business Rules impose some form of constraint and help enforce and maintain overall data integrity. The difference between them pertains to where and how they are established.

Database-oriented Business Rules are those that impose constraints that can be established within the *logical* design of the database. In other words, you impose these constraints by modifying elements within a Field Specification or the symbols in a relationship diagram. As long as a constraint can be *meaningfully* and *clearly* established by either of these means, the statement from which the constraint is derived is a database-oriented Business Rule. For example, say you have a VENDORS table and define the following Business Rule for the VENDSTATE field in that table:

> "We conduct business exclusively with vendors from the Pacific Northwest."

This Business Rule limits the values that can be entered into the VENDSTATE field to "WA," "OR," "ID," and "MT." The constraint imposed by this Business Rule can be meaningfully established by modifying the Range of Values element in the Field Specifications for the VENDSTATE field, as shown in Figure 11-2.

Application-oriented Business Rules are statements that impose constraints that *cannot* be established by modifying a Field Specification or

Logical Elements

Type of Key:	☒ Non	☐ Primary	**Comparisons Allowed:**			
	☐ Foreign	☐ Alternate	☒ Same Field	☒ =	☐ >	☐ >=
Uniqueness:	☒ Non-Unique	☐ Unique	☐ Other Fields	☐ ≠	☐ <	☐ <=
Required Value:	☐ No	☒ Yes	**Operations Allowed:**			
Null Support:	☐ Nulls Allowed ☒ No Nulls		☐ Same Field	☐ +	☐ x	
Edit Rule:	☒ Enter Now, Edits Allowed		☐ Other Fields	☐ -	☐ ÷	
	☐ Enter Now, Edits Not Allowed		**Values Entered By:**	☒ User	☐ System	
	☐ Enter Later, Edits Allowed		**Default Value:**	None		
	☐ Enter Later, Edits Not Allowed		**Range of Values:**	ID, MT, OR, WA		

Figure 11-2. *Representing a constraint imposed by a database-oriented Business Rule.*

relationship diagram; they must be established within the *physical* design of the database or within the design of a *database application*. (The term "database application" is used here to refer to programs written in some RDBMS software that allow users to use the database easily and perform a number of predefined tasks relative to the function of the organization.) This type of Business Rule is more meaningfully and clearly defined within either of those environments.

Here is an example of a typical application-oriented Business Rule:

> "A customer with a 'Preferred' status receives a 15 percent discount on all purchases."

This Business Rule determines the amount of discount applied to a customer's purchases, based on a particular status. The constraint cannot be meaningfully established in the logical design for two reasons: there is no field in which to store the discount amount (the amount is a result of a calculation, and calculated fields are not allowed in a table), and there is no way to indicate the criterion used—the customer's status—to determine the discount. Therefore, this Business Rule must be established within the *physical* design of the database or the design of the *database application*.

❖ **Note** Although some application-oriented Business Rules may be discussed in this chapter, the manner in which they are defined and established within the physical design of the database or the design of the database application is particular to each software package, and this topic is beyond the scope of this book.

Although both types of Business Rules are important, your main focus during this stage of the database design process will be on database-oriented Business Rules.

❖ **Note** Throughout the remainder of the book, database-oriented Business Rules are referred to simply as *Business Rules.*

Categories of Business Rules

Business Rules are divided into two categories that make them easier to understand and define: *field-specific* and *relationship-specific.*

Field-Specific Business Rules

Business Rules under this category impose constraints on the elements of a Field Specification for a particular field. Some rules will affect only one element; other rules will affect several elements. For example, this Business Rule only affects one element:

"Order dates are to be displayed in long form, such as 'January 10, 1996.'"

This rule affects the Display Format element of the ORDER DATE field in an ORDERS table. To establish this rule, you modify the Display

Format element of the Field Specifications for the ORDER DATE field to indicate the manner in which the date should be displayed.

In contrast, the following rule affects more than one element:

"We must be able to store a zip code for each of our Canadian customers."

The Data Type, Character Support, and Display Format elements of the Field Specifications for the CUSTZIPCODE field in a CUSTOMERS table are affected by this rule. Canadian zip codes include letters, so you must make the following modifications to the Field Specifications in order to impose the constraints defined by this rule:

1. Change the Data Type setting to "Alphanumeric."

2. Include "Letters" under the Character Support element.

3. Modify the Display Format element to ensure that the letters in Canadian zip codes will be capitalized.

Each of these changes is shown in Figure 11-3.

Relationship-Specific Business Rules

Constraints imposed by relationship-specific business rules affect the characteristics of a relationship between a particular pair of tables.

Physical Elements				
Data Type:	Alphanumeric		**Length:**	6
Character Support:			**Decimal Places:**	Not Applicable
☒ Letters (A-Z)	☐ Extended (. , / $ # %)		**Input Mask:**	Not Applicable
☒ Numbers (0-9)	☐ Special (© ® ™ Σ)		**Display Format:**	Upper case letters where applicable.

Figure 11-3. *Establishing a field-specific Business Rule for CUSTZIPCODE.*

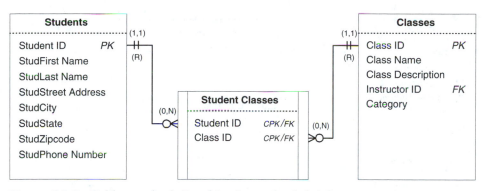

Figure 11-4. *Tables and relationships in a school database.*

For instance, assume you're working with the tables and relationships shown in Figure 11-4.

Say you determine that there must be a limit to the number of students for each class. So you define the following Business Rule:

> "Each class must have a minimum of five students but cannot have more than twenty."

This Business Rule affects the Degree of Participation between the CLASSES and STUDENT CLASSES tables. In order to enforce the constraint defined by this rule, you must modify the relationship diagram to show that a single record in the CLASSES table *must* be related to at least five—but no more than twenty—records in the STUDENT CLASSES table. (Depending on your point of view, you could also infer from this Business Rule that the Type of Participation for the CLASSES table is now Mandatory; a class will remain listed in the CLASSES table if and only if there are at least five students registered for the class.) Figure 11-5 shows the modifications that need to be made to the relationship diagram.

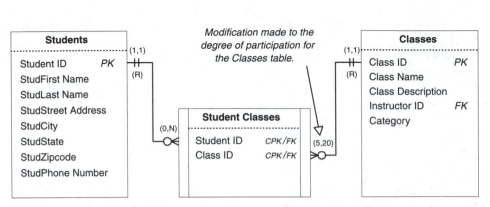

Figure 11-5. *Establishing a relationship-specific Business Rule.*

Defining and Establishing Business Rules

During this stage of the design process, you'll define and establish Business Rules for the database. Remember that these rules must be based on the manner in which your organization perceives and uses its data, which (as you well know) will depend on the way the organization functions or conducts its business. The best approach to this task is to define and establish the field-specific Business Rules first, followed by the relationship-specific Business Rules. This approach helps you to remain focused on the type of rule you're defining. It also keeps you from jumping back and forth between different types of Business Rules, which can often lead to confusion and some amount of frustration.

Working with Users and Management

Once again, you'll work with the representative group of users and management. Schedule new meetings with them so that you can work together to define and establish the appropriate Business Rules for the database. Working as a group enables you to make certain that the constraints imposed by the Business Rules you define are meaningful and that there is no confusion or ambiguity as to the necessity of imposing each constraint. If there is some doubt about a constraint, you can discuss the effect it will have on the field or relationship involved, the advantages and disadvantages of imposing the constraint, and then decide whether to keep the rule or disregard it completely based on the results of the discussion.

Defining and Establishing Field-Specific Business Rules

We begin the process of establishing Business Rules for the database by working with the field-specific Business Rules. The procedure for defining and establishing these rules involves the following steps:

1. Select a table.

2. Review each field and determine whether you need to impose any constraints on it.

3. Define the necessary Business Rules for the field.

4. Establish the rules by modifying the appropriate Field Specification elements.

5. Determine what actions test the rule.

6. Record the rule on the Business Rule Specification sheet.

You'll use this procedure for each table within the database. A detailed breakdown of this process follows.

Step 1. Select a table.

It doesn't matter which table you start with—you'll eventually take each table through this entire procedure. If you choose a table with an "easy" structure, you'll be able to ease into the process and get accustomed to it before you work on tables that have a more "complex" structure. (Here an "easy" table is one that contains fields that you are relatively familiar with; a "complex" table contains fields that you are not as familiar with and must examine carefully.)

Think about the subject the table represents. Then, pose these questions:

> "How is the information regarding this subject used by the organization?"

> "What relationships does the table itself have with other tables in the database?"

If necessary, consult the final table list and read the description for this table, and refer to any relationship diagrams that include this table. The answers to these questions will be useful while you're defining Business Rules, and focusing on the table in this manner prepares you for the next step.

Step 2. Review each field and determine whether there are any constraints that should be imposed on it.

Examine the Field Specifications sheet for each field and determine whether a constraint should be applied to any of its elements. As you review the specification sheet, think about the table in the manner described in the Step 1. Then, pose this question:

> "Based on how the table is used within the database, is a constraint necessary for any element within this specification?"

If the answer is no, move on to the next field. However, if the answer is yes, go on to the next step. For example, assume you're working with the CustCounty field in a CUSTOMERS table, and you

Logical Elements

Type of Key:	☒ Non	☐ Primary	**Comparisons Allowed:**			
	☐ Foreign	☐ Alternate	☐ Same Field	☐ =	☐ >	☐ >=
Uniqueness:	☒ Non-Unique	☐ Unique	☐ Other Fields	☐ ≠	☐ <	☐ <=
Required Value:	☒ No	☐ Yes	**Operations Allowed:**			
Null Support:	☒ Nulls Allowed	☐ No Nulls	☐ Same Field	☐ +	☐ x	
Edit Rule:	☐ Enter Now, Edits Allowed		☐ Other Fields	☐ -	☐ ÷	
	☐ Enter Now, Edits Not Allowed		**Values Entered By:**	☒ User	☐ System	
	☒ Enter Later, Edits Allowed		**Default Value:**			
	☐ Enter Later, Edits Not Allowed		**Range of Values:**	King, Kitsap		

Figure 11-6. *Current settings for the Logical Elements of the CustCounty field.*

have just posed the question about the need for a constraint. Furthermore, assume that the Logical Elements for this field are set as shown in Figure 11-6.

Moving on to the next step is warranted if you receive an answer such as this one:

> "Well, the boss wants to begin tracking our customers by county, so we must make certain we record a county for every customer. In fact, we've just added Pierce County and Snohomish County to our sales region, so it'll be *imperative* that the county names be recorded."

This response clearly is a yes, so you will go on to define the Business Rules in the next step.

Step 3. Define the necessary Business Rules for the field.

To define the appropriate Business Rules for the CUSTCOUNTY field, identify the constraints implied by the response in Step 2 and transform each constraint into a Business Rule.

From the responses in Step 2 you can infer that two constraints need to be made to the CUSTCOUNTY field: a county name is required for each customer, and two more county names need to be *added* to the current list of county names that can be entered into this field. To transform these constraints into Business Rules, you might start with statements such as

"A county must be associated with each customer."

"The only counties that can be entered into this field are King, Kitsap, Pierce, and Snohomish."

Once you've defined the appropriate Business Rules, you can move on to Step 4.

Step 4. Establish the rules by modifying the appropriate Field Specification elements.

Take each Business Rule you defined in Step 3 and establish it by modifying the appropriate elements on the Field Specification sheet. (Remember that some Business Rules may affect more than one element.) First, however, you must identify which elements of the Field Specification Worksheet are affected by a particular Business Rule. For example, consider the first Business Rule defined for the CUST-COUNTY field in Step 3:

"A county must be associated with each customer."

You can deduce that the Required Value, Null Support, and Edit Rule elements will be affected by this rule because the rule explicitly states that a county "must be associated" with a customer. Therefore Required Value will be set to "Yes," Null Support will be set to "No Nulls," and Edit Rule will be set to "Enter Now, Edits Allowed."

As you can see, you must examine each Business Rule very carefully in order to determine which elements of the Field Specifications will be affected by the constraint it imposes. When you first begin to define Business Rules, it's best to have a Field Specification sheet handy to remind you of the elements that can be affected by a Business Rule. As you become more experienced at establishing Business Rules, the elements will come to mind easily.

Now consider the remaining Business Rule in the example:

> "The only counties that can be entered into this field are King, Kitsap, Pierce, and Snohomish."

This Business Rule affects the Range of Values element. The new entry for Range of Values will be "King, Kitsap, Pierce, and Snohomish." Figure 11-7 shows the modifications made to the Field Specification sheet for the CUSTCOUNTY field.

Step 5. Determine what actions test the rule.

The constraint imposed by a Business Rule is tested when a user tries to perform one of three actions: *inserting* a record into the

Logical Elements

Type of Key:	[X] Non	[ ] Primary	**Comparisons Allowed:**			
	[ ] Foreign	[ ] Alternate	[ ] Same Field	[ ] =	[ ] >	[ ] >=
Uniqueness:	[X] Non-Unique	[ ] Unique	[ ] Other Fields	[ ] ≠	[ ] <	[ ] <=
Required Value:	[ ] No	[X] Yes	**Operations Allowed:**			
Null Support:	[ ] Nulls Allowed	[X] No Nulls	[ ] Same Field	[ ] +	[ ] x	
Edit Rule:	[X] Enter Now, Edits Allowed		[ ] Other Fields	[ ] -	[ ] ÷	
	[ ] Enter Now, Edits Not Allowed		**Values Entered By:**	[X] User	[ ] System	
	[ ] Enter Later, Edits Allowed		**Default Value:**			
	[ ] Enter Later, Edits Not Allowed		**Range of Values:**	King, Kitsap, Pierce, Snohomish		

Figure 11-7. *Revised settings for the Logical Elements of the CUSTCOUNTY field.*

table or an entry into a field, *deleting* a record from the table or a value within a field, or *updating* a field's value. Now that you've established a Business Rule and understand the constraint it will impose, determine what actions test the rule by identifying when a violation of the rule is most likely to occur. Asking yourself the following questions will make it easier to make a decision:

"Will this rule be violated if I enter a new record into this table?"

"Will this rule be violated if I *do not* enter a new record into this table?"

"Will this rule be violated if I delete a record from this table?"

"Will this rule be violated if I enter a value into this field?"

"Will this rule be violated if I *do not* enter a value into this field?"

"Will this rule be violated if I update the value of this field?"

"Will this rule be violated if I delete the value of this field?"

Once you've determined the actions that will trigger a violation of the rule, make note of them; you'll use them in the next step. This information will help an individual or team to establish this rule in the most effective manner possible when implementing the database in an RDBMS program.

The business rule for the CUSTCOUNTY field will be tested if a user tries to *insert* a value into the field, because the value must be within a specific range of values. The rule will also be tested if a user tries to *delete* a value in the CUSTCOUNTY field, because that value cannot be Null.

Step 6. Record the rule on the Business Rule Specification sheet.

In order to document your Business Rules for future reference, create a Business Rule Specification sheet for each rule—regardless of its type or category. The Business Rule specification sheet provides three advantages:

- *It allows you to document every database-oriented Business Rule.* You can use this specification sheet to make certain that you have appropriately defined and properly established each rule.

- *It allows you to document every application-oriented Business Rule.* Although you cannot *establish* this type of rule within the logical design of the database, you can at least indicate its basic elements. The information you document for this type of business rule will prove invaluable to the individual or team of individuals who will implement the database within a particular RDBMS or who will create the application program that is used to work with the database.

- *It provides a standard method for recording all Business Rules.* Business Rules are easier to track and maintain if they are recorded in a consistent manner. Using a uniform format also makes it easier to troubleshoot Business Rules because each aspect of the rule is recorded.

The Business Rule Specification sheet contains the following items:

- *Statement.* This is the text of the Business Rule itself. It should be clear yet succinct and should convey the required constraints without any confusion or ambiguity. Here's an example of a well-framed statement:

"A booking agent cannot be assigned to more than twenty-five entertainers."

- *Constraint.* This is a brief explanation of how the constraint applies to the tables and fields. For instance, you can use the following explanation for the constraint imposed by the Business Rule in the above example:

"This Business Rule limits the number of records in the ENTERTAINERS table that can be associated with a single record in the AGENTS table to twenty-five records."

- *Type.* The type of rule you are defining is indicated here. As you know, the options are database-oriented and application-oriented.

- *Category.* Here is where you indicate the category of the rule you are defining. The two options here are field-specific and relationship-specific.

- *Tested On.* The constraint imposed by a Business Rule is tested when a user tries to perform one of three actions: *inserting* a record into the table or entry into a field, *deleting* a record from the table or a value within a field, or *updating* a field's value. The action that is tested by this business rule is indicated here.

- *Structures Affected.* Depending on the type of Business Rule, the constraint will affect either a field or a relationship. Here is where you indicate the name of the field affected by the Business Rule or the names of the tables involved in the relationship affected by the rule.

- *Field Elements Affected.* If the Business Rule pertains to a field, it can affect one or more elements of that field's specifications. This is where you can indicate the elements affected by the constraint.

- *Relationship Characteristics Affected.* A Business Rule that pertains to a relationship will affect one of the relationship's characteristics. You indicate the characteristic that is affected here.

- *Action Taken.* Here you indicate the modifications you've made to the elements of a Field Specification or to a relationship diagram. It is very important that the statement you enter here be as clear and unambiguous as possible. Should a problem occur as a result of enforcing this Business Rule, this statement serves as accurate documentation of the steps you have taken to establish the rule. You can use this statement to make certain that these steps were actually carried out and that the rule has been properly established.

Now fill out a Business Rule Specification sheet for the rule you established in Step 4. Figure 11-8 shows a completed Business Rule Specification sheet documenting the Business Rules established for the CUSTCOUNTY field.

Defining and Establishing Relationship-Specific Business Rules

After defining and establishing field-specific Business Rules, the next order of business is to tackle the Business Rules for relationships. The procedure for performing this task involves the following steps:

1. Select a pair of tables that share a relationship.

2. Review each relationship characteristic and determine whether a constraint is warranted by the way the organization functions or conducts its business.

Business Rule Specification

Statement: A county must be associated with each customer.

Constraint: An entry must be made into the CustCounty field; it cannot be Null.

Type: [x] Database Oriented   **Category:** [x] Field Specific   **Tested On:** [x] Insert   [ ] Update
     [ ] Application Oriented   [ ] Relationship Specific   [x] Delete

---

Structures Affected

Field Names
CUST COUNTY

Table Names

Field Elements Affected

Physical Elements

Data Type	[ ]	Decimal Places	[ ]
Character Support	[ ]	Input Mask	[ ]
Length	[ ]	Display Format	[ ]

General Elements

Uniqueness	[ ]	Comparisons Allowed	[ ]
Required Value	[x]	Operations Allowed	[ ]
Null Support	[x]	Values Entered By	[ ]
Edit Rule	[x]	Default Value	[ ]
		Range of Values	[ ]

Relationship Characteristics Affected

Deletion Rule [ ]   Type of Participation [ ]   Degree Of Participation [ ]

Action Taken
Required Value was set to "Yes", Null Support was set to "No Nulls", and Edit Rule was set to "Enter Now, Edits Allowed".

Figure 11-8. *An example of a Business Rule Specification sheet.*

3. Define the necessary Business Rule.

4. Establish the rule by modifying the relationship characteristic.

5. Determine what actions will test the rule.

6. Record the rule on the Business Rule Specification sheet.

As you can see, this procedure is similar to the one used for field-specific Business Rules. Here is a detailed breakdown of each step:

Step 1. Select a pair of tables that share a relationship

Because you'll take each relationship through this procedure, the pair of tables you start with is unimportant. Once you select a pair of tables, review the relationship diagram used to illustrate their relationship. Then think about what the tables represent and why they are related, and pose the following questions:

"What kind of information do these tables provide?"

"Why is the relationship between these two tables important?"

The answer to these questions will be helpful in defining any necessary Business Rules for the relationship, and keeping them in mind will prepare you for the next step.

Step 2. Review each relationship characteristic and determine whether a constraint is warranted by the way the organization functions or conducts its business.

Examine each relationship characteristic and determine whether some form of constraint is necessary. As you review the characteristic, remember the answers to the questions posed in Step 1. Now ask the following question:

"Is there a limitation that should be imposed on this characteristic based on the way the organization functions or conducts its business?"

If the answer is yes, then go to the next step. If the answer is no, then review the next table relationship characteristic and perform this step once again. For example, assume you're defining a database for a small dance studio, and you're reviewing the relationship

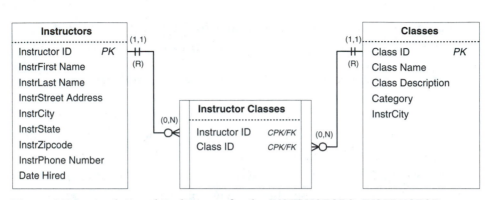

Figure 11-9. *A relationship diagram for the INSTRUCTORS, INSTRUCTOR CLASSES, and CLASSES tables.*

diagram shown in Figure 11-9. The Degree of Participation between the INSTRUCTORS and INSTRUCTOR CLASSES tables is currently under consideration.

Now you pose a question regarding degree of participation:

> "Is there some limitation that should be imposed on the degree of participation between these tables based on the way the school functions or conducts its business?"

You can move to the next step if you receive an answer such as this one:

> "Yes, there is. We require all instructors to teach at least one class. However, we limit them to teaching no more than eight classes."

This response will be used as that basis of defining a Business Rule in the next step.

Step 3. Define the necessary Business Rule.

Next define an appropriate Business Rule based on the response you received in Step 2. Identify the constraint implied by the response, and transform it into a Business Rule. For example, consider the response from Step 2 regarding the degree of participation of the tables in the dance studio database:

> "Yes, there is. We require all instructors to teach at least one class. However, we limit them to teaching no more than eight classes."

As you can see, you can infer two constraints from this response: the minimum number of classes an instructor can teach is one, and the maximum number is eight. Now you can transform these constraints into a Business Rule. You might use a statement such as this one:

> "An instructor must teach one class but no more than eight classes."

After you've defined the rule, you can continue with the next step.

Step 4. Establish the rule by modifying the relationship characteristic.

Establish the Business Rule you just defined by modifying the appropriate symbols in the relationship diagram. Before you make the modifications, you must determine which table is affected by the constraint. First consider the Business Rule statement:

> "An instructor must teach one class, but no more than eight classes."

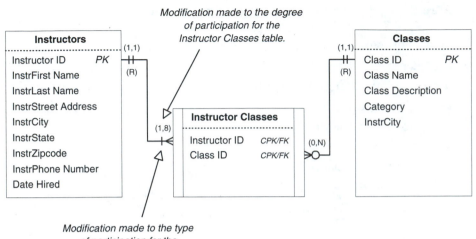

Figure 11-10. *Relationship diagram modifications made to establish the new Business Rule.*

Next identify which table receives the limitation. In this instance, the limit is on the *number of classes* an instructor can teach. Therefore the modification is made to the Degree of Participation characteristic of the INSTRUCTOR CLASSES table. This rule also affects the Type of Participation characteristic of the INSTRUCTOR CLASSES table. The Type of Participation is now Mandatory because a single record in the INSTRUCTORS table *must* be associated with at least one record in the INSTRUCTOR CLASSES table. Figure 11-10 shows the necessary modifications to the relationship diagram based on this Business Rule.

Step 5. Determine what actions will test the rule.

As you know, a Business Rule can be tested if a user tries to insert, delete, or update a record in a table or a value in a field. Now that you've established the Business Rule and understand how it affects the relationship, determine the actions by which the rule will be tested. You can determine this by identifying when a violation of the rule is most likely to occur. Use the following questions to help you make your decision:

"Are there circumstances under which this rule will be violated if I enter a new record into this table?"

"Will this rule be violated if I *do not* enter a new record into this table?"

"Will this rule be violated if I delete a record from this table?"

Once you have determined the actions that will trigger the test, make note of them; you'll use them in the next step. This information will help the individual or team of individuals who is implementing the database to establish this rule in the most effective manner possible.

Here's an important point to note: If you determine that a rule will be violated when you *delete* a record, then you must alter the current deletion rule for the relationship accordingly or add a new deletion rule to the relationship.

In Chapter 10 you learned that there is no need to worry about deleting records in the subordinate or "many" side of the relationship because there can be no adverse effects from doing so. We must now amend this assertion by stating that an exception to this assertion occurs if deleting a record on the subordinate or "many" side of the relationship would violate a required Business Rule. In this instance, the only option available is a restrict deletion rule. *Make certain* you keep this in mind when you're determining when a rule will be tested.

The constraint imposed by the Business Rule in the dance studio database will be tested if a user tries to *insert* a record into the INSTRUCTOR CLASSES table because the maximum number of records that can be associated with a particular instructor is eight.

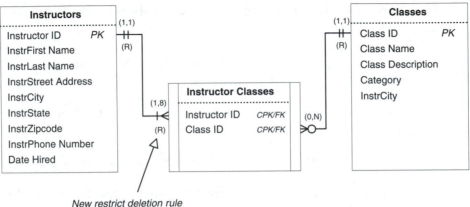

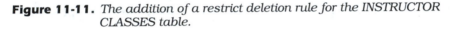

*New restrict deletion rule
added to the relationship for the
Instructor Classes table.*

Figure 11-11. *The addition of a restrict deletion rule for the INSTRUCTOR CLASSES table.*

The rule will also be tested if a user tries to *delete* a record from the INSTRUCTOR CLASSES table because the minimum number of records that *must* be associated with a particular instructor is one. Because the rule will be violated if the user tries to delete a record from the INSTRUCTOR CLASSES table, you need to add a restrict deletion rule for this table to the relationship. Figure 11-11 shows the modification made to the relationship diagram for the dance studio database.

Step 6. Record the rule on the Business Rule Specification sheet.

Finally, fill out a Business Rule Specification sheet for the Business Rule you established in Step 4. Figure 11-12 shows a completed Business Rule Specification sheet for the rule established for the dance studio tables.

Business Rule Specification

Statement: An instructor must teach one class, but no more than eight classes.

Constraint: The participation of INSTRUCTORS within the relationship is Mandatory. Also, a single
record in INSTRUCTORS can be related to only eight records in INSTRUCTOR CLASSES.

Type: [x] Database Oriented   **Category:** [ ] Field Specific   **Tested On:** [x] Insert   [ ] Update
[ ] Application Oriented   [x] Relationship Specific   [x] Delete

Structures Affected

┌ **Field Names** ───────────────────── ┌ **Table Names** ─────────────
INSTRUCTORS
INSTRUCTOR CLASSES

Field Elements Affected

┌ **Physical Elements** ───────────   ┌ **General Elements** ──────────────

Data Type	[ ]	Decimal Places	[ ]	Uniqueness	[ ]	Comparisons Allowed	[ ]
Character Support	[ ]	Input Mask	[ ]	Required Value	[ ]	Operations Allowed	[ ]
Length	[ ]	Display Format	[ ]	Null Support	[ ]	Values Entered By	[ ]
				Edit Rule	[ ]	Default Value	[ ]
						Range of Values	[ ]

┌ **Relationship Characteristics Affected** ──────────────────

Deletion Rule [x]   **Type of Participation** [x]   **Degree Of Participation** [x]

┌ **Action Taken** ──────────
Type of Participation for the INSTRUCTOR CLASSES table was changed to Mandatory.
The Degree of Participation for the INSTRUCTORS CLASSES table was changed to (1,8).
New Restrict Deletion Rule added to the relationship for the INSTRUCTOR CLASSES table.

Figure 11-12. *An example of a completed Business Rule Specification sheet.*

Validation Tables

As you define field-specific Business Rules, there will be instances in which a rule affects the range of values element of the Field Specifications for a particular field; it commonly *limits* the range of values to a *specific* set of valid entries. In many cases, the set of values is made up of a relatively fixed number of entries with values that will rarely change. You could attempt to enumerate each item in the Range of Values element in the Field Specifications sheet, but you would probably run out of room very quickly. Also this set of entries may be difficult to implement within the RDBMS or hard for a user to commit to memory. You can avoid these problems by storing the set of entries in a *validation table*.

What Are Validation Tables?

As you learned in Chapter 3, a *validation table* is a table that holds data specifically used to implement data integrity. Data in a validation table is rarely modified, and it is not very often that records are added or deleted once the table is populated with the required data. Validation tables usually (but not always) comprise two fields: one is assigned the role of the Primary key and is used to help enforce data integrity; the other field is simply a Non-key field used to store a set of values required by some other field in the database. Figure 11-13 shows two examples of validation tables.

In this chapter, you'll learn how the first field is used in support of enforcing a Business Rule. You'll learn how the Non-key field is used later in Chapter 12.

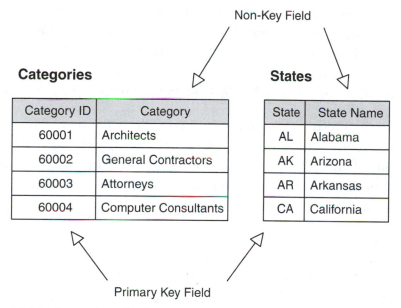

Figure 11-13. *Examples of validation tables.*

Using Validation Tables to Support Business Rules

When a Business Rule limits the range of values of a particular field, you can enforce the constraint by using a validation table; the value for the field will then be drawn from an appropriate field in the validation table. Establishing the Business Rule involves two steps: defining a relationship between the parent table of the field affected by the rule and the validation table, and making a modification to the Range of Values element of the Field Specifications for the affected field in the parent table.

For example, assume you're working with the SuppState field of a SUPPLIERS table, and you've defined the following Business Rule:

> "All suppliers must be from the eleven contiguous western United States, Alaska, or Hawaii."

This rule imposes a constraint on the Range of Values element of the SUPPSTATE field specifications. It limits the values that can be inserted into the field to "AK, AZ, CA, CO, HI, ID, MT, NM, NV, OR, UT, WA, and WY." It should be evident that an easy and efficient way to establish this rule is by using a STATES validation table.

Consider the tables shown in Figure 11-14. (Note the new symbol that is used to represent a validation table.) The SUPPLIERS table stores all the requisite data on the suppliers engaged by the organization. The STATES table is a new validation table that will store the names and abbreviations of the specified states.

In order to establish the Business Rule, the first step is to establish a relationship between these tables. As you can see, there is a one-to-many relationship between the STATES and SUPPLIERS tables—a single record in STATES can be associated with one or more SUPPLIERS, but a single record in SUPPLIERS will be associated with only *one* record in STATES. You already know that a one-to-many relationship is established by taking a copy of the Primary key on the "one" side and inserting it into the "many" side, where it becomes a Foreign key. Although the SUPPLIERS table already has a field named SUPPSTATE, it will be replaced by the STATE field from the STATES validation table.

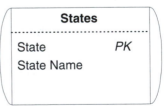

Figure 11-14. *The SUPPLIERS table and the STATES validation table.*

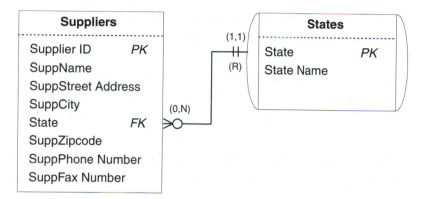

Figure 11-15. *A relationship established between the SUPPLIERS and STATES tables.*

(This modification is justified because it is in accordance with the Elements of the Ideal Field and is consistent with the manner in which one-to-many relationships are established.) Figure 11-15 shows the relationship established between these two tables.

Now that the State field is a Foreign key in the Suppliers table, make certain that it conforms with the Elements of a Foreign key, as outlined in Chapter 10. After you're finished, set the characteristics for the relationship in the following manner:

- *Deletion Rule.* Set a restrict deletion rule for this relationship. You *do not* want to delete a state in the STATES table that is referenced by records in the SUPPLIERS table.

- *Type of Participation.* This is set to "Optional" for the SUPPLIERS table and "Mandatory" for the STATES table. Although it's unnecessary for there to be any records in the SUPPLIERS table in order to enter a new state in the STATES table, there must be records in the STATES table before you can enter records into the SUPPLIERS table. In this way, data integrity is enforced.

- *Degree of Participation.* This is set to "(0,N)" for the STATES table and "(1,1)" for the SUPPLIERS table. It's not necessary for a single record in the STATES table to be associated with any records in the SUPPLIERS table; you may be waiting to engage your first supplier in Alaska. On the other hand, a single record in the STATES table *can* be associated with one or more records in the SUPPLIERS table. In the case of the SUPPLIERS table, a single record in that table *must* be related to only one record in the STATES table.

Next modify the Range of Values element of the Field Specifications for the STATE field in the SUPPLIERS table. The entry for this element should now be "Any value within the STATE field of the STATES table." Figure 11-16 shows the Logical Elements settings of the STATE field in the SUPPLIERS table.

Now that you've established the Business Rule, you must decide when it should be tested. Whenever you use a validation table to enforce a Business Rule, you typically want to test the rule if a user attempts to *insert* a new value into the field or *update* an existing value within the field. In either case, the rule will be violated if the user attempts to use a value that does not exist in the validation table.

Logical Elements

Type of Key:	☐ Non ☒ Foreign	☐ Primary ☐ Alternate	**Comparisons Allowed:**			
			☒ Same Field	☒ =	☐ >	☐ >=
Uniqueness:	☒ Non-Unique	☐ Unique	☐ Other Fields	☐ ≠	☐ <	☐ <=
Required Value:	☐ No	☒ Yes	**Operations Allowed:**			
Null Support:	☐ Nulls Allowed	☒ No Nulls	☐ Same Field	☐ +	☐ x	
Edit Rule:	☒ Enter Now, Edits Allowed		☐ Other Fields	☐ -	☐ ÷	
	☐ Enter Now, Edits Not Allowed		**Values Entered By:** ☒ User ☐ System			
	☐ Enter Later, Edits Allowed		**Default Value:**			
	☐ Enter Later, Edits Not Allowed		**Range of Values:** Any value within the State field of the STATES table.			

Figure 11-16. *Logical Elements for the STATE field in the SUPPLIERS table.*

Business Rule Specification

Statement: All suppliers must be from the eleven contiguous western United States, Alaska, or Hawaii.

Constraint: Entries for the State field in the SUPPLIERS table are limited to existing values of the State field in the STATES table.

Type: [x] Database Oriented   **Category:** [x] Field Specific   **Tested On:** [x] Insert   [x] Update
[ ] Application Oriented   [ ] Relationship Specific   [ ] Delete

Structures Affected

Field Names
STATE

Table Names
SUPPLIERS
STATES

Field Elements Affected

Physical Elements

Data Type	[ ]	Decimal Places	[ ]
Character Support	[ ]	Input Mask	[ ]
Length	[ ]	Display Format	[ ]

General Elements

Uniqueness	[ ]	Comparisons Allowed	[ ]
Required Value	[ ]	Operations Allowed	[ ]
Null Support	[ ]	Values Entered By	[ ]
Edit Rule	[ ]	Default Value	[ ]
		Range of Values	[x]

Relationship Characteristics Affected

Deletion Rule [x]   **Type of Participation** [x]   **Degree Of Participation** [x]

Action Taken

Range of Values set to "Any value within the State field of the STATES table." Type of Participation: STATES is Mandatory, SUPPLIERS is Optional. Degree of Participation: SUPPLIERS is (0,N), STATES is (1,1). Restrict Deletion Rule defined for the relationship between SUPPLIERS and STATES.

Figure 11-17. *A completed Business Rule Specification sheet for the example Business Rule.*

Finally, complete a Business Rule Specification sheet for the Business Rule you've just established with the validation table. Be sure to indicate the modifications you've made to *both* the field and the new relationship. Figure 11-17 shows the completed Business Rule Specification sheet for the example Business Rule.

Reviewing the Business Rule Specification Sheets

Once you've established the Business Rules you believe to be appropriate, review their specification sheets. Carefully examine the specification sheet and make certain that the rule has been properly established and that all the appropriate areas on the sheet are clearly marked. If you find an error, make the necessary modifications and review it once more. Repeat this process until you've reviewed every Business Rule.

Business Rules are an important component of the database. Along with contributing to overall data integrity, Business Rules impose integrity constraints that are specific to the organization. As you've seen, these rules help to ensure the validity and consistency of the data within the context of the manner in which the organization functions or conducts its business. Furthermore, these rules will affect the manner in which the database is implemented in an RDBMS and how it works with the application program used to work with the database.

It's important to understand that you will revisit these rules quite often. As you review the final structure, for example, you may determine that additional Business Rules are necessary. You may discover that several of the rules will not provide the results you had initially envisioned, and thus they need to be modified. It's also possible to determine that some of the rules aren't necessary after all. (In this instance, be absolutely sure to examine the rules carefully *before* you remove them.)

Keep in mind that the Business Rules you define now are bound to require modifications in the future; you will most likely need to *add* Business Rules in due course because of changes in the way the organization functions or conducts its business. The need to modify existing Business Rules or develop new ones comes up naturally—the organization inevitably grows and matures, and so does the manner in which it acts upon or reacts to external forces. These forces affect the manner in which the organization perceives and uses its data, which, in turn, changes the nature of the organization's requirements in terms of Business Rules.

The task of defining and establishing Business Rules is—as are so many other tasks within the database design process—ongoing. Don't be discouraged if you have to perform this task several times. Your efforts will pay great dividends in the long run.

CASE STUDY

Now it's time to establish Business Rules for Mike's database. You schedule a meeting with Mike and his staff to review the tables and relationships in their database. The first order of business is to define and establish field-specific Business Rules.

You begin the process by reviewing the PRODUCTS table. As you begin to examine each field, you try to determine whether any constraints are required. Upon reviewing the CATEGORY field, you remember that there was some question as to the values that could be entered into the field. (Refer to the Case Study in Chapter 9.) After some discussion with Mike and his staff, you compile a list of categories. Then Mike decides that the values for the CATEGORY field should be limited to those on this list to make certain that the staff does not arbitrarily invent new categories. Because Mike wants to limit the values that can be entered in the CATEGORY field, you define an appropriate Business Rule to properly establish the constraint. The new rule is stated as follows:

"Invalid product categories are not allowed."

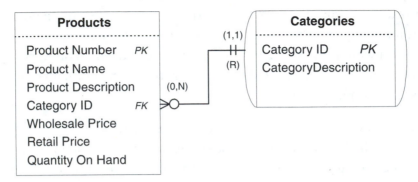

Figure 11-18. *A relationship diagram for the PRODUCTS and CATEGORIES tables.*

Because there are a number of items in the list of possible categories, you decide that the best way to establish this rule is to create and use a CATEGORIES validation table. So you create the table and establish a relationship between it and the PRODUCTS table. After you establish the relationship, you make the appropriate settings to its characteristics. The new validation table, relationship, and its table relationship characteristics are shown in the diagram depicted in Figure 11-18.

These are the settings you've made for the table relationship characteristics:

- There is a restrict deletion rule for the relationship.

- The type of participation for the CATEGORIES table is set to "Mandatory."

- The type of participation for the PRODUCTS table is set to "Optional."

- The degree of participation for CATEGORIES is set to "(1,1)."

- The degree of participation for PRODUCTS is set to "(O,N)."

Remember that by establishing this relationship, you've replaced the existing CATEGORY field in the PRODUCTS table with a copy of the CATEGORY ID field from the new CATEGORIES table. Because the CATEGORY

Logical Elements

Type of Key:	☐ Non	☐ Primary	**Comparisons Allowed:**
	☒ Foreign	☐ Alternate	☒ Same Field ☒ = ☐ > ☐ >=
Uniqueness:	☒ Non-Unique	☐ Unique	☐ Other Fields ☐ ≠ ☐ < ☐ <=
Required Value:	☐ No	☒ Yes	**Operations Allowed:**
Null Support:	☐ Nulls Allowed	☒ No Nulls	☐ Same Field ☐ + ☒ x
Edit Rule:	☒ Enter Now, Edits Allowed		☐ Other Fields ☐ - ☐ ÷
	☐ Enter Now, Edits Not Allowed		**Values Entered By:** ☒ User ☐ System
	☐ Enter Later, Edits Allowed		**Default Value:**
	☐ Enter Later, Edits Not Allowed		**Range of Values:** Any value within the

Category ID field of the CATEGORIES table.

Figure 11-19. *Logical Elements settings for the* CATEGORY ID *field in the PROD-UCTS table.*

ID field in the PRODUCTS table is a Foreign key, you now make certain that it conforms to the *Elements* of a Foreign key and make the appropriate modifications to its Field Specifications. Then you modify the Range of Values element to read "Any value within the CATEGORY ID field in the CATEGORIES table." Figure 11-19 shows the Logical Elements settings of the Field Specifications for the CATEGORY ID field in the PRODUCTS table.

Now you must decide when the rule should be tested. As you already know, you typically want to test a rule established with a validation table if the user attempts to insert a value into the field or update an existing value within the field.

Finally, you complete a Business Rule Specification sheet for this new Business Rule. This specification sheet will reflect the modifications you've made to the Field Specifications for the CATEGORY ID field as well as the characteristics of the relationship between the CATEGORIES and PRODUCTS tables. Figure 11-20 shows the completed Business Rule Specification sheet.

You repeat this process for the remaining fields in this table, as well as the fields in the remaining tables. After you're finished, you move on to the next task.

Business Rule Specification

Statement: Invalid product categories are not allowed.

Constraint: Entries for the Category ID field in the PRODUCTS table are limited to existing values of the Category ID field in the CATEGORIES table.

Type: [x] Database Oriented   **Category:** [x] Field Specific   **Tested On:** [x] Insert   [x] Update
       [ ] Application Oriented   [ ] Relationship Specific   [ ] Delete

Structures Affected

Field Names

CATEGORYID

Table Names

PRODUCTS
CATEGORIES

Field Elements Affected

Physical Elements

Data Type	[ ]	Decimal Places	[ ]
Character Support	[ ]	Input Mask	[ ]
Length	[ ]	Display Format	[ ]

General Elements

Uniqueness	[ ]	Comparisons Allowed	[ ]
Required Value	[ ]	Operations Allowed	[ ]
Null Support	[ ]	Values Entered By	[ ]
Edit Rule	[ ]	Default Value	[ ]
		Range of Values	[x]

Relationship Characteristics Affected

Deletion Rule [x]   **Type of Participation** [x]   **Degree Of Participation** [x]

Action Taken

Range of Values set to "Any value within the Category ID field of the CATEGORIES table." Type of Participation: CATEGORIES is Mandatory, PRODUCTS is Optional. Degree of Participation: PRODUCTS is (0,N), CATEGORIES is (1,1). Restrict Deletion Rule defined for the relationship between PRODUCTS and CATEGORIES.

Figure 11-20. *The completed Business Rule Specification sheet for the CATEGO-RIES and PRODUCTS tables.*

The next order of business is to establish relationship-specific Business Rules. You begin by reviewing the relationship between the EMPLOYEES and INVOICES tables, and you review the relationship diagram to

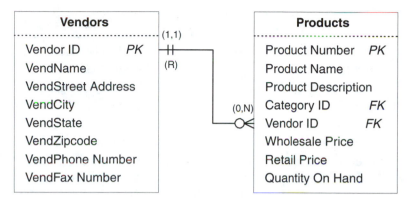

Figure 11-21. *A relationship diagram for the VENDORS and PRODUCTS tables.*

determine whether any constraints are necessary. Everything seems to be in order, so you move to the next relationship, that between the VENDORS and PRODUCTS tables, as shown in Figure 11-21.

As you and Mike discuss whether there are any constraints that should be imposed on this relationship, Mike determines that there should be a constraint on the PRODUCTS table. He wants to make sure that every vendor in the VENDORS table is associated with *at least* one product; he figures that it's unnecessary to keep data on a vendor who's not supplying him with any products. So you define the following Business Rule for this constraint:

"Every vendor must supply at least one product."

Now you establish the Business Rule by modifying the appropriate relationship characteristics. In this instance, you modify the type of participation for the PRODUCTS table so that it is set to "Mandatory," and you modify the degree of participation for PRODUCTS table to "(1,N)." Then you add a new restrict deletion rule to the relationship for the PRODUCTS table. These changes are shown in Figure 11-22.

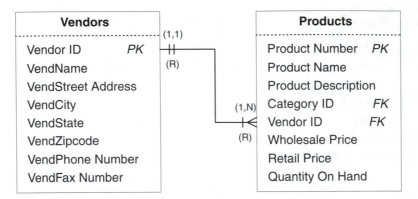

Figure 11-22. *A revised relationship diagram for the VENDORS and PRODUCTS tables.*

Because of the nature of the Business Rule, you already know that it will be tested if a user attempts to insert a record into the PRODUCTS table or delete a record from the PRODUCTS table. So you fill out a Business Rule Specification sheet for this rule, which is shown in Figure 11-23.

Now you repeat this process for the remaining table relationships. When you're finished, the process is complete. You're now ready for the next stage of the database design process.

Summary

This chapter opens with a definition of *Business Rules*. You learned that a Business Rule is a constraint imposed on a field or a table relationship that it is based on the way the organization perceives and uses its data, and it is derived from the manner in which the organization functions or conducts its business. You now know that there are two major types of Business Rules: *database-oriented* and *application-oriented*. Although our focus here is on database-oriented Business

---

Business Rule Specification

Statement: Every vendor must supply at least one product.

Constraint: A single record in the VENDORS table *must* be associated with at least *one* record in the PRODUCTS table.

Type: [x] Database Oriented   **Category:** [ ] Field Specific   **Tested On:** [x] Insert   [ ] Update
[ ] Application Oriented   [x] Relationship Specific   [x] Delete

Structures Affected

Field Names

Table Names
VENDORS
PRODUCTS

Field Elements Affected

Physical Elements

Data Type	[ ]	Decimal Places	[ ]
Character Support	[ ]	Input Mask	[ ]
Length	[ ]	Display Format	[ ]

General Elements

Uniqueness	[ ]	Comparisons Allowed	[ ]
Required Value	[ ]	Operations Allowed	[ ]
Null Support	[ ]	Values Entered By	[ ]
Edit Rule	[ ]	Default Value	[ ]
		Range of Values	[ ]

Relationship Characteristics Affected

Deletion Rule [x]   Type of Participation [x]   Degree Of Participation [x]

Action Taken
Type of Participation for PRODUCTS was changed to Mandatory.
The Degree of Participation for PRODUCTS was changed to (1,N).
New Restrict Deletion Rule defined for the PRODUCTS table.

Figure 11-23. *A completed Business Rule Specification sheet.*

Rules, you know that you can at least record the basic elements of application-oriented Business Rules for use later in the implementation process.

You then learned that database-oriented Business Rules are divided into two categories: *field-specific* Business Rules, which affect the elements of a Field Specification for a particular field; and *relationship-specific* Business Rules, which affect the characteristics of a relationship between a pair of tables.

The chapter continued with a discussion of defining and establishing Business Rules. Here you learned that you'll work with users and management to define the Business Rules required by the organization. Furthermore, you learned that it is best to establish the field-specific Business Rules first, followed by the relationship-specific Business Rules.

Next you learned the steps necessary to define and establish each type of business rule. You now know that, in general, you work with a field or relationship, review the field or relationship in light of the rule to determine whether any constraints are necessary, define the appropriate Business Rule, establish the rule by modifying the appropriate Field Specification elements or table relationship characteristics, decide when the rule should be tested, and complete a Business Rule Specification sheet for each Business Rule.

The chapter continues with a discussion on the elements of the Business Rule Specification sheet, and how each element on the sheet is defined. As you now know, using Business Rule Specification sheets allows you to document all of your rules and provides a standard method for recording and reviewing them.

We close the chapter by discussing *validation tables*. You learned that a validation table can be created and used in support of a Business Rule that limits the Range of Values for a particular field. In this manner, the validation table helps to enforce data integrity. You also learned that you need to establish new table relationships when you use validation tables, and that these relationships have the same types of characteristics as do any other types of table relationships in the database.

12

Views

*There is no object on earth which
cannot be looked at from a
cosmic point of view.*
—FYODOR MIKHAYLOVICH DOSTOYEVSKY

Topics Covered in This Chapter

What Are Views?

Anatomy of a View

Determining and Establishing Views

Case Study

Summary

What Are Views?

As you learned in Chapter 3, a *View* is a *virtual table* that comprises
the fields of one or more tables in the database; it can also include
fields from other views. The reason a View is called a virtual table is
because it does not store or contain data—it draws its data from the
tables or Views upon which it is based. Because a View does not store
data, only its *structure* is saved in the database, and it is re-created
each time it is accessed.

> ❖ **Note** The manner in which Views are implemented is particu-
> lar to each RDBMS, and thus it is beyond the scope of this book.

Views are valuable for the following reasons:

- *They can be used to work with data from two or more tables.*
  During the database design process, you established a relationship between a particular pair of tables because the
  subjects they represent bear some connection to one another.
  A view provides the mechanism that allows you to work with
  the data from both tables simultaneously. Views also allow
  you to work with multiple tables, as in the case of a relationship that includes a linking table.

- *They reflect the most up-to-date information.* Because a View
  does not store or contain its own data, it is re-created every
  time it is accessed. This means that the data displayed by the
  View exhibits the most current changes to the data in its base
  tables.

- *They can be fitted to the specific needs of an individual or
  group of individuals.* Views can be set up to suit any set of
  requirements, such as providing the data for a particular
  report or providing a means of viewing specific data that is
  common to several departments within an organization.

- *They can be used to help enforce data integrity.* You can define
  a *validation view* that works in the same manner as a validation table—its purpose is to provide a valid range of values for
  another field in the database.

- *They can be used for security or confidentiality purposes.* You
  can determine which fields are available to a particular user
  or group of users by defining a View that *excludes* certain
  fields of the tables upon which the View is based.

If Views are skillfully defined, they are an invaluable asset to a database application program once the database has been implemented in
an RDBMS software program. Views can help you control the manner
in which data is entered, modified, retrieved, and displayed.

Anatomy of a View

Views can be based on a single table, multiple tables, other Views, or a combination of tables and Views, and they can use the fields from the structures they comprise. The structures that compose the View are referred to as "base tables" or "base Views."

> ❖ **Note** In order to avoid confusion or ambiguity, tables and Views that are used to define a View will be referred to collectively as "base tables." The diagram illustrating the structure of a View will use the appropriate symbols to distinguish an actual table from a View.

There are three categories of Views: *data Views*, *aggregate Views*, and *validation Views*.

Data Views

Data Views are used to examine and manipulate data from base tables. Depending on the purpose of the View, certain fields from the base tables are used to create the View's structure. For example, say you wanted a list of employee names and phone numbers to be available to everyone in the organization. You can construct an EMPLOYEE PHONE LIST View based on the EMPLOYEES table using just the EMPLOYEE ID, EMPFIRST NAME, EMPLAST NAME, and EMPPHONE NUMBER fields. Figure 12-1 shows a diagram of such a View. (Note the new symbol used to indicate a View.)

Every time the EMPLOYEE PHONE LIST View is accessed, it will be recreated and will reflect the latest changes made to the data in the EMPLOYEES table. Figure 12-2 shows how the data for the View might be displayed.

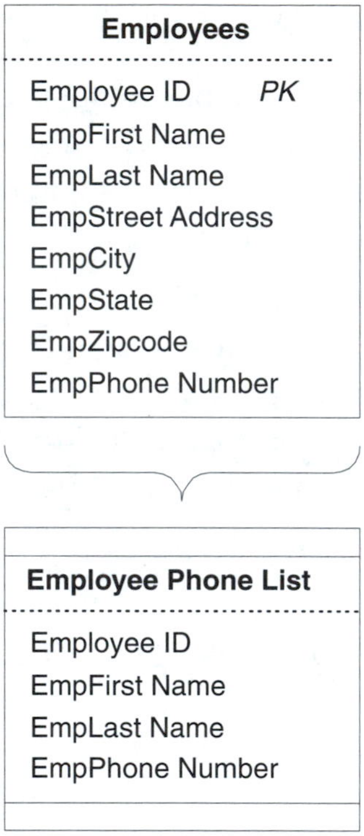

Figure 12-1. *The EMPLOYEE PHONE LIST View.*

Employee Phone List

Employee ID	EmpFirst Name	EmpLast Name	EmpPhone Number
100	Zachary	Erlich	553-3992
101	Susan	McLain	790-3992
102	Joe	Rosales	551-4993
103	Alastair	Black	227-4992
104	Teresa	Ford	525-2993
105	Stuart	Lockhart	248-4953

Figure 12-2. *Data displayed by the EMPLOYEE PHONE LIST View.*

Data in a single-table data View can be modified at any time; the changes to the data are passed through the view and into the base table. But you cannot modify the value of a field if such a change is disallowed by a particular field specification element or constrained by a Business Rule. For example, you cannot delete a last name from the data displayed by the View if the Null Support element of the Field Specification for the EMPLAST NAME field is set to "No Nulls."

You can create a data View that is based on two or more tables as well. The only requirement is that the tables used to create the View bear a relationship to each other. For example, say you want to create a View called CLASS ROSTER that shows the name of each class and the students that are currently registered to attend it. In order to create this View, you must use the tables shown in Figure 12-3. The tables are part of a database used to operate a local school.

These tables contain the fields necessary to create the CLASS ROSTER View. They also fulfill the requirement that the tables used to create a multitable View must bear some relationship to each other. Create the CLASS ROSTER View by using the CLASS NAME field from the CLASSES table and the STUDFIRST NAME and STUDLAST NAME fields from the STUDENTS table. The appropriate student names will appear for each class

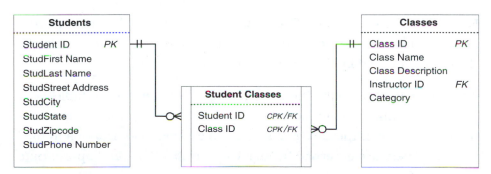

Figure 12-3. *Tables needed to create the CLASS ROSTER View.*

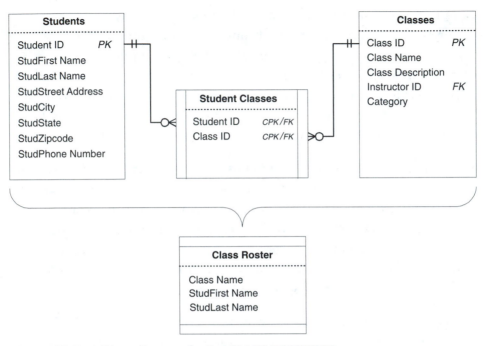

Figure 12-4. *A View diagram for the CLASS ROSTER View.*

because CLASSES and STUDENTS are related (and therefore connected) through the STUDENT CLASSES linking table. Figure 12-4 shows a View diagram for the CLASS ROSTER View. Note that no changes have been made to either of the base tables.

Every time the CLASS ROSTER View is accessed, it will be re-created and will draw the most current data from its base tables. A *sample* of the data displayed by this View is shown in Figure 12-5.

Although you can modify the values of most fields in a multitable View, you cannot modify the Primary key field of any table comprised by the View. As in the case of a single-table View, modifications to the value of a field are governed by its Field Specifications and appropriate Business Rules.

Class Roster

Class Name	StudFirst Name	StudLast Name
Advanced Calculus	Martin	Applebee
Advanced Calculus	Gina	Carter
Advanced Calculus	Joe	Rosales
Advanced Calculus	Sara	Ulrich
Advanced Music Theory	Mike	Hernandez
Advanced Music Theory	Susan	McLain
Advanced Music Theory	Lee	Turner
American History	Gina	Carter
American History	Susan	McLain
American History	Gregory	Piercy
American History	Joe	Rosales

Figure 12-5. *Data displayed by the CLASS ROSTER View.*

You should have noticed that there is redundant data displayed in the CLASS ROSTER View. This is the result of merging a record from the CLASSES table with a record from the STUDENTS table; the number of times a particular CLASS NAME is displayed is equal to the number of students that are registered to attend that class. This apparent redundancy is acceptable because the data *is not* being physically stored—rather, it is being drawn from the base tables where it is stored in accordance with the rules of proper database design. It is common for data from multitable Views to be displayed in this fashion.

Another point you may have noted is that a View does not contain a Primary key. It lacks a Primary key because it is not a table; true tables store data and require a Primary key to serve as a unique identifier for each of their records. Nonetheless, a Primary key from a base table can be used in a View, and it retains its characteristics regardless of how it is being accessed. Therefore, if a Primary key of a base table is included in the View, you must make certain that you treat it as you would a Primary key within a table—its value cannot be Null, and its value must be unique. Make certain you do not have any Primary key indicators within the View symbol when you diagram a View.

Aggregate Views

The purpose of this type of View is to display information that is the result of aggregating a particular set of data in a specific manner. An *aggregate View* includes one or more calculated fields that incorporate the functions that aggregate the data, and one or more data fields (drawn from the View's base tables) to group the aggregated data. The most common aggregate functions executed against a set of data includes *sum*, *average* (arithmetic mean), *minimum*, *maximum*, and *count*.

For example, say you wanted to know how many students are registered for each class. Using the tables from the school example shown in Figure 12-3, you can create an aggregate View called CLASS REGISTRATION that provides this information. Use the CLASS NAME field from the CLASSES table and create a calculated field called TOTAL STUDENTS REGISTERED, which counts the number of students per class. (When you work with a calculated field, make certain that you give it a name that is meaningful and will distinguish it from other calculated fields in the View.) The calculated field will use a count function to count the number of STUDENT ID's in the STUDENT CLASSES table that are associated with each CLASS ID in the STUDENT CLASSES table. (Later, you'll learn how to document a View and record the expression used by a calculated field.) Figure 12-6 shows a diagram for the new CLASS REGISTRATION View.

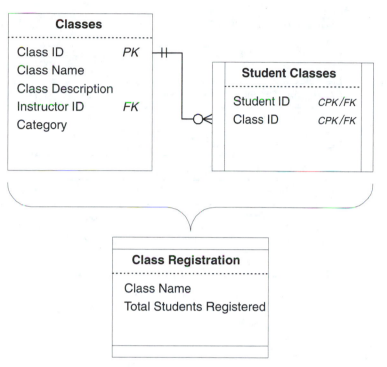

Figure 12-6. *View diagram for the CLASS REGISTRATION View.*

Every time the CLASS REGISTRATION View is accessed, it will be re-created and will access the most current data from the CLASSES and STUDENT CLASSES tables. A sample of the data displayed by the View is shown in Figure 12-7.

Data cannot be modified in an aggregate View for two reasons: calculated fields are noneditable, and the data fields are used for grouping purposes only. This type of View is best used as the basis of a report or as a means of providing various types of statistical information. You'll learn later that you can apply filtering criteria to this (or any) View in order to control and restrict the data displayed by the View.

Class Registration

Class Name	Total Students Registered
Advanced Calculus	325
Advanced Music Theory	389
Business Administration	450
Computers in Business	484
English Literature	388
Introduction to Biology	382
Introduction to Database Design	420
Pan-American Studies	325

Figure 12-7. *Data displayed by the CLASS REGISTRATION View.*

Validation Views

Validation Views are similar to validation tables in that they are used to implement data integrity. When the Range of Values of a particular field is limited by a Business Rule, you can enforce the constraint just as easily with a validation View as you can with a validation table. The difference between the two lies in their construction—you must explicitly define a validation table because it will store its own data, whereas a validation View is constructed with fields from base tables and draws its data from those tables as well. As with any other View, you can create a validation View from a single table, multiple tables, other Views, or a combination of both tables and Views. However, it's common that validation Views are built from a single table and comprise only two or three fields, just as their Validation table counterparts do.

As an example, say you are designing a database for a small contractor and you're working with the tables shown in Figure 12-8.

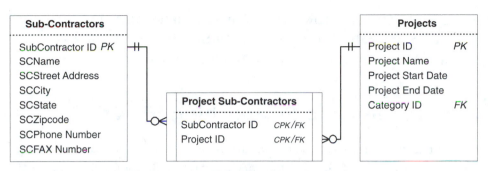

Figure 12-8. *Tables from a Contractors database.*

Although there is a relationship between the SUB-CONTRACTORS table and PROJECT SUB-CONTRACTORS table, you want to restrict the access users have to the data in the SUB-CONTRACTORS table. The only fields you believe users should have access to are SUBCONTRACTOR ID, SCNAME, SCPHONE NUMBER, and SCFAX NUMBER fields. So you create an APPROVED SUB-CONTRACTORS View to provide the range of values for the SUBCONTRACTOR ID field in the PROJECT SUB-CONTRACTORS table. A diagram of the tables, including the new View, is shown in Figure 12-9.

The APPROVED SUB-CONTRACTORS VIEW now provides the appropriate values for the SUBCONTRACTOR ID field in the PROJECT SUB-CONTRACTORS table, while restricting users' access to the data

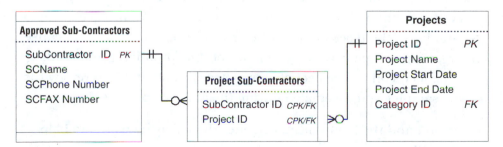

Figure 12-9. *Revised Contractors database structure.*

in the SUB-CONTRACTORS *table*. Also, the relationship characteristics that exist for the SUB-CONTRACTORS table are still enforced through the APPROVED SUB-CONTRACTORS view.

Determining and Establishing Views

As you can see, Views can be a substantial asset to the database. During this stage of the database design process, you'll define a fundamental set of Views for the database. Your definition of Views won't stop here—you'll create more Views when you implement the database in an RDBMS and create a database application program. In these instances, Views are used as a tool to support particular aspects of the implementation or application program. However, the Views you create during the database design process will focus strictly on data access and information retrieval issues.

Working with Users and Management

You'll work once again with the organization's representative group of users and management to identify the types of Views required by the organization. After identifying the Views you will establish and document them, and then you and the group will review the Views to make certain that they were properly defined.

Before you conduct your first meeting with the group, review the notes you've taken throughout the entire design process. Your objective is to get an idea of the types of Views the organization might need. Because an organization spends a large amount of time producing and reading reports, focus on that aspect of your notes. You should also review the report samples you assembled during the analysis process.

When you and the group meet, consider the following points to help you identify View requirements:

- *Review your notes with the group.* In many instances, an idea for a new or required View will be sparked by a topic currently under discussion. For example, someone may realize a need for a View during a discussion of mission objectives.

- *Review the data-entry, report, and presentation samples you gathered during the early stages of the design process.* Examining these samples, especially summary-style reports, could easily illuminate the need for certain types of Views.

- *Examine the tables and the subjects they represent.* Some individuals in the group may identify the need for a View based solely on a specific subject. If someone mentions a subject such as Employees, it may cause someone else to say: "We definitely need a View that restricts certain employee data for confidentiality reasons."

- *Analyze the table relationships.* You'll most likely identify a number of multitable Views that should be created for many of the relationships. Several of these Views will coincide with Views you identified for the report samples.

- *Study the Business Rules.* As you already know, a rule that imposes a constraint on the Range of Values for a particular field can be enforced with a validation View.

You and the group should be able to identify a number of Views by going over the items on this list. After you've identified as many of the required Views as possible, your next task is to construct them.

Establishing Views

Create each View that you've identified using the appropriate tables and fields. Review the relationship diagrams to identify which tables and fields will be included in the View structure. When you've determined what you need, establish the View and record it in a View diagram.

Customer Call List

City	Customer Name	Phone Number	Last Purchase
Bothell	Sara Anderson	542-0039	05/16/96
	Jim Booth	367-4495	02/11/96
	Larry Currey	445-3394	02/06/96
Bellevue	Jim Davis	545-9932	05/10/96
	Larry Lang	545-3384	01/22/96
	Sandra Wasser	367-2293	06/30/96
Edmonds	Julia Black	223-9943	04/12/96
Lynnwood	Mary McLain	562-1274	02/28/96
	Barbara Reeves	445-2094	03/07/96

Figure 12-10. *Report sample requiring a View.*

For example, say you've determined that you can use a View for the report shown in Figure 12-10; the name of the new View will be CUSTOMER CALL LIST.

The notes you've taken throughout the design process become useful once again. You reviewed this report during the analysis stage of the design process, and you've noted that this report represents information about customers and their orders; it is from the order data that you can determine when the last purchase was made by a particular customer. Now review the relationship diagram for the CUSTOMERS and ORDERS tables; you'll use fields from these tables to create the

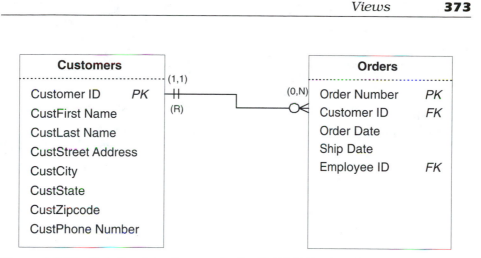

Figure 12-11. *Relationship diagram for the CUSTOMERS and ORDERS tables.*

CUSTOMER CALL LIST View. The relationship diagram for these tables is shown in Figure 12-11.

After examining the diagram, you determine you need to use five fields to build this View: CustFirst Name, CustLast Name, CustPhone Number, and CustCity from the CUSTOMERS table, and Order Date from the ORDERS table. Now establish the CUSTOMER CALL LIST View by assigning the fields to the View and then recording them in a View diagram. Your diagram should look like the one in Figure 12-12.

Using Calculated Fields Where Appropriate

Earlier in the database design process, you learned that tables cannot contain *calculated fields* for a number of good reasons. But one of the characteristics of a View that makes it so useful is that it *can* contain calculated fields. Remember that calculated fields will display the result of a concatenation, expression, or aggregate function; this makes them an extremely flexible structure to include in a View.

For example, consider the new CUSTOMER CALL LIST View. Although you have the fields you need for the View, you'll have to make a minor

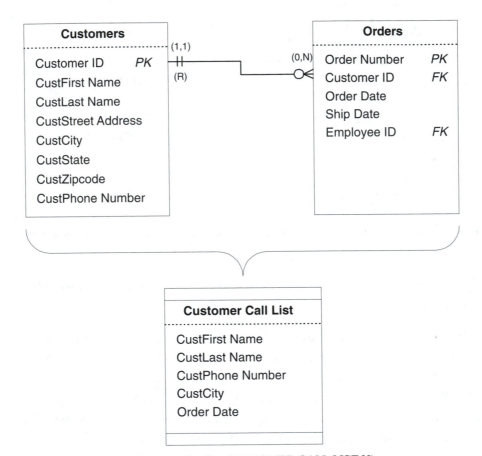

Figure 12-12. *View diagram for the CUSTOMER CALL LIST View.*

modification in order for the View to display the appropriate data. As required in the example, this View must display the date of the last purchase made by each customer. In order to retrieve the proper date, you'll have to add a calculated field to the View. The calculation will be based on the ORDER DATE field, and it will use the Maximum function (commonly known as *Max()*) to retrieve the correct date. Name the new field LAST PURCHASE DATE and add it to the CUSTOMER CALL LIST View diagram. The expression that is used to retrieve the appropriate date is

Max(ORDER DATE)

Later in this section, you'll learn where and how to record this expression.

Another calculated field you might use in this View is one that concatenates CUSTFIRST NAME and CUSTLAST NAME so that the complete customer name is displayed as "Hernandez, Michael." Create a calculated field called CUSTOMER NAME and add it to the CUSTOMER CALL LIST View diagram. "'CUSTLAST NAME & ', ' & CUSTFIRST NAME'" is the expression you'll use to display the name in the desired manner, and you'll soon properly record the concatenation as well. Because you're using the CUSTOMER NAME calculated field to display the customer name, remove the CUSTFIRST NAME and CUSTLAST NAME fields from the View.

When you've completed the changes to the View diagram, it should look like the one shown in Figure 12-13.

As you've just learned, calculated fields can be used to enhance the information presented by a View, so they are quite an asset. Earlier in this chapter, you also learned that calculated fields are particularly crucial in aggregate Views. A good rule of thumb to follow with calculated fields is to use them if they will provide pertinent and meaningful information, or if they will enhance the manner in which the data is used by the View.

One of the best sources for calculated fields that can be useful in a View is the *calculated field list* you compiled earlier in the database design process. (Refer to Chapter 6.) You'll find that many of the fields on this list can be used in the Views you create for the database.

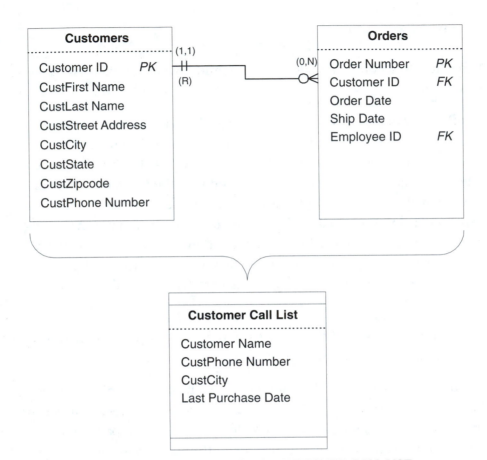

Figure 12-13. *Revised View diagram for the CUSTOMER CALL LIST.*

Imposing Criteria to Filter the Data

Views have another characteristic that makes them extremely useful: you can impose criteria against one or more fields in the View to filter the records it displays. For example, say that the CUSTOMER CALL LIST View included the CUSTSTATE field. Although the View would continue to display the set of records it did before, you would see the state each customer lives in as well. However, assume you wanted the View to show a very specific set of records—for instance, just the records of those customers who live in the state of Washington. You could set a criterion against the CUSTSTATE field that would filter the data so that only records of customers from Washington would be displayed by the View.

In database work, the word "criterion" refers to an expression that is tested against the value in a particular field. A record is included in the View if the value of the field meets the criterion. Continuing the example, you would use the following expression to filter the records for the CUSTOMER CALL LIST View:

CUSTSTATE = "WA"

Now the View will display only customers from Washington. If you wanted to filter the records further to show only those customers who live in specific cities, add a criterion such as

CUSTCITY In ("Bellevue," "Olympia," "Redmond," "Seattle," "Spokane," "Tacoma")

The View will now display Washington State customers who live in the cities specified in the expression. You may wonder why both criteria are necessary—the criterion for the CUSTCITY field should retrieve the appropriate records by itself. The trouble is that many cities are named for other cities, so that cities in two or three different states could have the same name. For example, there is a "Portland, Oregon," and a "Portland, Maine," both named after Portland, England. The point to remember is that you must use your best judgment when establishing criteria for a View—use the *minimal* criteria that will cause the View to display the records you require.

When you use criterion in a View, you must make certain that the field being tested in the criterion is included in the View's structure. If the field is not included in the View, you have no way of imposing the criterion. This is an important point to remember because it is true when you logically define a View as well as when you implement the View in an RDBMS.

The one problem with applying a filter to a View is that there is no way to indicate it on a View diagram. Therefore you must record it on a View Specifications sheet.

Using a View Specifications Sheet to Record the View

Each View diagram you create *must* be accompanied by a *View Specifications sheet*. It is on this sheet that you will record the characteristics of the View. The View Specifications sheet contains the following items:

- *Name.* Here is where you indicate the name of the View. Before you record the name, however, test it against the *guidelines for creating table names* you learned in Chapter 7. These guidelines govern the naming of Views as well, with *one* exception: the name of a View can implicitly or explicitly identify more than one subject. This is due to the fact that Views can be constructed from two or more tables, so they do, indeed, represent more than one subject.

- *Type.* Indicate here whether the View type is data, aggregate, or validation.

- *Base Tables.* For this item you indicate the names of the tables used to construct the View. Although the tables are shown on the View diagram, they are also included here as a matter of convenience. Field names are not included in the View Specifications because they are better recorded and displayed in the View diagram.

- *Calculated Field Expressions.* Here is where you record the expressions for the calculated fields you included in the View. As you record the name of the calculated field, test it against the guidelines for creating field names you learned in Chapter 7. Calculated field names are governed by these guidelines with two exceptions: you can implicitly or explicitly identify more than one characteristic in a name, and you can use the plural form of the name. But when you name a calculated field, it is still desirable to use the singular form of the name if possible.

- *Filters.* This item is used to record the criteria that will be used to filter the records displayed by the View. Here you'll record both the field being tested and the expression used to test it.

> ❖ **Note** When you fill out the Calculated Field Expressions and Filters sections of a View Specification sheet, use the expressions with which you are most familiar. You'll modify them as necessary when you implement the database in an RDBMS.

Fill out a View Specifications sheet for each View you create and attach the sheet to the proper View diagram. Both of these items will serve to fully document the View. Figure 12-14 shows a completed View Specifications sheet for the CUSTOMER CALL LIST View. (Keep in mind that the View has been updated to include the CUSTSTATE field.)

Reviewing the Documentation for Each View

Once you've completed the task of establishing and documenting each View, review your Views once more—ensuring the quality of the information provided by each View is well worth the effort. As you review each View, keep the following points in mind:

- *Make certain that the View is properly constructed.* Think about the information the View should provide. Are you establishing the correct type of View for the required information? Are the appropriate base tables used to construct the View? Are all the necessary fields included in the View's structure?

View Specifications

Name:	Customer Call List	**Type:** ☐ Data ☒ Aggregate ☐ Validation

Description: This View provides information that allows us to execute follow-up calls to our customers in Washington. Also indicated is the date of the customer's last purchase.

Base Tables

CUSTOMERS
ORDERS

Calculated Field Expressions

Name	Expression
CUSTOMERNAME	CUSTFIRST NAME & " " & CUSTLAST NAME
LAST PURCHASEDATE	MAX(ORDER DATE)

Filters

Field Name	Condition
CUSTSTATE	= "WA"
CUSTCITY	In ("Bellevue," "Olympia," "Redmond," "Seattle," "Spokane," "Tacoma")

Figure 12-14. *Completed View Specifications sheet for the CUSTOMER CALL LIST View.*

- *Make certain that the calculated fields you've created are suitable for the View.* Do they provide pertinent and meaningful information? Do they serve to enhance the manner in which the data is displayed?

- *Make certain that the filters will retrieve the required records.* First of all, do you need a filter for this View? If the answer is yes, do you know exactly which records you want the View to display? Does the filter work correctly?

- *Above all, make certain that you have a View diagram and View Specifications sheet for each View.* This documentation will be very useful when you finally implement the database in an RDBMS.

CASE STUDY

Your work on Mike's database is finally nearing an end. You meet with Mike and his staff to determine whether there is a need to establish Views for the database. The agenda you've set up for the meeting involves the following steps:

1. Review the notes you've compiled during the design process.

2. Review each of the various samples you gathered during the early stages of the design process.

3. Examine the subjects represented by the tables in the database.

4. Analyze the table relationships.

5. Review and study the Business Rules.

As the meeting progresses, you identify several Views that you need to construct, including a PREFERRED CUSTOMERS View and a VENDOR PRODUCT COUNT View. The first View will provide the name and phone number of each customer who has a "Preferred" status, and the second View will provide information on the total number of different products each vendor supplies.

You use the CUSTOMERS table to establish the PREFERRED CUSTOMERS View. The only fields you need for the View are CustomerID, CustFirst Name, CustLast Name, CustHome Phone, and Status. But before you construct the View, Mike asks if there's any way to display the first name and last name together. You respond that it can be done, so you create a calculated field called Customer Name that concatenates both of the fields together. This field replaces the CustFirst Name and CustLast Name fields. Figure 12-15 shows the View diagram for the PREFERRED CUSTOMERS View.

Figure 12-15. *View diagram for the PREFERRED CUSTOMERS View.*

After you create the View diagram, you make note of the expression that will be used to filter the data for the View, which is

STATUS = "Preferred."

Then you complete the View Specifications sheet for the PREFERRED CUSTOMERS View, as shown in Figure 12-16.

Now you create the VENDOR PRODUCT COUNT View using the VENDORS and PRODUCTS tables as the base tables. You use the VENDOR NAME field from the VENDORS table to display the names of the vendors. Next you create a calculated field called PRODUCT COUNT to display the total number of products each vendor supplies; your calculated field uses this expression to calculate the total:

Count(PRODUCT NAME).

You then create a diagram for the View, which is shown in Figure 12-17.

After determining that a filter is unnecessary for this View, you finish documenting the View by completing the View Specifications sheet shown in Figure 12-18.

You then repeat this process for every View you've identified for Mike's database.

Summary

We began this chapter with a definition of a View, and you learned that it is a virtual table that does not contain or store data. Views are useful for several reasons, such as that they let you work with data from multiple tables, help enforce data integrity, and keep data secure or confidential.

View Specifications

Name:	Preferred Customers	**Type:** ☒ Data ☐ Aggregate ☐ Validation	

Description: This View provides the names and phone numbers of our Preferred customers.
We use this information in support of the services we provide to these customers.

Base Tables

CUSTOMERS

Calculated Field Expressions

Name	Expression
CUSTOMERNAME	CustLast Name & ", " & CustFirst Name

Filters

Field Name	Condition
STATUS	= "Preferred"

Figure 12-16. *The View Specification sheet for the PREFERRED CUSTOMERS View.*

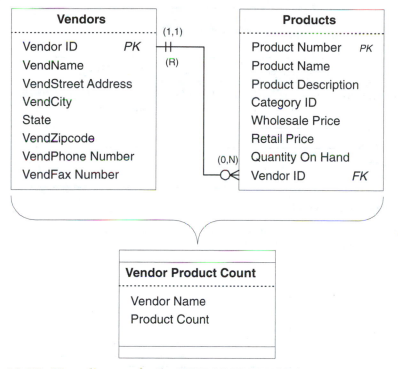

Figure 12-17. *View diagram for the VENDOR PRODUCT Count View.*

We then discussed the three types of Views: *data, aggregate,* and *validation.* You learned that each type of View can be based on one or more tables, other Views, or a combination of both. Views are recreated every time they are accessed and will display the most current data from the base tables. As you now know, there must be relationships between tables in a multitable View, and the characteristics of those relationships are carried forth through the view. Data can be modified in most Views, and all modifications to data are passed through the View to the base tables. You also learned that *validation Views* work in the same manner as validation tables do, but they have distinct advantages over validation tables; for instance, they can incorporate data from multiple tables.

View Specifications

| **Name:** | Vendor Product Count | **Type:** | ☐ Data | ☒ Aggregate | ☐ Validation |

Description: This View tells us how many products are supplied by each vendor. This information will help us determine which vendors we might need to drop.

Base Tables

VENDORS
PRODUCTS

Calculated Field Expressions

Name	Expression
PRODUCTCOUNT	Count(PRODUCTNAME)

Filters

Field Name	Condition

Figure 12-18. *View Specifications sheet for the VENDOR PRODUCT COUNT View.*

The chapter then continues with a discussion on determining and establishing Views for the database. Here you learned several specific points to keep in mind while you work with users and management to identify the organization's View requirements. Next we discussed how to establish a View, and you learned how to create a *View diagram* to document the View. Now you know how to select fields from the base tables and assign them to the View.

We then discussed how to use calculated fields in a View. You learned that they are used to provide pertinent information and enhance how the data is displayed in the View. You also learned that calculated fields are especially crucial in aggregate Views. Each calculated field uses an expression to derive the value it displays. Next you saw how to apply a filter to a View in order to retrieve a specific set of records. Records will be displayed by the View only if they meet the criterion imposed against one or more fields in the View. Each criterion is framed as an expression and is used to test the values of a particular field.

The chapter closes with a discussion of the View Specifications sheet. Here you learned how to document the characteristics of the View, such as its name and type. You also learned about the items that compose the View specifications sheet and how they are used to record the View's characteristics.

13

Reviewing Data Integrity

*When you have eliminated the
impossible, whatever remains,
however improbable, must be the truth.*
—SHERLOCK HOLMES,
THE SIGN OF FOUR

Topics Covered in This Chapter

Why You Should Review Data Integrity

Reviewing and Refining Data Integrity

Assembling the Database Documentation

Case Study—Wrap Up

Summary

You are now at the final stage of the database design process. You've accomplished many things since you started the process. Thus far you have

- perceived the advantages of the relational database model and how it compares to other database models.

- created a mission statement for a new database.

- defined mission objectives for the new database.

- performed a complete analysis of an old database.

- identified the organization's information requirements.

- defined all the appropriate table structures.

- assigned a Primary key to each table.

- established Field Specifications for each field.

- established table relationships.

- defined and established Business Rules.

- defined all the appropriate Views.

- established overall data integrity.

For all intents and purposes, your new database is complete. Nevertheless it would be to your advantage to perform one final review of the overall data integrity of your database.

Why You Should Review Data Integrity

You're probably wondering why you should review the database structure one last time, especially considering that you've paid attention to every detail and have focused on data integrity throughout the entire design process. The answer is simple: You want to make certain that the data integrity you've been so careful to establish is absolutely as sound as possible. As you well know, a crack in the integrity could result in inconsistent data or inaccurate information. However improbable, it is possible that you may have overlooked something. The peace of mind you gain from knowing that you have a solidly designed database is well worth the time and effort of this final review.

❖ **Note** Remember: Garbage in, garbage out!

Reviewing and Refining Data Integrity

Reviewing data integrity is a simple task if you take a modular approach. In other words, sequentially review each component of overall data integrity: table-level, field-level, and relationship-level integrity and Business Rules. If you have carefully followed the design method presented in this book, you should encounter very few problems here. The following sections briefly outline the points you should keep in mind as you conduct the review and contain references to earlier chapters in case you encounter any problems.

At the Table Level

In order to ensure that table-level integrity has been properly established, review each table and make certain that the table conforms with all of the following points:

- There are no duplicate fields in the table.
- There are no calculated fields in the table.
- There are no multivalued fields in the table.
- There are no multipart fields in the table.
- There are no duplicate records in the table.
- Every record in the table is identified by a Primary key value.
- Each Primary key conforms to the Elements of a Primary key.

If you believe you have problems with any of these items, resolve them using the techniques and concepts discussed in Chapters 6, 7, and 8.

At the Field Level

You can ensure that field-level integrity has been properly established by making certain that

- each field conforms to the Elements of the Ideal Field.
- a set of Field Specifications has been defined for each field.

Field-level integrity problems can be resolved with the techniques discussed in Chapter 9.

At the Relationship Level

Examine each table relationship to ensure that relationship-level integrity has been properly established. Make certain that

- the table relationship is properly established.

- the appropriate deletion rule has been established.

- the type of participation has been correctly identified.

- the proper degree of participation has been established.

If you identify a problem with a relationship, use the techniques in Chapter 10 to resolve it.

At the Level of Business Rules

Ensuring that the Business Rules are sound can be achieved by making certain that

- each rule imposes a *meaningful* constraint.

- the proper category has been determined for the rule.

- each rule is properly defined and established.

- the appropriate Field Specification elements or table relationship characteristics have been properly modified.

- the appropriate validation tables have been established.

- a Business Rule Specification sheet has been completed for each rule.

If you encounter problems with any of your Business Rules, refer to Chapter 11 for the techniques necessary to solve them.

At the Level of Views

Although Views are not directly connected to any component of data integrity, you should review all of your View structures nevertheless. As you examine each View, make certain that

- each View contains the base tables necessary to provide the required information.

- each View has been assigned the appropriate fields.

- each calculated field provides pertinent information or enhances the manner in which the data is displayed.

- each filter returns the appropriate set of records.

- each View has a View diagram.

- each View is accompanied by a View Specifications sheet.

If you encounter problems with any View, resolve them by using the techniques discussed in Chapter 12.

Once you've completed this entire review, you can be confident that the database structure is sound, the data within the database is consistent and valid, and the information you retrieve from the database will be accurate.

Assembling the Database Documentation

Throughout the database design process, you've generated a number of lists, specification sheets, and diagrams used to record various aspects of the database design. You should now assemble them into a central repository, preferably in a set of binders. (Incidentally, you could generate and store these documents using a computer program.) The design repository should consist of the following sets of documents:

final table list	relationship diagrams
Field Specifications sheets	Business Rule Specifications sheets
calculated field list	View diagrams
table structure diagrams	View Specifications sheets

Two additional sets of items you may consider keeping with this documentation are the notes you compiled during the design process and the samples you gathered during the analysis stage of the design process. Each can be kept in a separate appendix at the end of the documentation.

All of these items constitute the complete set of documentation for the logical design of the database. The design documentation is vital for three reasons:

1. *It provides a complete record of the structure of the database.* Every aspect of the logical structure of the database can be found in the documentation. Almost any question concerning the database can be answered by referring to the documentation.

2. *It provides a complete set of specifications and instructions on how the database should be created during the implementation process.* This documentation is similar to an architect's blueprints: it indicates how the database is to be constructed. It also identifies the integrity that needs to be established for the database. Because the database design is not directed to a particular RDBMS, the individuals implementing the database have full latitude concerning the manner in which the database is physically implemented, without affecting the design.

3. *Should it seem necessary to modify the database structure during the implementation process, the design documentation can be used to determine the effects and consequences of any modifications.* Any modifications you make to the database structure should be the result of an *informed* decision. Reference to the documentation will make certain that the proposed modifications do not have an adverse effect on the database structure.

Done at Last!

Now that you've completed the integrity review and assembled all of the documentation for the database, the logical database design process is complete. You can rest assured that you have a properly designed database and that its implementation will proceed smoothly. On to the next client and the next database design!

CASE STUDY—WRAP UP

This is your last meeting with Mike and his staff. Your objective is to review his database and its integrity one final time. Although you're confident that you will not find any problems, you want to give the database one final quality-control review.

During the meeting, you review each of the database structures to ensure that they are in accordance with the various elements that govern them. Then you review each component of overall data integrity to make certain that table-level, field-level, and relationship-level integrity as well as Business Rules have been properly established. Finally you gather all of the documentation you've generated throughout the design process. After you've assembled all of the documentation into a set of binders, you give them to Mike and declare that his database is now complete. Mike expresses his thanks and gratitude for a job well done and promises your check will be in the mail by the fifteenth of the month. You express your thanks to Mike and his staff, say your "good-byes" and depart for new horizons. As you leave, Mike stares in your direction; one final thought occurs to him.

"Now, if I could just get you to implement my database for me. . . ."

Summary

The chapter opens with a list of the accomplishments you've made since you began the database design process. It then continues with a discussion of why you should review overall data integrity one final time. This is followed by a brief discussion of the points to keep in mind as you review each component of overall data integrity. We close the chapter by discussing the importance of the documentation you've assembled during the entire design process.

Part III

Other Database Design Issues

14

Bad Design—What Not To Do

Mistakes are always initial.
—CESARE PAVESE

Topics Covered in This Chapter

Flat-File Design

Spreadsheet Design

Dealing with the Spreadsheet View Mind-set

Database Design Based on the Database Software

A Final Thought

Summary

You may have wondered why this chapter appears at the end of the book as opposed to at the beginning. The reason is simple: Now that you've learned how to design a database properly, you can appreciate the dangers presented by a poorly designed database. Furthermore, you will be able to determine for yourself why a particular design is bad—you'll look at the design and be able to identify the problems with the structure immediately. Also you now possess the knowledge needed to determine possible solutions to these problems.

In this chapter, you'll see the three most common design approaches that lead to poorly structured databases. The discussions are brief because they are only meant to illustrate types of design you should avoid. It should now be obvious that the way to resolve an improperly designed database is to take it through the complete design process you've just learned.

Flat-File Design

The flat-file design is common in databases that have been designed to be implemented in nonrelational database programs. A flat-file design is fraught with problems, as you can see by examining the structure in Figure 14-1.

This diagram represents the structure of a *single* table. (Imagine how the rest of the tables are structured!) As you can see, this structure certainly suffers from redundant data and inconsistent data. Also there is little data integrity built into the structure. Although you have probably noticed the problems yourself, here are just a few, this table contains:

Table Structures

Customer Orders

Order Number	Customer Phone	Item 3 Extension
Order Date	Item 1	Item 2
Ship Date	Quantity 1	Quantity 2
Order Amount	Price 1	Price 2
Sales Rep Name	Item 1 Extension	Item 2 Extension
Customer Number	Item 3	
Customer Name	Quantity 3	
Customer Address	Price 3	

Figure 14-1. *An example of a flat-file structure.*

- *Multipart fields.* SALES REP NAME includes the sales rep's first and last name, CUSTOMER NAME includes the customer's first and last name, and CUSTOMER ADDRESS includes the customer's street address, city, state, and zip code.

- *Calculated fields.* The ORDER AMOUNT field contains a value that is most likely calculated by hand, especially if the customer is ordering more than three items. The ITEM # EXTENSION fields are all calculated fields containing an expression that multiplies the QUANTITY # field by THE PRICE # field.

- *Unnecessary duplicate fields.* Each of the fields pertaining to a particular item are duplicates. For example, the ITEM 1, ITEM 2, and ITEM 3 fields are unnecessary duplicate fields.

- *No true Primary key.* There is no field or group of fields that can uniquely identify a single record in this table. The ORDER NUMBER field is not a Primary key in this table; if a customer orders more than three items, the user will have to enter another record into the table using the *same* ORDER NUMBER.

- *The table represents more than one subject.* Customers, orders, and items are represented by this table. (Depending on your point of view, it also represents Sales Reps.)

Now that you know the elements of good database design, you're sure to avoid a design such as this.

Spreadsheet Design

A spreadsheet is certainly a good tool if used properly and for the purpose for which it was designed. It has many suitable applications within an organization. But contrary to popular myth, a spreadsheet *does not* make a good relational database. If your organization has a need to collect, store, maintain, and manipulate various types of data,

	A	B	C
1	Store 100 (344-0029)		Store 103 (554-2993)
2	Manager: Mike Hernandez		Manager: Diannia Piercy
3	Asst. Mgr: Bob McNeal and		Asst. Mgr: Terri Sharpe
4	Suzi Thompson		
5	Store 101 (445-3928)		Store 104 (773-1837)
6	Manager: Abe Hernandez		Manager: Gary Holcomb
7	Asst. Mgr: Steve McMahn		Asst. Mgr: Barbara Cooper
8			and Jan Eckstadt
9	Store 102 (433-4872)		Store 105 (344-2883)
10	Manager: Susan McLain		Manager: Caroline Coie
11	Asst. Mgr: Carol Schaeffer		Asst. Mgr: Leroy Bonnicksen

Figure 14-2. *An example of a typical spreadsheet "database."*

then use the proper tool for the job by designing and implementing a real database. For example, consider the spreadsheet in Figure 14-2.

This spreadsheet is being used to keep track of branch stores for a particular organization. You can see that there are problems with the quality of this system, including

- *Duplicate fields.* Each field on this spreadsheet is a duplicate field. If you take the fields at face value, there are basically three fields in each instance: STORE NUMBER, MANAGER NAME, and ASSISTANT MANAGER NAME.

- *Multipart fields.* Each field holds two values. The first field stores the store number and phone number, the second field stores the manager's first and last name, and the third field stores the assistant manager's first and last name.

- *Multivalued fields.* The ASSISTANT MANAGER field is a multivalued field because there can be more than one assistant manager assigned to a particular store.

- *This type of database is difficult to use.* Data-oriented tasks that can be performed with ease in an RDBMS program are tedious and time-consuming to carry out in a spreadsheet. For example, it would be a lengthy job to create a list containing only the name of each store manager and his or her phone number.

After seeing the problems with a simple spreadsheet "database" such as this one, you can imagine the types of problems you would encounter with a more complex "database." If you're currently using a spreadsheet as a database, you would improve quality, speed, and versatility if you remove the database from the spreadsheet, take it through the entire database design process, and implement it an a suitable RDBMS software.

Dealing with the Spreadsheet View Mind-set

When you begin to work with a true database and RDBMS program, you must break away from a "spreadsheet mind-set." In other words, you'll have to resign yourself to the fact that certain ways of viewing the data are now unavailable—you can no longer use typical spreadsheet layouts. For example, consider the typical spreadsheet report shown in Figure 14-3.

Using a database program, you cannot produce a report with this type of layout because of the manner in which the data is stored. In a spreadsheet, the data is stored exactly as you see it on the report. If you were to use a database, the data used for this report would be stored in four separate fields of the table. Figure 14-4 shows an example of a database report you could generate for the same data.

The database presentation is not the same as the spreadsheet presentation, but it is just as clear.

Branch Stores

Bellevue

| Store 201 | Store 211 | Store 118 |
| Manager: Mike Hernandez | Manager: George Chavez | Manager: Joyce Williams |

Redmond

| Store 322 | Store 27 | Store 75 |
| Manager: Jose Aguilar | Manager: Mark Rosales | Manager: Chris Weber |

Seattle

| Store 105 | Store 187 | Store 200 |
| Manager: Frank Lerum | Manager: Susan McLain | Manager: Linda Teller |

Figure 14-3. *An example of a typical spreadsheet report.*

The point to remember is that you'll have to adjust the manner in which you think about working with the data in your database. In the end, there are far more advantages to storing and using your data in an actual database than trying to use a spreadsheet in a similar manner. A database gives you much more control over data integrity and the consistency and validity of the data. It also provides an almost unlimited number of ways to retrieve the data, enabling you to obtain a wide variety of information.

Branch Stores

Bellevue		Seattle	
Store 201	Manager: Mike Hernandez	Store 105	Manager: Frank Lerum
Store 211	Manager: George Chavez	Store 187	Manager: Susan McLain
Store 118	Manager: Joyce Williams	Store 200	Manager: Linda Teller

Redmond	
Store 322	Manager: Jose Aguilar
Store 27	Manager: Mark Rosales
Store 75	Manager: Chris Weber

Figure 14-4. *An example of a typical database report.*

Database Design Based on the Database Software

An RDBMS does not provide a basis or procedure, or even a reason for designing a database in a particular fashion—it only provides the tools that are needed to implement a design. In contrast, a formal database design method provides both the principles and rationale necessary to define a database properly and effectively.

Many people fall into the trap of creating a database design based on the RDBMS software they will use for its implementation. Using the software program's tools, you may create a database that "works," but you may have a poor design without knowing it. Designing a database in this manner results in improper structural design, insufficient data integrity, and problems with inconsistent data and inaccurate information. Without a good understanding of proper database design principles, you will inadvertently let the software dictate the design of the database as opposed to driving the design strictly from the organization's information requirements. This is still true even if you are quite adept at using the tools and programming language of the RDBMS software.

A Final Thought

Through years of teaching database design and instructing people on how to use various RDBMS software programs, I've observed an interesting phenomenon: People who are familiar with the fundamental principles of proper database design have a better comprehension of the RDBMS software and the tools it provides than those who know little at all about database design. I believe this is due to the fact that the people who know database design are able to understand why certain tools are provided in the RDBMS and how they are properly used. For this reason—as well as the many others presented in this book—it is to your distinct advantage to learn and understand good database design techniques. This book does not map the only road, but it is, I believe, the straightest, surest and most easily traveled.

Summary

This chapter contrasts relational database design with weaker, less effective design formats. First we looked at flat-file design. You learned that there are numerous fatal problems with this approach, and that it should be completely avoided. We then examined spreadsheet design and you were shown some differences in versatility as well as in managing data integrity. The chapter closes with a discussion on designing a database using RDBMS software. You learned that this type of design was perilously dependent on your familiarity and skill level with the software. Unlike a good database design method, designing around an RDBMS does not provide you with principles and rationale for designing a proper database structure. Superficially, in the short run, the software product looks as good—it just doesn't work as well in the long run as the design method discussed in this book.

15

Bending or Breaking the Rules

Nature never breaks her own laws.
—LEONARDO DA VINCI

Topics Covered in This Chapter

When May You Bend or Break the Rules?

Documenting Your Actions

Summary

I always advocate following proper database design techniques. As you've already learned, there are numerous reasons for doing so. But first and foremost you should use a good design method to ensure the integrity of the database. I cannot overstate how important this is. You now know the consequences of improperly established data integrity. So "following the rules" is of paramount importance.

When May You Bend or Break the Rules?

There are only two specific circumstances under which it is at all permissible to bend or break the rules of proper database design. Unless either of these is an inescapable imperative, you should use proper database design techniques when designing your database.

Designing an Analytical Database

As you learned in Chapter 1, an *analytical database* is used to store and track historical and time-dependent data. This type of database often contains calculated fields within some of its table structures. The expressions used in many of these fields are meant to record the state of a particular set of data at a given moment in time; other fields store the results of aggregate functions.

As you may have surmised from its description, this type of database violates proper database design because its tables contain calculated fields. (Refer to Chapter 7.) In this *particular* instance, the violation is acceptable because of the manner in which the data in the database is being used. I recommend that you *properly* design the database first and then break the rules only after judicious consideration—you should make a deliberate decision to break a rule and understand why doing so is necessary in the specific instance.

Improving Processing Performance

This is by far the most common reason that people feel compelled to bend or break the rules. Whenever multitable queries or complex reports are slow to process, many believe that the solution to the problem is to alter the underlying table structures. They would have you modify a table in such a way that it includes *every* field necessary for the query or report. While this modification does indeed increase the speed at which the query or report will be processed, it also introduces a number of new problems, such as unnecessary duplicate fields and redundant data. This is clearly not a welcome solution, because it violates proper database design.

Unfortunately, real life is not as ideal as we would like it to be. So you will sometimes find you must decide between improving processing performance or holding to proper design principles.

Is It Worth It?

In order to make this decision, ask yourself: "Is the increase in speed worth the risk to quality?" As you well know, consequences, like ripples in a pond, will spread from altering the structure in this manner. Here are a few of the ill effects you will have to try to counter:

- *Inconsistent data.* This is caused by the introduction of unnecessary duplicate fields. It will be your responsibility to ensure that the data in these fields is synchronized; if the value in a particular duplicate field is modified, the same modification must be made for the remaining duplicate fields.

- *Redundant data.* Redundant data is also caused by unnecessary duplicate fields. When you edit a particular value in a field containing redundant data, you must be sure to make the same modification for each occurrence of that value.

- *Impaired data integrity.* Bending or breaking the rules often violates one or more components of overall data integrity, such as table-level integrity and relationship-level integrity. It will be your responsibility to compensate for the lack of integrity—in whatever way it is manifested—as best as you can.

Improving Performance by Other Means First

On the other hand, if you want to pursue this course of action in order to improve processing performance, *do it only as a last resort*. Before you do it, try to improve performance by other means first. There are a number of alternatives you can employ, such as

- *enhancing or upgrading the hardware.* In spite of the cost involved, this is still the easiest way to increase processing performance. A faster CPU, more memory, and a printer that better meets your requirements will all help to greatly decrease the time it takes to process a complex query or report. Using a larger hard drive will also help increase the retrieval speed for disk-intensive queries. Larger hard drives incorporate technology that produces extremely fast disk-access times.

- *fine-tuning the operating system software.* Make certain that the operating system is optimized for peak performance. This is especially important for networked computers. Processing performance can be greatly enhanced by working with the settings of the network's configuration options. The types of modifications you make to the operating system in general will depend on the type of *software* you're using for the operating system. So you'll have to refer to the software's documentation to learn what types of modifications you can make.

- *reviewing the database structure.* Make absolutely certain that the database is properly designed. It makes quite a difference. Poorly designed databases actually contribute to poor processing performance.

- *reviewing the implementation of the database.* Examine how the database has been implemented in the RDBMS software. Make certain you've taken full advantage of the RDBMS's capabilities and defined the database as efficiently and completely as possible.

- *reviewing the application program used to work with the database.* Here's another area you should examine very closely. Is the application program well-written? Does it make the best use of the tools provided by the RDBMS? Are the application's components well-defined? In some cases, a report may print more slowly because of the report design used by the application programmer—there may be more effective ways to generate the same report. Queries may run slowly because they are improperly defined. Make certain that each query is defined correctly and in the most efficient way possible.

If you believe you must depart from proper database design techniques, carefully examine your situation. As noted above, it's occasionally acceptable to suspend the rules *if* you are designing an analytical database. Just make certain you carefully design the database and that you relax the rules only for very specific reasons.

Documenting Your Actions

If you've taken all of these actions and still come to the conclusion that you need to bend or break the rules, then *you must document each rule you break and each action you take!* Documenting your changes is important because it will compel you to think about the consequences of what you are about to do. It also provides a means of recording the changes you make to the database structure. Should you decide later that the modifications did not provide a significant increase in processing performance, you can use the documentation as a guide to reverse the modifications you initially made.

The items that should be recorded include

- *the reason you're by-passing the rules.* You're departing from proper design in order to increase processing performance, or to decrease the time it takes to print a specific statistical report. List all the reasons.

- *the design principle you are violating.* If you record how you're altering the database design, you can reverse these changes later should you determine that performance did not significantly improve. You might indicate that you're altering the structure of a table, for example.

- *identify the aspect of the database that you're modifying.* Indicate here which particular field, table, relationship, or View you are going to alter. Once again, this information will be valuable should you decide to reverse the modifications.

- *the method by which you make the modifications.* Once you determine which item you need to modify, record the exact modifications you make to that item. For example, if you need to modify a relationship, note the exact changes you make to its characteristics.

- *the anticipated affects on the database and the application program.* Any modifications you make to the database are going to affect the applications based on it. For example, altering the structure of a particular table can affect data integrity, View structures, data entry forms and reports built upon the table (either partially or totally), and macros or programming code that refer to the table. List every effect.

Add this document with the documentation you compiled for the database. Even if you reverse the changes later, the record could prevent you from yielding to a future impulse to make the same changes.

Summary

The chapter opens by examining the two circumstances under which you might feel compelled to depart from proper database design techniques. You learned that you may need to break the rules if you are designing an analytical database. However, you should design the database properly first, and then make deliberate decisions to break or bend specific rules. The most common reason for departing from proper design techniques is to improve processing performance. Although this *is not* a satisfactory reason for breaking the rules, there are times when circumstances dictate that such changes must be considered.

We then continue with a discussion on the alternate measures you can take to improve processing performance, such as enhancing or upgrading the hardware and reviewing the implementation of the database. You learned that you should do all you can to improve performance first and depart from proper design techniques only as a last resort. The chapter then closes with a list of items you should record if you need to break the rules.

In Closing

*I'm not a teacher: only a
fellow-traveller of whom you asked
the way. I pointed ahead—ahead of
myself as well as you.*
—GEORGE BERNARD SHAW

I've always believed that you shouldn't have to be a rocket scientist in
order to design a database properly. It should be a relatively straightforward task that can be performed by anyone possessing a good
amount of common sense. As long as you follow a good database
design method, you should be able to design a sound and reliable database structure.

You now possess the knowledge and skills necessary to design a relational database. You know how to define the necessary structures,
establish table relationships, and implement various levels of data
integrity. If you encounter improperly or poorly designed structures,
you now know how to improve them.

Learning about database design is an ever-continuing process. You
can learn enough to design the types of databases you require, you
can turn it into a profession, or you can even make it a lifelong study.
Whatever your approach, you'll encounter one inescapable fact: The
more you learn, the more you realize you don't know it all! But don't
be discouraged—this is true of any major subject you endeavor to
learn, such as music, art, philosophy, or rocket science.

I sincerely hope you've enjoyed reading this book as much as I've
enjoyed writing it. I know that most technical books of this nature can
be a little dry, so I tried to inject a little humor every now and then,

particularly in the interview and meeting dialogues. Those of you who thought the conversations were realistic are quite perceptive—they were very loosely based on a number of conversations I've had with my clients over the years.

As a parting piece of advice, let me leave you with two words: Always learn. Never be afraid or intimidated or reluctant to learn something new. Learning opens the door to fresh ideas, different concepts, and new perceptions. It encourages participation and communication between individuals and broadens everyone's horizons.

Learning is a journey that begins with but one step. You've taken the first step by reading this book. Now you will continue your journey by learning about other facets of database management.

My book ends here, but your journey is just beginning. . . . .

Recommended Reading

Should you be interested in pursuing an in-depth study of database technology, here are my recommendations for books on this subject. Keep in mind that these books are going to be challenging to read. The authors of these books presume that you have a fair amount of background in computers and programming.

Fleming, Candace C., and Barbara von Halle, *Handbook of Relational Database Design*. Reading, Mass.: Addsion Wesley Longman. The authors discuss the logical design of a relational database as well as its implementation in an RDBMS such as DB2. The book includes chapters on logical data modeling, normalization, Business Rules, SQL, and indexing methods.

Connolly, Thomas, Carolyn Begg, and Anne Strachan, *Database Systems*. Reading, Mass.: Addison Wesley Longman. This book encompasses a wide range of topics, from designing and implementing a database to using SQL and implementing security. The authors include detailed discussions of topics such as the history and types of database systems, entity-relationship modeling, normalization, database languages, and database administration.

Date, C. J. *An Introduction to Database Systems (Sixth Edition)*. Reading, Mass.: Addison Wesley Longman. This is one of the most comprehensive and in-depth treatments of database technology to date. It is a widely regarded and respected study of the relational database model. The topics in this book include database system architectures, the relational model, data integrity, relational algebra and relational calculus, SQL, normalization, security, optimization, and object-oriented systems.

Codd, E. F. *The Relational Model for Database Management: Version 2.* Reading, Mass.: Addison Wesley Longman. This is the definitive book on the relational database model by the model's creator, Dr. E. F. Codd. Everything you would want to know about the relational database model is in this book. Topics include structure-oriented and data-oriented features, domains, joins, database operations, Views, functions, distributed database management, and extending the relational model. Dr. Codd also includes a chapter entitled "Claimed Alternatives to the Relational Model" and presents his comments and rebuttals to these alternatives.

Bowman, Judith, Sandra Emerson, and Marcy Darnovsky. *The Practical SQL Handbook (2nd ed.)*. Reading, Mass.: Addison Wesley Longman. This is a good book on SQL that is very thorough and has plenty of examples. Each command is fully discussed, and there is even an appendix showing the manner in which you would execute SQL statements in DB2, Informix, Ingres, Oracle, SQL/DS, and Sybase. The Authors discuss designing and creating a database, working with data in the database, retrieving data from multiple tables, working with Views, and security issues.

Learning SQL. Wellesley Software Englewood Cliffs, NJ: Prentice Hall. If your only intent is to acquire a working knowledge of SQL, this is the book for you. The authors take a "workbook" approach to the subjext; they briefly discuss a concept or command and then provide several exercises for you to test your new knowledge. Topics include defining and populating tables, selecting rows from a table, built-in functions, joining tables, Views, and security.

 **B**

Sample Designs

The sample designs provided here are meant to serve as *ideas* for databases you may want or need to create. I emphasize the word "ideas" because five people can look at the same design and come up with five distinct variations based on their needs, backgrounds, and personal points of view.

I intentionally omitted all but the Primary and Foreign key fields from each table because I did not want to greatly influence you in any way as to how the tables should be populated. I also omitted a majority of the relationship characteristics for the same reason. Should you see a design that you might be able to use, run it through the entire database design process and treat it like an existing database. At the end of the process, you should have a database that suits your needs.

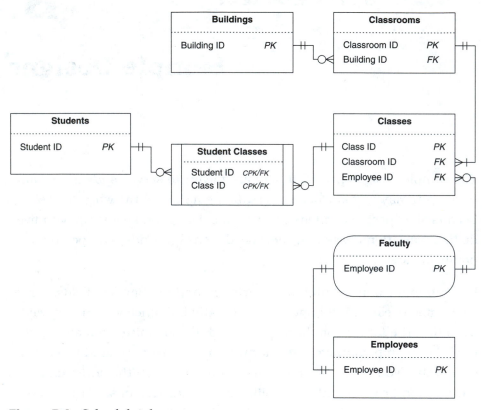

Figure B-1. *School database.*

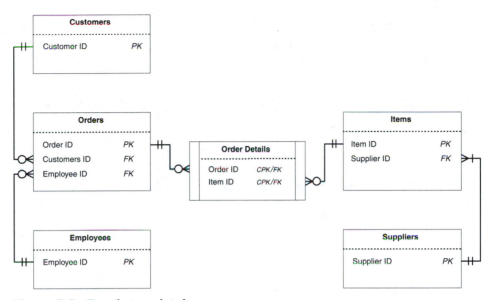

Figure B-2. *Retail store database.*

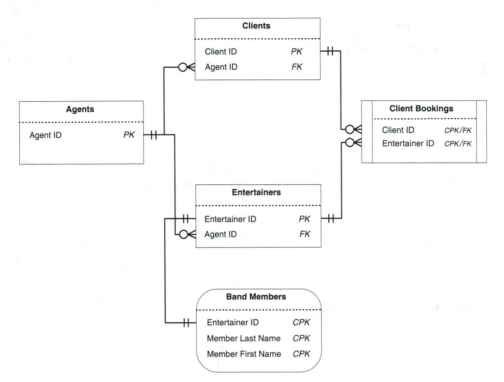

Figure B-3. *Entertainment agency database.*

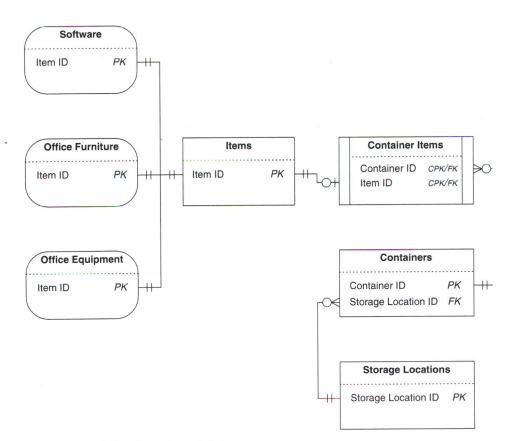

Figure B-4. *Office inventory database.*

Diagram Symbols

The symbols used to diagram table and view structures, table relationships, and relationship characteristics, and key designations are presented here for quick and easy reference.

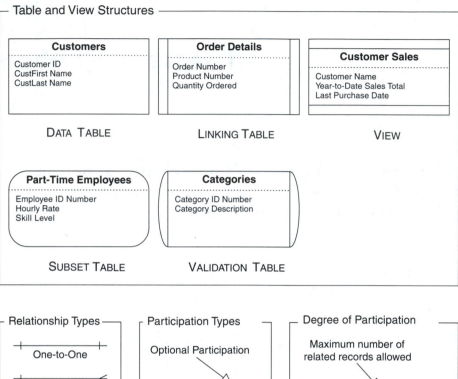

Table and View Structures

Customers
Customer ID
CustFirst Name
CustLast Name

DATA TABLE

Order Details
Order Number
Product Number
Quantity Ordered

LINKING TABLE

Customer Sales
Customer Name
Year-to-Date Sales Total
Last Purchase Date

VIEW

Part-Time Employees
Employee ID Number
Hourly Rate
Skill Level

SUBSET TABLE

Categories
Category ID Number
Category Description

VALIDATION TABLE

Relationship Types

One-to-One

One-to-Many

Many-to-Many

Participation Types

Optional Participation

Mandatory Participation

Degree of Participation

Maximum number of
related records allowed

(1,8)

Minimum number of
related records allowed

Deletion Rules

(C) Cascade

(R) Restrict

Key Designations

AK Alternate Key	**CCK** Composite Candidate Key	**FK** Foreign Key
CK Candidate Key	**CPK** Composite Primary Key	**PK** Primary Key

D

Documentation Forms

Blank copies of the Field Specifications sheet, Business Rule Specification sheet, and View Specifications sheet are provided here for you to copy and use on your database projects.

Field Specifications

General Elements

Field Name:	**Parent Table:**
Label:	

Shared By: **Alias(es):**

Description:

Physical Elements

Data Type: **Length:**

Character Support: **Decimal Places:**

☐ Letters (A-Z)   ☐ Extended (. , / $ # %)   **Input Mask:**

☐ Numbers (0-9)   ☐ Special   (© ® ™ Σ)   **Display Format:**

Logical Elements

Type of Key: ☐ Non   ☐ Primary   **Comparisons Allowed:**
                    ☐ Foreign   ☐ Alternate   ☐ Same Field   ☐ =   ☐ >   ☐ >=

Uniqueness: ☐ Non-Unique ☐ Unique   ☐ Other Fields ☐ ≠   ☐ <   ☐ <=

Required Value: ☐ No   ☐ Yes   **Operations Allowed:**

Null Support: ☐ Nulls Allowed ☐ No Nulls   ☐ Same Field   ☐ +   ☐ x

Edit Rule: ☐ Enter Now, Edits Allowed   ☐ Other Fields ☐ -   ☐ ÷

                    ☐ Enter Now, Edits Not Allowed   **Values Entered By:**   ☐ User   ☐ System

                    ☐ Enter Later, Edits Allowed   **Default Value:**

                    ☐ Enter Later, Edits Not Allowed **Range of Values:**

Specification Information

Specification Type: ☐ Unique   ☐ Generic   ☐ Replica

Based on Existing Specification: ☐ No   ☐ Yes

Source Specification:

Business Rule Specification

Statement:

Constraint:

Type: ☐ Database Oriented   Category: ☐ Field Specific   Tested On: ☐ Insert   ☐ Update
☐ Application Oriented   ☐ Relationship Specific   ☐ Delete

Structures Affected

Field Names _____   Table Names _____

Field Elements Affected

Physical Elements _____   General Elements _____

Data Type	☐	Decimal Places	☐	Uniqueness	☐	Comparisons Allowed	☐
Character Support	☐	Input Mask	☐	Required Value	☐	Operations Allowed	☐
Length	☐	Display Format	☐	Null Support	☐	Values Entered By	☐
				Edit Rule	☐	Default Value	☐
						Range of Values	☐

Relationship Characteristics Affected

Deletion Rule ☐   **Type of Participation** ☐   **Degree Of Participation** ☐

Action Taken

View Specifications

Name:	Type:	☐ Data	☐ Aggregate	☐ Validation

Description:

Base Tables

Calculated Field Expressions

Name	Expression
CUSTOMER NAME	

Filters

Field Name	Condition

References

Codd, E. F. (1990) Relational Philosopher *DBMS*, December 1990, 34–40, 60

———(1990) *The Relational Model for Database Management Version 2.* Reading, Mass.: Addison-Wesley.

Connolly, Thomas, Carolyn Begg, and Anne Strachan. (1996) *Database System: A Practical Approach to Design, Implementation and Management.* Wokingham, England: Addison-Wesley.

Date, C. J. (1994) According to Date: Many Happy Returns! *Database Programming and Design*, September 1994, 19–22.

Fleming, Candace C., and Barbara von Halle. (1989) *Handbook of Relational Database Design* Reading, Mass.: Addison-Wesley.

Kalman, David. (1994) Moving Forward with Relational *DBMS*, October 1994, 62–74, 109.

Kroenke, David M. (1995) *Database Processing Fundamentals, Design, and Implementation, 5th ed.* Englewood Cliffs, N.J.: Prentice Hall.

McGoveran, David. (1994) The Relational Model Turns 25 *DBMS*, October 1994, 46–61.

Index